Human Rights and Gender Violence

TRANSLATING INTERNATIONAL LAW INTO LOCAL JUSTICE

Sally Engle Merry

The University of Chicago Press | Chicago and London

The University of Chicago Press, Chicago 60637
The University of Chicago Press, Ltd., London
© 2006 by The University of Chicago
All rights reserved. Published 2006
Printed in the United States of America

15 14 13 12 11 10 09 08 07   3 4 5

ISBN: 0-226-52073-0 (cloth)
ISBN: 0-226-52074-9 (paper)

Library of Congress Cataloging-in-Publication Data

Merry, Sally Engle, 1944–
    Human rights and gender violence : translating international law into local justice /
Sally Engle Merry.
        p.   cm. — (Chicago series in law and society)
    Includes bibliographical references and index.
    ISBN 0-226-52073-0 (cloth : alk. paper) — ISBN 0-226-520749 (pbk. : alk. paper)
    1. Women — Violence against. 2. Women — Legal status, laws, etc. 3. Human rights.
4. Culture and law. 5. Culture conflict. I. Title. II. Series.
HQ1237.M47 2006
362.88′082 — dc22

2005011951

Human Rights and Gender Violence

CHICAGO SERIES IN LAW AND SOCIETY

Edited by William M. O'Barr and John M. Conley

Contents

Acknowledgments

This book is a collaborative process that has benefited enormously from countless discussions over the last five years with human rights lawyers and activists, NGO leaders, women at the grassroots, and academic colleagues. The generosity of spirit and commitment to social justice displayed by activists I interviewed in India, China, Fiji, Hong Kong, Hawai'i, and Massachusetts was inspirational, and for their insights and patience with my endless curiosity and questions, I am deeply thankful. They demonstrated an impressive commitment to women's safety and well-being in many parts of the world. I am also grateful to the many transnational activists, from NGO leaders to CEDAW Committee members, who talked to me and helped me understand their practice and their commitment to the project of improving the global position of women. To my colleagues who have read portions or all of this book or discussed it with me, I am also very grateful. Peggy Levitt, Ellen Lutz, and Nan Stein read a draft of the manuscript and provided invaluable comments. I also benefited greatly from discussions and comments from Kamari Clarke, Jane Collier, Thomas Cushman, Mark Goodale, Susan Hirsch, Michael Ignatieff, Lidwein Kapteijns, Michael Krauss, Mindie Lazarus-Black, Laura Nader, Harriet Samuels, Austin Sarat, Hanna Beate Schöpp-Schilling, Alan Smart, Sidney Tarrow, Franz and Keebet Van Benda-Beckman, Cheryl Welch, and Robert Weller. During the research period I was a Fellow at the Carr Center for Human Rights Policy at the Kennedy School at Harvard University and greatly appreciate the intellectual intensity of the environment and the support of my colleagues there. Teaching a course on human rights with Thomas Cushman while I was writing this book has been a valuable learning experience for me.

As this book shows, international work always requires funding, and I was fortunate to have the generous support of the National Science Foundation. The Cultural Anthropology Program and the Law and Social Sciences Program awarded me grant #BCS-9904441. A Mellon New Directions Fellowship provided support for another semester of research and writing as well as for curriculum development in human rights. Wellesley College has always created a very supportive and stimulating teaching and research environment. It also generously provided funding for three excellent research assistants: Justine Hanson, Rachel Stern, and Eleanor Kleiber, all three recent graduates from Wellesley College. These students contributed in significant ways to the book.

I have received invaluable insights from colleagues and audiences at lectures, conferences, and workshops where I have presented portions of this work. I lectured on this material at New York University Law School, New York University Department of Anthropology, Columbia Law School, Carr Center for Human Rights Policy at Harvard, University of Pennsylvania anthropology department, University of Hawai'i political science department, University of Hawai'i women's studies department, the Max Planck Institute for Social Anthropology in Halle, Germany, Emory University anthropology department, the Social Science Research Council, Brandeis University, University of North Carolina Law School, Edinburgh University, University of Wisconsin, China Law Society in Beijing, Chinese Academy of Social Sciences in Beijing, University of the South Pacific in Suva, Fiji, and at conferences of the American Anthropological Association, the Law and Society Association, and the Law, Culture, and Humanities Association in addition to several small conferences and workshops. Many people have made significant contributions to my thinking, showing me again that scholarship is a shared and cumulative process.

Parts of this book were published in earlier articles, although all have been substantially revised here. Parts of chapters 3 and 4 were published in "Constructing a Global Law—Violence against Women and the Human Rights System," *Law and Social Inquiry* 28, no. 4 (2003): 941–79; sections of chapter 6 were published as parts of longer articles: "Rights Talk and the Experience of Law: Implementing Women's Human Rights to Protection from Violence," *Human Rights Quarterly* 25, no. 2 (2003): 343–81, and "The Female Inheritance Movement in Hong Kong: Theorizing the Local/Global Interface," coauthored with Rachel E. Stern, *Current Anthropology* 46, no. 3 (2005): 387–409.

My family has always been supportive, putting up with my frequent research trips and endless hours at the computer screen. My children, now in their twenties, are used to a mother who loves to write books, and my husband continues to encourage me in this passion. My sister, who is herself a transnational activist, has tried to keep me from being too confined to the ivory tower in my work. To all of them, without whom I could not keep writing, I am enormously grateful.

Wellesley, MA
December 2004

Introduction: Culture and Transnationalism

The transnational circulation of people and ideas is transforming the world we live in, but grasping its full complexity is extraordinarily difficult. To do so, it is essential to focus on specific places where transnational flows are happening. The international human rights movement against violence to women provides a valuable site for understanding how new categories of meaning emerge and are applied to social practices around the world. These meanings are often enthusiastically appropriated by regional, national, and local social movements and used to criticize everyday practices of violence. In order for human rights ideas to be effective, however, they need to be translated into local terms and situated within local contexts of power and meaning. They need, in other words, to be remade in the vernacular. How does this happen? Do people in local communities reframe human rights ideas to fit into their system of cultural meanings? Do they resist ideas that seem unfamiliar? Examining this process is crucial to understanding the way human rights act in the contemporary world.

Remaking human rights in the vernacular is difficult. Local communities often conceive of social justice in quite different terms from human rights activists. They generally lack knowledge of relevant documents and provisions of the human rights system. Global human rights reformers, on the other hand, are typically rooted in a transnational legal culture remote from the myriad local social situations in which human rights are violated. Nevertheless, global human rights law has become an important resource for local social movements.

This book explores how global law is translated into the vernacular, highlighting the role of activists who serve as intermediaries between different sets of cultural understandings of gender, violence, and justice.

Gender violence provides an ideal issue for examining this process. As a human rights violation, gender violence is a relative newcomer, but since the 1990s it has become the centerpiece of women's human rights. Strenuous activism by nongovernmental organizations (NGOs) along with a series of major world conferences on women in the 1980s and 1990s defined violence against women as a human rights violation. But establishing women's rights as human rights is still an uphill struggle. Because violence against women refers to bodily injury as do other human rights violations such as torture, it is a relatively straightforward violation. Like torture, it is about injury, pain, and death. But in many parts of the world it appears to be an everyday, normal problem rather than a violation of human rights. Moreover, because gender violence is deeply embedded in systems of kinship, religion, warfare, and nationalism, its prevention requires major social changes in communities, families, and nations. Powerful local groups often resist these changes.

The relevance of human rights for the campaign against violence toward women has taken on new importance as human rights have become the major global approach to social justice. Since the 1980s, human rights concepts have gained increasing international credibility and support at the same time as a growing body of treaties and resolutions have strengthened their international legal basis. The global human rights system is now deeply transnational, no longer rooted exclusively in the West. It takes place in global settings with representatives from nations and NGOs around the world. Activists from many countries enthusiastically adopt this language and translate it for grassroots people. Vulnerable people take up human rights ideas in a wide variety of local contexts because they offer hope to subordinated groups. An Indo-Fijian lawyer told me, for example, that she had experienced racism and discrimination in Fiji and in New Zealand and only the international human rights system gave her the tools and consciousness to fight back. In the New Territories of Hong Kong, women were denied the right to inherit property under a law passed by the British colonial government and legitimated as ancient Chinese custom. The international human rights language of women's rights and sex discrimination proved critical to overturning this legislation.

Yet the idea that everyday violence against women is a human rights violation has not been easy to establish, nor has it moved readily from transnational to local settings. There are fissures between the global settings where human rights ideas are codified into documents and the local communities where the subjects of these rights live and work. Human rights ideas, embedded in cultural assumptions about the nature of the person, the community, and the state, do not translate easily from one setting to another. If human rights ideas are to have an impact, they need to become part of the consciousness of ordinary people around the world. Considerable research on law and everyday social life shows that law's power to shape society depends not on punishment alone but on becoming embedded in everyday social practices, shaping the rules people carry in their heads (e.g., Merry 1990; Sarat and Kearns 1993; Ewick and Silbey 1998). Yet, there is a great distance between the global sites where these ideas are formulated and the specific situations in which they are deployed. We know relatively little about how individuals in various social and cultural contexts come to see themselves in terms of human rights.

Nor do ideas and approaches move readily the other way, from local to global settings. Global sites are a bricolage of issues and ideas brought to the table by national actors. But transnational actors, and even some national elites, are often uninterested in local social practices or too busy to understand them in their complicated contexts. Discussions in transnational settings rarely deal with local situations in context. There is an inevitable tension between general principles and particular situations. Transnational reformers must adhere to a set of standards that apply to all societies if they are to gain legitimacy. Moreover, they have neither the time nor the desire to tailor these standards to the particularities of each individual country, ethnic group, or regional situation. National and local actors often feel frustrated at the lack of attention to their individual situations.

The division between transnational elites and local actors is based less on culture or tradition than on tensions between a transnational community that envisions a unified modernity and national and local actors for whom particular histories and contexts are important. Intermediaries such as NGO and social movement activists play a critical role in interpreting the cultural world of transnational modernity for local claimants. They appropriate, translate, and remake transnational discourses into the vernacular. At the same time, they take local stories and frame them in national and international human rights language. Activists often participate in two cultural spheres at the same time, translating between them with a kind of double consciousness.

This book examines the interface between global and local activism, showing how ideas about violence against women as a human rights violation are produced in global conferences in New York and Geneva and appropriated in local community centers in Hawai'i, Delhi, Beijing, Fiji, and Hong Kong. It shows the power of human rights ideas for transnational and local social movements and their contribution to gradually rethinking gender inequality around the world. It explains how human rights create a political space for reform using a language legitimated by a global consensus on standards. But this political space comes with a price. Human rights promote ideas of individual autonomy, equality, choice, and secularism even when these ideas differ from prevailing cultural norms and practices. Human rights ideas displace alternative visions of social justice that are less individualistic and more focused on communities and responsibilities, possibly contributing to the cultural homogenization of local communities. The localization of human rights is part of the vastly unequal global distribution of power and resources that channels how ideas develop in global settings and are picked up or rejected in local places.

I thought about these questions as I sat in the grand conference room of the United Nations in New York listening to the delegation from Fiji present its first report to the committee monitoring the Convention on the Elimination of All Forms of Discrimination against Women, or CEDAW. Government and NGO representatives had flown halfway around the world for this hearing. It was January 2002 and they found it chilly. As the government delegation presented its report to the CEDAW monitoring committee, made up of 23 experts on gender issues from around the world, some tension developed over a Fijian practice called *bulubulu,* a traditional village custom for reconciling differences. The conflict illustrated for me the challenges of communicating across the fault line separating the transnational human rights community from local and national spaces. The Fiji country report noted that bulubulu was being used to take rape cases out of court. The committee asked the government delegation when they were going to eliminate this custom. The government minister told me later that bulubulu was essential to Fijian village life and could not be given up. At first I was startled by this defense of bulubulu, but after reading the report again and doing some research in Fiji, I realized that the concern expressed in the report was not about the custom itself but about how its use undermined the legal process. The problem suddenly seemed more complicated than just eliminating the custom. Why did the experts assume that the custom itself was the problem rather than its application to court cases? And why did they focus on culture and religion rather than economic or political conditions that might affect the way the custom functions?

After watching many CEDAW hearings, I decided that the experts concluded that the custom was the problem because they see "customs" as harmful practices rooted in traditional culture. The experts do not have the time to investigate when and how customs such as bulubulu are better able to protect women from rape than the courts or how these customs intersect with state legal systems in new ways. Their task is to apply the law of the Convention. There is a general assumption that problems such as violence against women are the responsibility of the state and that local culture is an excuse for noncompliance. The divide between transnational, national, and local activists is exacerbated by the various ways culture is defined.

There are several conundrums in applying human rights to local places. First, human rights law is committed to setting universal standards using legal rationality, yet this stance impedes adapting those standards to the particulars of local context. This perspective explains why local conditions often seem irrelevant to global debates. Second, human rights ideas are more readily adopted if they are packaged in familiar terms, but they are more transformative if they challenge existing assumptions about power and relationships. Activists who use human rights for local social movements face a paradox. Rights need to be presented in local cultural terms in order to be persuasive, but they must challenge existing relations of power in order to be effective. Third, to have local impact, human rights ideas need to be framed in terms of local values and images, but in order to receive funding, a wider audience, and international legitimacy, they have to be framed in terms of transnational rights principles. Fourth, to promote individual rights–consciousness, institutions have to implement rights effectively. However, if there is little rights consciousness, there will be less pressure on institutions to take rights seriously.

Fifth, the human rights system challenges states' authority over their citizens at the same time as it reinforces states' power. In some ways, the emergence of the human rights system has weakened state sovereignty. In the aftermath of the Holocaust, states are no longer trusted by the international community to govern their own citizens without international oversight. On the other hand, the focus of much human rights activism is the state. Sometimes the state is the human rights violator, when it subjects its citizens to torture or extrajudicial killings, for example. Ironically it is also the agent for carrying out human rights reforms in many cases. Social and economic rights, such as the right to development or the right to adequate housing, require state action, as does the provision of many civil and political rights. Campaigns against sex trafficking encourage increasing policing of borders and control of immigration. Thus, human rights activism ends up demanding more state regulation and services.

The first part of this book examines UN deliberations and the way the texts of human rights law are formed. It describes how a global set of cultural understandings about gender, violence, and the family emerge from major world conferences, UN Commission meetings, special inquiry procedures, and the work of treaty bodies that supervise human rights conventions. The second part explores the extent to which this international discourse is appropriated in a variety of national contexts. The countries I examine differ enormously in size and in many other features. All participate in the UN system in some way; all but the United States have ratified CEDAW; and all have local feminist movements demanding change. But differences in history, colonial experience, NGO activism, governmental structure, and resources have an enormous impact on how international ideas and regulations are adopted. I examine how programs and laws dealing with violence against women are transplanted from one society to another and how international documents concerning violence against women are localized. This is a comparative study of a transnational movement and its legal basis rather than an in-depth examination of a single country. There are good ethnographic studies of the local adoption of global human rights (e.g., Speed and Collier 2000; Goodale 2002; Tate 2005); here I trace the links between global production and local appropriation. It examines how human rights law works in practice.

Theorizing the Global-Local Interface

The global-local divide is often conceptualized as the opposition between rights and culture, or even civilization and culture. Those who resist human rights often claim to be defending culture. For example, male lineage heads in the rural New Territories of Hong Kong claimed that giving women rights to inherit land would destroy the social fabric. Fijian politicians worried that restricting the use of bulubulu might undermine Fijian culture. However, as considerable work within anthropology and sociology has demonstrated, these arguments depend on a very narrow understanding of culture and the political misuse of this concept (see especially Wilson 1996; Cowan, Dembour, and Wilson 2001: 6–7; An-Naʿim and Hammond 2002: 13–14). Amartya Sen provides an eloquent critique of this notion of culture in his advocacy of a human rights approach to development (1999: 240–46). As Cowan, Dembour, and Wilson point out, a more flexible and contested model of culture provides a better way of understanding the practice of human rights both in global sites such as international meetings and local sites where these ideas are picked up and used by social movements and nongovernmental organizations (2001: 13–14).

Even as anthropologists and others have repudiated the idea of culture as a consensual, interconnected system of beliefs and values, the idea has taken on new life in the public sphere, particularly with reference to the global South.

For example, in 2002, I was interviewed by a local radio station about an incident in Pakistan that resulted in the gang rape of a young woman, an assault apparently authorized by a local tribal council. The interviewer, who was looking for someone to speak on the radio show, wanted to know if I was willing to defend the council's actions. I explained that I considered this an inexcusable act, that many Pakistani women's rights and human rights groups and the Pakistani press had condemned the rape, and that it was connected to local political struggles. The woman was of a subordinate group in the village and attacked by members of the dominant landowning group. I said it should not be seen as an expression of Pakistani "culture." Indeed, it was the local imam, an Islamic religious leader, who talked about the incident in his Friday sermon and made it known to the world, condemning the actions as unfitting for a *panchayat* (tribal council) and for Islam.[1]

The interviewer was distressed. She wanted me to defend the value of respecting Pakistani culture at all costs, despite the sentence of rape. When I told her that I could not do that, she wanted to know if I knew of any other anthropologists who would. I could think of none, but I began to wonder what she thought about anthropologists and their views of culture. She apparently assumed that anthropologists made no moral judgments about "cultures" and failed to recognize the contestation and changes taking place within contemporary local communities around the world. Apparently cultures have no contact with the expansion of capitalism, the arming of various groups by transnational superpowers using them for proxy wars, or the cultural possibilities of human rights as an emancipatory discourse. I found this interviewer's view of culture wrong-headed and her opinion of anthropology discouraging.

But she was clearly reflecting a wider public opinion. Her view was echoed by US and UK news coverage of the event. The Omaha *World Herald* editorialized that "Pakistan may be an ally of the United States in the fight against terrorism, but Americans should have no illusions about how deeply into rural and backward portions of the nation the veneer of civilized law and order extends. . . . This abhorrent action may make it easier to understand how Islamic militants, even terrorists, can sprout and grow in some parts of the country" (2002: 68). A journalist in London pointed out that the UK press did not report any surprise in Pakistan over the event, in contrast to the outrage it described in Belgium when 19 men raped or abused an 11-year-old child (Shamsie 2002: 7). She also reports being asked to discuss the case on a radio show and explain "the culture behind it." She rejected the idea that Pakistan is a nation with a culture of rape that does nothing until international human rights groups take up the case. Instead, she sees Pakistan as a country in which there is a grim struggle

8

between progressive factions and those who want to return to more repressive gender regimes. The Pakistani press did express a great deal of outrage about the incident. Fourteen men were arrested soon after the rape, quickly tried in an antiterrorist court, and six were sentenced to death only nine weeks after the incident (*Press Trust of India,* Sept. 1, 2002), although they were released in 2005. The Minister for Women visited the remote village and gave a substantial check to the affected family (*Press Trust of India,* July 5, 2002.)

To view this incident as symptomatic of Pakistani culture is analogous to seeing the Enron thefts as characteristic of American culture. When corporate executives in the United States steal millions of dollars through accounting fraud, we do not criticize American culture as a whole. We recognize that these actions come from the greed of a few along with sloppy institutional arrangements that allow them to get away with it. Similarly, the actions of a single tribal council in Pakistan do not characterize the entire country, as if it were a homogeneous entity. Although Pakistan and many of its communities do have practices and laws that subordinate women and subject them to violence, these are neither universal nor uncontested. Pakistan as a "culture" can be indicted by this particular council's authorization of rape only if culture is understood as a homogenous entity whose rules evoke universal compliance. Despite widespread critiques (see Wilson 1996; Walley 1997; Sen 1999; Cowan, Dembour, and Wilson 2001; An-Naʿim and Hammond 2002; Weissman 2004), this essentialized concept of culture remains a powerful idea within popular culture.

An essentialized understanding of culture contributed to the universalism-relativism debate of the 1990s. This debate focused on the clash between maintaining global standards of social justice and respecting local cultural practices (see Renteln 1988, 1990; An-Naʿim 1990; Leary 1990; Howard 1995; Pollis 1996; Preis 1996; Hatch 1997; Messer 1997; Turner 1997; Zechenter 1997; Bauer and Bell 1999; Merry 2001b; Donnelley 2003). Universalists insisted that their principles applied to all cultures while relativists argued that tolerance of cultural difference trumped universal standards (itself a universalistic claim, of course). When universalists criticized relativists as moral nihilists, they assumed that relativists accepted all the practices of a society, including the oppression of women and other vulnerable groups. When relativists asserted tolerance for difference, they usually defended cultures as wholes. Relativists focused on the dilemmas of people living in isolated villages rather than those of people living in urban areas or facing war, displacement, or economic change. They defended the isolated, homogeneous, and consensual society, not the way of life of the urban poor or displaced refugees. Yet, relatively few communities live in such isolation; at a minimum most face intrusions by outsiders eager to seize their land and resources. One legacy of this view that a culture must be accepted in total is a reluctance to challenge any practices. Within anthropology, Nancy Scheper-Hughes worries about the troubling passivity of anthropologists in the face of human rights violations and abuses based on a cultural relativism that slides into moral relativism (1995: 410).

Seeing culture as contested and as a mode of legitimating claims to power and authority dramatically shifts the way we understand the universalism-relativism debate (see further Cowan, Dembour, and Wilson 2001: 4–15). It undermines those who resist changes that would benefit weaker groups in the name of preserving "culture," and it encourages human rights activists to pay attention to local cultural practices. This view of culture emphasizes that culture is hybrid and porous and that the pervasive struggles over cultural values within local communities are competitions over power. More recent anthropological scholarship explores processes by which human rights ideas are mobilized locally, adapted, and transformed and, in turn, how they shape local political struggles. As Cowan, Dembour, and Wilson point out, "Rather than seeing universalism and cultural relativism as alternatives which one must choose, once and for all, one should see the tension between the positions as part of the continuous process of negotiating ever-changing and interrelated global and local norms" (2001: 6). Culture in this sense does not serve as a barrier to human rights mobilization but as a context that defines relationships and meanings and constructs the possibilities of action.

Seeing culture as open to change emphasizes struggles over cultural values within local communities and encourages attention to local cultural practices as resources for change. An example from Australia illustrates this complex understanding of culture. At a conference on culture and violence against women held in Sydney, Australia in 2002, representatives from an Australian Aboriginal group dealing with violence against women displayed a brochure they had developed for battered women that was richly decorated with the swirls and spots of Aboriginal art. They drew on the artistic traditions of Aboriginal peoples to tailor information about how to seek help for battering in a way that might appeal to other Aboriginal women. But this is not the only way to localize imported practices. Representatives from another Aboriginal group described their efforts to protect young Aboriginal men from harassment in shopping malls in Sydney. They had developed a tee shirt. The back of the tee shirt listed the legal rights of people in public spaces while the front displayed several stylized faces, some apparently Aboriginal, and the phrase, "It's public space, Get Outta My Face" (presentation from Wirringa Baiya/Tranby Aboriginal Cooperative College, Feb. 22, 2002, Sydney). As the Aboriginal presenter pointed out, "get outta my face" is a phrase commonly used by young Aboriginal people and therefore the one the young people chose for the tee shirt. The words and images were not those of Aboriginal art but of African Americans. The young people, facing racism in Australia, chose a phrase from the transnational language of resistance to racism. They localized their claims to rights with transnational images. This example shows the creativity and flexibility of culture in its mobilization by local activists. Appropriating signs and sentiments is fundamental to the way culture works within contemporary globalization.

Moreover, local cultural practices are far more fluid and open to change than the essentialized model suggests. For example, Nyamu-Musembi shows how local norms and practices in Kenya offer opportunities as well as barriers to gender equality and that the production of local custom is a dynamic and changing process, even when it specifies inheritance practices (2002: 133–34). She concludes, "a genuine engagement with practice at the local level is powerful in dislodging both the abolitionist imagination of the local as the repository of unchanging patriarchal values and the defensive relativist portrayal of local norms as bounded, immutable, and well settled" (2002: 145). Abdullah's analysis of women's groups in Nigeria shows how over time they change their approaches to women's rights, including their willingness to invoke human rights, depending on the shift from military to civilian government, economic crises, and the growth of religious fundamentalism (2002). These studies present a complex and fluid understanding of culture.

Deconstructing Culture

Although culture is a term on everyone's lips, people rarely talk about what they mean by it. The term has many meanings in the contemporary world. It is often seen as the basis of national, ethnic, or religious identities. Culture is sometimes romanticized as the opposite of globalization, resolutely local and distinct. It sometimes refers to rural villages and minority communities where life is understood to be governed by fixed traditions. Within white settler states such as the United States and Canada, it offers an apparently benign way of describing immigrant minorities, racializing these populations while appearing to describe differences in terms of values and beliefs (Razack 1998, 2004; Volpp 2000). In international human rights meetings, culture often refers to traditions and customs: ways of doing things that are justified by their roots in the past. There is a whiff of the notion of the primitive about this usage of the term culture. It is not what modern urbanites do but what governs life in the countryside. As I observed UN meetings, I found that transnational elites often located culture "out there" in villages and rural areas rather than "in here" in their offices and conference rooms. Culture more often describes the developing world than the developed one. Culture was often juxtaposed to civilization during the civilizing mission of imperialism, and this history has left a legacy in contemporary thinking.[2]

Culture is also celebrated as heritage. A report from a meeting of the Regional Office of South Asia of UNICEF in 1999 reflects this complicated set of meanings. The report says that South Asia has a vibrant women's movement with networks and a considerable body of knowledge. But there is a need to change belief systems and modes of interaction and to recognize and promote basic rights. "Often cultural traditions provide justifications to preserve discriminatory practices. UNICEF must always review and challenge such practices that reinforce inequity based on gender, class and caste. Such a position should not be construed as a rejection of the richness and diversity of age-old cultural heritage in the region" (UNICEF 1999: 5–6). There is a dual voice that runs through this document as well as others: violence against women is a product of traditional cultural practices, which must be changed, but cultural heritage is something to treasure.

There is a critical need for conceptual clarification of culture in human rights practice. Insofar as human rights relies on an essentialized model of culture, it does not take advantage of the potential of local cultural practices for change. Practices labeled harmful and traditional are rarely viewed as part of wider systems of kinship and community, yet they are deeply embedded in patterns of family and religion. A more dynamic understanding of culture foregrounds the importance of translators to the human rights process and the possibilities for change in local cultural practices.

Anthropologists have spent the past century theorizing culture and how it changes. This framework defines culture as historically produced in particular locations under the influence of local, national, and global forces and events. Cultures consist of repertoires of ideas and practices that are not homogeneous but continually changing because of contradictions among them or because new ideas and institutions are adopted by members. They typically incorporate contested values and practices. Cultures are not contained within stable borders but are open to new ideas and permeable to influences from other cultural systems, although not all borders are equally porous. Cultural discourses legitimate or challenge authority and justify relations of power.

Of the myriad ways culture is imagined in transnational human rights discussions, two of the most common ones reflect an essentialized concept of culture. After describing these views, I show how an anthropological conception of culture offers a valuable framework for understanding the historical and contextual features of specific social arrangements and the possibilities for change within local communities.

CULTURE AS TRADITION

Within the discourse of human rights activism, culture is often used as a synonym for tradition. Labeling a culture as traditional evokes an evolutionary vision of change from a primitive form to something like civilization. In the evolutionary model, all cultures are positioned on a continuum from primitive to modern. Variations are exclusively temporal. So-called traditional societies are at an earlier evolutionary stage than modern ones, which are more evolved and more civilized. Culture in this sense is not used to describe the affluent countries of the global North but the poor countries of the global South, particularly isolated and rural areas. When it does appear in discussions of European or North American countries, it refers to the ways of life of immigrant communities and/or racial minorities (see Razack 1998; Volpp 2000). In the colonial era, this definition of culture was used to describe backward peoples who were to be educated and civilized by Christianity, wage labor, and formal education.

Although some human rights activists refer to "good" cultural practices and "harmful" cultural practices and a few feminist scholars examine cultural practices that protect women from violence (Green 1999), many who write about women's right to protection from violence identify culture and tradition as the source of the problem (Bunch 1990, 1997; Cook 1993, 1994a). A concern about traditional harmful practices and the role of culture in subordinating women is enshrined in the major documents concerning women's rights, such as the Convention on the Elimination of All Forms of Discrimination against Women (CEDAW). Using these documents, the human rights process seeks to replace cultural practices that are discriminatory with other cultural practices rooted in modern ideas of gender equality. Thus, like the colonial state, they seek to move ethnically defined subjects into the realm of rights-bearing modernity (see Comaroff and Comaroff 1997; Comaroff 1998). This effort sometimes demonizes culture as it seeks to save individuals from its oppressive effects.

Female genital cutting (also called female genital mutilation) is the poster child for this understanding of culture. There has been an enormous international effort to eliminate this practice over the last two decades (see Gunning 1991–92, 1999; Walley 1997; Cerna and Wallace 1999; Boyle 2002). At least since 1958, when the World Health Organization at the request of the UN Economic and Social Council carried out a study of ritual operations, this practice has been the subject of international scrutiny.[3] It is typically described as a "harmful traditional practice" or a "harmful cultural practice."

Traditions, however, are often newly created for political purposes or borrowed from others, as Hobsbawm and Ranger showed in their study of the elaboration of British royal ceremonies in colonial Africa (1983). They may take on symbolic roles of defining identity and community, particularly in modern societies. Especially in postcolonial societies, what is called tradition is located within modernity and created by it (Menon 2000: 76). Modernity defines what counts as tradition. Although the language of civilization is rarely articulated in human rights discussions or documents, notions of what it means to be a civilized nation linger, particularly in the field of international law. Nineteenth-century narratives of evolution and concepts of racial difference have been smuggled into prevailing theoretical models by maintaining the binary distinction between tradition and modernity. These terms subtly juxtapose modernity and savagery and locate culture in the domain of the latter and civilization in the former.

CULTURE AS NATIONAL ESSENCE

A second common understanding of culture is as national essence or identity. This concept of culture grows out of the German romantic tradition of the nineteenth century. Confronted with the claims to universal civilization of England and France, Germans began to draw a distinction between the external trappings of civilization and the inward, spiritual reality of culture (Kuper 1999b: 25–26). German romantics asserted the importance of a distinct culture, or *Kultur,* which formed the spiritual essence of their society. Each people, or *Volk,* has its own history and culture that expresses its genius. This includes its language, its laws, and its religion. The cosmopolitan elite corrupts it, while foreign technological and material values undermine it. The peasantry holds the purest *Volksgeist,* or culture. The German conception reflected a nationalist movement seeking to unite the Germans as a culturally and ethnically similar people (Kuper 1999b: 8).[4] Norbert Elias traces the source of the Germanic concept of Kultur to Germany's nineteenth-century opposition to the civilizational claims of England and France (1978 [1939]: 3–9). France and England thought that their distinctive social and cultural patterns should be broadcast globally, to become the standard for the world. While Kultur emphasizes national distinctiveness, civilization emphasizes what is common to all human beings: "It expresses the self-assurance of peoples whose national boundaries and national identity have for centuries been so fully established that they have ceased to be the subject of any particular discussion, peoples which have long expanded outside their borders and colonized beyond them" (Elias 1978 [1939]: 5). Civilization encouraged a continual expansion of empire, while Kultur fostered national self-definition and a demarcation of difference from other groups.[5]

Culture as national essence is fundamental to claims to indigenous sovereignty and ethnonationalism, often in resistance to human rights. In 1993, when Lee Kuan Yew of Singapore claimed that human rights failed to incorporate Asian values, he drew on this understanding of culture. With support from several other Asian leaders, he argued that Asian values differed from Western conceptions of human rights (see Bauer and Bell 1999: 3–23; Sen 1999).[6] In some ways, the Asian values argument replays the German romantic resistance to French and English claims to civilization. Indeed, one critic of the Asian values argument notes that it falls into Orientalist notions of a communitarian East, with communal values, and an individualistic West (Tatsuo 1999).

Although the Asian values argument is less often articulated now, it represents one of many ways that leaders assert that human rights violate the fundamental cultural principles of a nation or a religion and therefore cannot be adopted (see Chanock 2002: 41). Women's rights are often opposed by those who claim to defend culture. Challenging women's subordinate position in the family or the workplace threatens to disrupt a wide range of patriarchal privileges. Those who stand to lose will often argue that providing these rights will cause social chaos and disturb established hierarchies. Thinking of culture as national essence provides governments with an excuse not to intervene more energetically to protect human rights since they can defend their resistance as the protection of the national identity. As a representative from Sweden asked at the 2001 meeting of the UN Commission on the Status of Women, "Cultural diversity is a treasure of the modern world, but how can we avoid using these arguments to justify human rights violations of women and girls?" (see Nagengast and Turner 1997; Zechenter 1997). And as the prominent African women's activist Florence Butegwa observes, "African women and men need to join others who actively wonder and ask why it is only when women want to bring about change for their own benefit do culture and custom become sacred and unchangeable" (2002: 123).

CULTURE AS CONTENTIOUS

The prevailing understanding of culture within contemporary anthropology envisions a far more fluid and changing set of values and practices than either of these conceptions. Over the last two decades, anthropology has elaborated a conception of culture as unbounded, contested, and connected to relations of power, as the product of historical influences rather than evolutionary change. Cultural practices must be understood in context, so that their meaning and impact change as their context shifts. Comaroff and Comaroff suggest interrogating the "production, in imaginative and material practice, of those compound political, economic, and cultural forms by means of which human beings create community and locality and identity, especially on evanescent terrains; by means of which, in the face of material and moral constraint, they fabricate social realities and power relations and impose themselves on their lived environments; by means of which space and time are made and remade, and the boundaries of the local and the global are actualized" (1999: 295). This conception emphasizes the active making of culture, society, and institutions and the grounding of this action in specific places and moments. Cultures consist not only of beliefs and values but also practices, habits, and commonsensical ways of doing things. They include institutional arrangements, political structures, and legal regulations. As institutions such as laws and policing change so do beliefs, values, and practices. Cultures are not homogeneous and "pure" but produced through hybridization or creolization.

The way culture is conceptualized determines how social change is imagined. If culture is fixed and unchanging, it is simply a barrier that needs to be removed through education. If culture is a set of practices and meanings shaped by institutional contexts, it is both malleable and embedded in structures of power. These different perspectives on culture affect policies concerning women. For example, in Uruguay's country report to the committee monitoring the Women's Convention, the government expressed regret that more women were not involved in politics but blamed cultural traditions, women's involvement in domestic tasks, and the differences in wages by gender. In contrast, facing the same absence of women politicians, Denmark offered funds to offset babysitting expenses when women attended meetings (CEDAWC/DEN/5, 3 July 2000: 16). In the first case, the barrier to change is theorized as cultural tradition; in the second case, as institutional arrangements of child care. The first model sees culture as fixed; the second assumes that the meanings of gender will change as institutional and legal arrangements change.

When a group's failure to abide by human rights principles is blamed on its "traditional culture," this ignores the complex and dynamic nature of culture. Organizations working at the grassroots are far more aware of the importance of local cultural practices as a resource than are the transnational elites meeting at global conferences. Local norms can be paths to change as well as barriers, as Nyamu-Musembi demonstrates in her study of women's property rights in Kenya (2002). Local actors creatively adopt human rights ideas, sometimes reshaping local social relationships. For example, Jane Cowan shows how the use of a human rights framework by Greeks living in Macedonia promoted the formation of a minority Greek identity (2001).

Culture defined only as tradition or as national essence implies that villages are full of culture but that there is no culture in the conference halls of New York and Geneva. Yet, culture is as important in shaping human rights conferences as it is in structuring village mortuary rituals. Thinking of those peoples formerly labeled "backward" as the only bearers of culture neglects the centrality of culture to the practice of human rights. UN meetings are deeply shaped by a culture of transnational modernity, one that specifies procedures for collaborative decision-making, conceptions of global social justice, and definitions of gender roles. Human rights law is itself primarily a cultural system. Its limited enforcement mechanisms mean that the impact of human rights law is a matter of persuasion rather than force, of cultural transformation rather than coercive change. Its documents create new cultural frameworks for conceptualizing social justice. It is ironic that the human rights system tends to promote its new cultural vision through a critique of culture.

WHO SPEAKS FOR CULTURE?

One way of disentangling the meanings of culture is to consider who speaks for a "culture" in international forums, national debates, and village forums. Those who worry about enhancing the cultural legitimacy of the international human rights system, such as Abdullahi An-Naʿim, advocate working with cultural insiders. With reference to promoting reforms in Islamic countries, he notes that "It is primarily the task of internal actors, supported and encouraged by external allies, to promote and sustain the necessary degree of official commitment and popular political support for a program for changing Shariʾa laws" (1994: 184). He argues that it is only those within the society or culture who can be fully persuasive. But what does it mean to be an "internal actor?" Is there a clear boundary between who is inside and outside a culture? In practice, these boundaries are fluid and shifting. Is a person born in one country who has been educated and works in another country an insider in the nation of his or her birth? Does the person born in one country who has spent her life living in another have less right to speak in her adopted country? The boundaries around cultures are never clear and unambiguous.

I became aware of this issue when I listened to a Nigerian woman describe widowhood rituals in Nigeria as human rights violations at the UN Human

Rights Commission in 2001. Speaking in the elegant conference hall of a UN building nestled among mountains in Geneva, she was part of a panel of non-governmental activists from an international human rights organization. She described the plight of widows in Nigeria and the humiliations widowhood rituals inflicted on women. Widows were forced to marry their dead husband's brother, blamed for their husband's death, and forced to undergo ordeals to determine their responsibility, such as drinking the water used to wash the corpse. They were forced to stay in a room alone and sit on ashes, expected to wear tattered clothes, fed on a broken plate, and sometimes prohibited from looking at the person who brings their food. Widows were expected to cry so loudly that their wails were audible to people outside the compound and were taunted by their in-laws if they failed. A widow may no longer be able to work the land she was given by her husband's family; she may not be supported by her husband's family; and she may lose her children. These practices are common mostly in rural areas, she said, and in the southern part of the country. She pointed out that women are equal to men in the Nigerian constitution but are not treated that way. She ended by observing that many NGOs in Nigeria are working hard to criticize the government and to train people in their rights because "this widowhood thing is so bad."[7]

Although the denial of access to a woman's lands and children after her husband's death was very troubling, I found myself surprised by this broad condemnation of rituals and cultural practices. As an anthropologist, I had come to value respect for cultural difference. As a student of colonialism, I found critiques of customs and rituals a familiar repeat of imperial arguments. What, I thought, had happened to the commitment to treat cultural differences with respect? Cultural relativism as an ethical stance was critically important to anthropologists in the early twentieth century as they fought against the colonial civilizing mission. Yet, here was a highly educated member of Nigerian society voicing the kinds of criticisms of cultural practices familiar from colonial rhetoric. I wondered again about the way the concept of culture was being deployed in human rights discourse and about practices of cultural representation in international forums. For whom did she speak? Did all the women in these villages condemn these practices? Were they applied equally to all widows? Were all villages the same? If culture were not seen as a consensual system determining all behavior but instead a repertoire of argument that allowed powerful people to control weaker ones, would that make a difference? Is there an intractable contradiction between respecting cultural difference and protecting vulnerable groups such as widows?

After the meeting, I sought out the speaker to ask her about her work. She

18

said that she was concerned with several violations of women's human rights, of which widowhood rituals were only one, but that they were a great problem for some women. They were particularly difficult for urban educated women like her. She is a lawyer, fluent in English, and living in a major urban center. She is employed by a US-based human rights NGO. When women in her class are widowed, they find themselves journeying to the village of their husbands where they are subjected to rituals by relatives who may not have liked the woman or the way she treated the family while her husband was alive. Village women, she told me, do not really mind these rituals.

This incident made me wonder who is an insider who can speak for a culture in international settings. In Geneva, this woman was speaking for all Nigerian women. For some in the audience, she probably represented all African women. Yet, there is a vast diversity among Nigerian women on the basis of education, social class, and language as well as region and religion. Widowhood clearly affects women in different social positions differently. But in the context of an international setting and universal principles, acknowledging such complexity would diminish the political impact of her statement. It is not that she claimed to speak for all Nigerian women, of course, but that she was positioned in the international forum as a spokesperson for her country and as representing the experiences and suffering of all Nigerian women. Like other postcolonial elites, she is viewed internationally as speaking for a national culture despite her own positioning within particular social class and ethnic frameworks.

Moreover, by telling the horrors of widowhood rituals as some experience them while implying that all Nigerian women experience them the same way, she is able to tell a more gripping story. Perhaps she assumed that the horrors of the rituals were more persuasive than the disabilities of the inheritance system, even though concerns about property rights and marriage choices after widowhood are issues of major concern for African feminists (Butegwa 2002; Nizioki 2002). Instead of offering a story about how cultural practices are used in struggles over class, education, urban mobility, and ruptures in kinship obligations, she told a story about the oppression of culture.

The issue of representation appears over and over in international forums. NGOs working in various countries hold panels in which the activists speak for their countries, whether about women and poverty, trafficking, or customs such as female genital cutting. The setting reinforces the idea that they are speaking for national "cultures" and that these national cultures are homogeneous. Thus, the holistic image of culture is smuggled into international discussions even as participants themselves recognize the dangers of overgeneralization. Just as the concept of culture needs to be interrogated and destabilized, so do assumptions about who speaks for culture.

Global Cultural Processes

Understanding the global-local interface requires attention to transnational cultural flows and their relationship to local cultural spaces (see Hannerz 1992; Sassen 1994, 1996, 1998; Appadurai 1996, 2001; Gupta and Ferguson 1997; Ong 1999). I distinguish three forms of global cultural flow that take place across and within global and local spaces. These processes are fundamental to the global production and local appropriation of human rights.

The first is *transnational consensus building.* This describes the global production of documents and resolutions that define human rights and social justice: major treaty conventions, policy documents that come out of global conferences, and resolutions and declarations of the UN General Assembly and its commissions such as the Commission on the Status of Women and the Human Rights Commission. In this process, representatives of states and civil society negotiate a consensus across differences in ideology, politics, and cultural practices. This requires a protracted and often excruciating debate about wording and sentence structure, but the result is a document legitimated by its unified transnational support. Debate circles around word choice rather than social science evidence. As representatives from governments work together over the years, a consensus on procedure emerges as well as some agreement on substance. While the negotiation process is often arcane and frustrating, it is amazing that national representatives who hold vastly different ideas about women's place in society talk together at all and reach some agreement. Chapter 2 describes this process in detail based on several international conferences I observed in the early 2000s.[8] Chapter 3 considers how one of these global documents, CEDAW, is actually implemented. Chapter 4 explores tensions between global legal standards and more local, contextualized understandings through a case study of Indian personal laws and Fijian reconciliation processes.

The second form of cultural flow is *transnational program transplants.* Social service programs and legal innovations created in one society are transplanted into another. All five countries I studied adopted the same repertoire of interventions more or less simultaneously, sometime between the mid 1980s and early 1990s. In addition to promoting counseling services and new laws for domestic violence and rape, they conducted surveys on the incidence of domestic violence and developed public education programs. Ironically, despite an interest in suiting programs to local contexts, in practice these repertoires were quite similar. Although activists tailored the programs to some extent, they were largely shaped by an international discourse of feminism and social work. Most of the activists who transplanted programs were connected to an international network that shares ideas through academic and professional research and publications, international conferences, and academic and activist meetings. For example, all of the transplanted programs saw gender violence as learned behavior and socially caused, not an expression of innate evil or natural male behavior. Chapter 5 compares the transplantation process in these five places.

The third cultural flow is the *localization of transnational knowledge* by national and local actors who participate in transnational events and bring home what they learn. These are the key players navigating the divide between transnational actors and local activists. NGO representatives, government representatives, movement leaders, and academics attend the large and vibrant NGO sessions that take place around the major UN conferences and commission meetings. They also attend international conferences on violence against women.[9] These events are important for information exchange and learning. Although NGO participation in such events is typically described as networking (see Keck and Sikkink 1998; Riles 2001), a central concern of participants is education and skills acquisition. These events take place in international settings but focus on providing knowledge from one local place to another. Individuals who move between these settings provide transnational knowledge to local and national activists and contribute local knowledge to transnational settings. They provide a critical link in localizing human rights. Chapter 6 presents two case studies that focus on the way local, poor, and relatively immobile women come to take on human rights ideas and the role of intermediary activists in facilitating this translation.

The UN creates opportunities for these exchanges by staging events at which information flows take place. For example, the periodic reports to CEDAW require consultation between government ministers and NGOs, whereas the global conferences and their planning meetings offer both governments and NGOs the chance to prepare reports collaboratively and for NGOs to lobby governments. The investigative activities of UN special rapporteurs and independent experts collect country-specific information that is subsequently made available to international audiences.

All three forms of global cultural flow are channeled by global inequalities of resources and power. Those with more resources can participate more often in conferences and events where information is exchanged. Wealthier countries send larger delegations to international conferences and can participate in more deliberations. Smaller countries, such as Fiji, often fail to send national representatives to UN meetings at all. Some of the smaller Pacific island states have not ratified UN conventions because they lack the resources to prepare reports and present them at UN meetings. Many of the NGOs in poorer countries are funded by the wealthier states of the global North as well as foundations rooted in these areas. As a professor in Delhi working on women's issues told me, the new ideas that come from these international cultural exchanges are welcome, but international funding for NGOs creates a parallel system of government within India that is unaccountable to its citizens. Global inequalities of power shape the kinds of cultural flows that take place even for feminist efforts to prevent violence against women.

Violence against Women as a Human Rights Violation

The emergence of violence against women as an important human rights issue illustrates how human rights are made. First discussed as a human rights violation in the1980s, concern about violence against women expanded enormously in the 1990s. The original meaning of violence against women — men's violence against their partners in the form of rape, assault, and murder— has expanded to include female genital mutilation/cutting, gender-based violence by police and military forces in armed conflict as well as in everyday life, violence against refugee women and asylum seekers, trafficking and prostitution, sexual harassment, forced pregnancy, forced abortion, forced sterilization, female foeticide and infanticide, early and forced marriage, honor killings, and widowhood violations (see Cook 1994a: 20; Keck and Sikkink 1998). Gender violence was not a major issue in the 1975 and 1980 global women's conferences, although it was explicitly mentioned in the 1980 Copenhagen document (Thomas 1999: 244–45). The Nairobi Forward-looking Strategies developed in 1985 identified reducing violence against women as a basic strategy for addressing the issue of peace (Report of the Secretary-General 1995: 125). The 1979 Convention on the Elimination of All Forms of Discrimination against Women did not mention violence against women, but the committee monitoring the convention developed an initial recommendation against violence in 1989 and in 1992 formulated a broader recommendation that defined gender-based violence as a form of discrimination. The 1992 statement placed violence against women squarely within the rubric of human rights and fundamental freedoms and made clear that states are obliged to eliminate violence perpetrated by public authorities and by private persons (Cook 1994b: 165; Report of the Secretary-General 1995: 131–32).

Yet, violence against women is not easily defined as a human rights violation. Many forms of domestic violence and sexual assault are perpetrated by private citizens rather than by states. Beginning in 1990, activists argued that a state's failure to protect women from violence is itself a human rights violation (Bunch 1990; Thomas and Beasley 1993). States are responsible for exercising "due diligence" in the protection of women from the violence of private individuals. States that fail to protect their members from violence in a discriminatory way violate their responsibilities toward these members (Bunch 1990; Thomas and Beasley 1993; Romany 1994). They have not exercised sufficient effort — due diligence — in protecting them. If assault or murder is prosecuted less avidly when it occurs against women in intimate relationships than under other circumstances, a state has discriminated on the basis of gender. The committee charged with enforcing CEDAW asserts that violence against women is a form of discrimination, defining gender-based violence as "a form of discrimination which seriously inhibits women's ability to enjoy rights and freedoms on a basis of equality with men" (CEDAW General Recommendation 19, n. 3). Some suggest viewing violence against women as a form of torture (Copelon 1994), a position supported by Amnesty International (2001). In 2003, Amnesty International USA initiated a major global campaign against violence toward women, using a human rights framework (www.amnestyusa.org/stopviolence/about.html). As anthropologist Sheila Dauer, director of Amnesty International USA's Women's Program says, "By providing the global human rights framework for the struggle, Amnesty International will show how international human rights standards cut across national boundaries, cultures and religions and how we can hold governments accountable to meet their obligations to protect women and girls from violence regardless of who commits it or where it is committed."[10]

At the 1993 UN Conference on Human Rights in Vienna, global activism by women's NGOs drew attention to the issue of violence against women (see Schuler 1992). A worldwide petition campaign gathered over 300,000 signatures from 123 countries, putting the issue of violence against women at the center of the conference (Friedman 1995: 27–31).[11] The concluding document, the Vienna Declaration and Programme of Action, formally recognized the human rights of women as "an inalienable integral and indivisible part of human rights" (Connors 1996: 27). In addition to working to eliminate violence against women in public and private life, this document advocated "the elimination of gender bias in the administration of justice and the eradication of any conflicts which may arise between the rights of women and the harmful effects of certain traditional or customary practices" (sec. II, B, par. 38, UN Doc A/Conf.157/24 [Oct. 1993], quoted in Thomas 1999: 249). The Vienna Declaration specifically called for the appointment of a special rapporteur on violence against women and the drafting of a declaration eliminating violence against women.[12] In 1994, the UN Commission on Human Rights condemned gender-based violence and appointed the requested rapporteur (Report of the Secretary-General 1995: 132). The Special Rapporteur on Violence against Women is mandated to collect information relating to violence against women, to recommend measures to remedy it, and to work with other members of the Commission on Human Rights.[13]

The Commission on the Status of Women developed the Declaration on the Elimination of Violence against Women in 1993 and the General Assembly adopted it unanimously. Although it has no binding force, this declaration does have the moral force of world consensus (Coomaraswamy and Kios 1999: 182). It is a comprehensive document that defines violence against women broadly to include physical, sexual, and psychological harm or threats of harm in public or private life (Article 1). It names gender-based violence as a violation of human rights and as an instance of sex discrimination and inequality (Connors 1996: 27–28). The declaration attributes the roots of gender violence to historically unequal power relations between men and women, arguing that it is socially constructed and historically justified rather than natural (Coomaraswamy and Kios 1999: 183). It prohibits invoking custom, tradition, or religious considerations to avoid its obligations and urges states to exercise "due diligence" to prevent, investigate, and punish acts of violence against women whether perpetrated by the state or private persons (Article 4; Van Bueren 1995: 753). This declaration was based on the general recommendation on violence against women produced by the CEDAW Committee.

The 1995 Platform for Action of the Fourth World Conference on Women in Beijing included a section on gender-based violence. Violence against women is defined broadly as "any act of gender-based violence that results in, or is likely to result in, physical, sexual or psychological harm or suffering to women, including threats of such acts, coercion or arbitrary deprivation of liberty, whether occurring in public or private life" (sec. D, 113). It includes any act of gender-based violence in the family or the community or perpetrated by the state that results in physical, sexual, psychological harm or suffering to women in private or public life, including acts of violence and sexual abuse during armed conflict, forced sterilization and abortion, and female infanticide. The text reads, "Violence against women both violates and impairs or nullifies the enjoyment by women of their human rights and fundamental freedoms. The long-standing failure to protect and promote those rights and freedoms in the case of violence against women is a matter of concern to all States and should be addressed" (Platform for Action, sec. D, 112). By declaring the right of women and girl children to protection from violence as a universal human right, the conference reasserted this dramatic expansion of human rights.

The Commission on the Status of Women considered violence against women in connection with racism and HIV/AIDS in 2001 and poverty and natural disasters in 2002. In 2003, it was again a central focus. The Commission on Human Rights has passed a unanimous resolution against violence toward women and another against trafficking in women annually since the mid-1990s. Several regional documents and agreements also condemn violence against women, such as the American Convention on Human Rights and its Additional Protocol in the Area of Economic, Social and Cultural Rights, the Inter-American Convention on the Prevention, Punishment and Eradication of Violence against Women (Convention of Belem do Para); the African Charter on Human and Peoples' Rights, and the 1999 Grand Baie Declaration and Plan of Action on Human Rights.

This global development of human rights declarations and concerns builds on extensive national and local social movements beginning in the 1970s. After two decades of work to mobilize state law to redefine battering as a crime, activists globalized their approaches through NGOs and the UN (see Keck and Sikkink 1998). Grass roots feminist movements in Europe, the United States, Australia (Silard 1994), Argentina (Oller 1994), Brazil (Thomas 1994), India (Bush 1992), the Virgin Islands (Morrow 1994), as well as many other parts of the world developed strategies to protect women from violence in the home based on a critique of male power within gendered relationships and using approaches such as shelters, support groups for victims, and criminalization of battering. The need for intervention is widely recognized in the global South as well as the global North (e.g., Ofei-Aboagye 1994; Green 1999; Weldon 2002). Since the early 1990s, this central concern of global feminism has become an international human rights issue.

VIOLENCE AGAINST WOMEN AND THE QUESTION OF CULTURE

Nowhere do issues of culture and rights seem more difficult than in the area of violence against women. While violence exists in a culture-free zone of injury and death, its meanings are deeply informed by social contexts. The substrate of violence against women is a universal space of pain and suffering that can be understood across cultural differences, but gender-based violence is embedded in cultural understandings of gender and sexuality as well as in the institutions of marriage, community, and state legal regulations of marriage, divorce, inheritance, and child custody. Its location in family and personal relationships has shielded this domain of violence from state scrutiny for a long time and at the same time has naturalized the practice. Thus, the violence against women movement offers a good case study of how activists and government officials handle the apparent contradictions between culture and rights.

Diminishing violence against women requires cultural transformation. Most societies draw a boundary between acceptable forms of violence against women, defined as discipline, and unacceptable forms, defined as abuse. The location of this boundary is a cultural construct that depends on relationships, contexts, and situations. Many societies accept violence as appropriate discipline for certain kinds of behavior. People who cross this boundary and use excessive violence may face penalties from their communities. Redrawing this boundary is at the heart of the human rights project concerning violence against women. Activists seek to redefine violence from discipline to abuse. In order to shift the boundary of appropriate violence, activists need to alter such fundamental institutions as marriage. Their opponents claim that this violence is a form of discipline essential to the preservation of marriage. Many religious and political leaders resist making the changes that are required to improve women's safety, often invoking the need to protect culture.[14] Arguments about preserving culture become the basis for defending male control over women. Consequently, feminist activists have little patience for cultural arguments, despite their commitment to cultural diversity.

Is it possible to find a space that respects cultural differences and at the same time protects women from violence? These often appear as opposite goals. Cultural beliefs and institutions often permit and encourage violence against women, and protecting women requires substantial shifts in beliefs about gender as well as changes in the institutions that govern women's lives such as marriage, divorce, education, and work opportunities. There is an inevitable collision between protecting women and preserving marriages. If the only way to provide security and safety for a woman is to allow her to separate from her violent husband, reducing violence against women will diminish the permanence of marriage. Reducing violence and rape demands changes in ideas and practices about sexuality, marriage, and the family. Consequently, human rights activists, social service reformers, and government policymakers constantly tack between the goals of respecting cultural diversity and protecting women's safety. They use pragmatic compromise and situationally determined decision-making. The case studies show how activists negotiate these turbulent waters as they adapt transnational approaches to specific local contexts.

The major international documents concerning violence against women are less negotiable. They condemn using cultural justifications for harming women. The 1993 Vienna Declaration stressed the importance of "the eradication of any conflicts which may arise between the rights of women and the harmful effects of certain traditional or customary practices, cultural prejudices and religious extremism" (Vienna Declaration and Programme of Action [A/conf.157/24/Part I: 19, par. 38]).[15] This paragraph does not explicitly condemn such customs and practices, however. The 1995 Platform for Action from the Beijing Fourth World Conference on Women took a stronger stand. It states: "Violence against women throughout the life cycle derives essentially from cultural patterns, in particular the harmful effects of certain traditional or customary practices and all acts of extremism linked to race, sex, language or religion that perpetuate the lower status accorded to women in the family, the workplace, the community and society" (United Nations 1995: sec. D, 118, p. 75). According to Strategic Objective D.1, governments should: "Condemn violence against women and refrain from invoking any custom, tradition or religious consideration to avoid their obligations with respect to its elimination as set out in the Declaration on the Elimination of Violence against Women" (Platform for Action D.1: 124 [a], p. 76). By urging governments to refrain from invoking culture as a defense, the platform goes beyond the 1993 document that asks governments to reconcile conflicts between rights and culture. The women's convention (CEDAW) uses similar language. CEDAW requires ratifying states to change cultural practices that subordinate women. General Recommendation 19 issued by the CEDAW Committee in 1992 says: "States should condemn violence against women, and should not invoke any custom, tradition, or religion or other consideration to avoid their obligation with respect to its elimination" (Cook 1994b: 167, citing CEDAW General Recommendation 19 at 1, U.N. Doc., CEDAW/C/1992/L.1/Add. 15 [1992]).

A prominent NGO based in Asia that helps NGOs develop shadow reports and attend CEDAW hearings concurs with this view that culture is often used as a justification for oppressing women. In a posting on the electronic listserve "Endviolence," managed by UNIFEM, Beng Hui, the information and communications officer for International Women's Rights Action Watch—Asia/Pacific (IWRAW-AP), writes from Kuala Lumpur in response to the question: What about situations where some women in a society consider a practice to be legitimate and others consider it violence?

In the view of IWRAW Asia Pacific, [ending] any belief, practice or policy that results in harm cannot be seen as violating the cultural right of any community/society. Thus, even if there are women within a community/society who accept cultural practices that result in the violation of fundamental human rights, we should speak out against this since we need to adhere to certain standards. This is especially necessary when persons who are being violated may not necessarily have the power to object. . . .

Given that 169 states (governments) have ratified the CEDAW Convention, women should utilise this treaty to demand that cultural practices which limit women's rights be eliminated. The recent amendment to the inheritance laws in Nepal is a good example of how governments can intervene to challenge and change negative cultural values and practices. Prior to the amendments, women had limited inheritance rights, i.e., linked to their marital status, because culture viewed that they should be dependant on their husbands for economic resources. While it is too early to know if this legal reform will result in changing cultural values, it is still useful to remember that governments CAN—and under CEDAW, ARE OBLIGATED TO—take action to eliminate all forms of discrimination against women, including those which have cultural origins. (end-violence@mail .edc.org, June 21, 2002)

HARMFUL TRADITIONAL PRACTICES

One of the basic conceptions in discussions of women's right to protection from violence is that of harmful traditional practices. Originally developed to describe female genital cutting, this term describes practices that have some cultural legitimacy yet are harmful to women. In their discussion of traditional practices harmful to women, Coomaraswamy and Kios refer to cultural and traditional practices interchangeably. They note, for example, that violence against women is inherent in patriarchal traditions and culture (1999: 190). Customs criticized as harmful traditional practices include widow immolation, prenatal sex selection and female infanticide as a result of son preference, child marriage, arranged or forced marriage, polygamy, seclusion and veiling, and food taboos for women. Female genital cutting is the central issue around which the conception of harmful cultural practices or harmful traditional practices has coalesced.[16] This practice has inspired Western critiques since the 1930s, initially focusing on health hazards but more recently on the gender oppression inherent in the practice (Boyle 2002).[17] Thus, genital cutting became the prototype of a practice justified by custom and culture and redefined as an act of violence and a breach of women's human rights (Bernard 1996: 79). Yet in the United States, domestic violence, rape in wartime, and stalking are not labeled as harmful cultural practices nor are forms of violence against women's bodies such as cosmetic surgery, dieting and the wearing of high heels.

Theorizing culture as an open and flexible system changes the debate about human rights and their localization and offers a more accurate framework for human rights activism. This conception of culture does not eliminate tensions between rights concepts and cultural beliefs. Nor does it resolve the gap between general principles and the complexities of local contexts. Given its global reach, the human rights system must articulate general principles and cannot treat each local situation as distinct. When transnational reformers confront the incredible complexity of local communities around the world, there is an inescapable tendency to simplify, to miss the nuances in each situation. But this concept of culture does focus attention on the capacity of local social arrangements to promote human rights ideals and the importance of framing universalistic reforms in local cultural terms.

Some feminist organizations adopt this perspective. For example, the theme of the 2002 Sixteen Days of Activism against Gender Violence, sponsored by the Center for Women's Global Leadership at Rutgers University, was "Creating a culture that says no to violence against women."[18] The campaign statement recognizes that culture has been used by individuals and institutions to support beliefs and practices that legitimize and perpetuate violence against women, but notes that culture is not static and that there are creative ways to challenge it. "It is important that we continue to critically explore and challenge the history and construction of claims that use culture as a justification for violence against women. We must also examine who has constructed or is constructing the cultural beliefs that legitimize violence against women and whose interests are served by these claims. We should question whose cultural views and values are being privileged and why."[19] Taking an ethnographic approach to the flows that constitute the transnational movement against violence toward women facilitates this understanding of culture.

Doing Deterritorialized Ethnography

The ethnographic study of global reform movements is an important challenge for contemporary anthropology. How can anthropology, with its historic focus on local places, comprehend these processes in which the local and global are inextricably intertwined? The distinctive contribution of anthropology has always been its focus on small-scale, more or less observable, social units and the cultural meanings and practices that constitute them. But is this model appropriate now? Where can we find these units as we look at the new political and cultural configurations produced by globalization and the flows of capital and culture across national boundaries? The challenge is to study placeless phenomena in a place, to find small interstices in global processes in which critical decisions are made, to track the information flows that constitute global discourses, and to mark the points at which competing discourses intersect in the myriad links between global and local conceptions and institutions. One answer is to locate sites where global, national, and local processes are revealed in the social life of small groups. My approach is to focus on a single issue, the movement against gender violence, in five local places in the Asia-Pacific region and in the deterritorialized world of UN conferences, transnational NGO activism, and academic, legal, and social service exchanges of ideas and practices.

This is an effort to do an ethnographic analysis of globalization, or at least a corner of it. It is probably the most methodologically challenging field research I have ever done. How does one go about examining the globalization of human rights approaches to violence against women? Where does the researcher go to look for this? How can one person, or even a team of people, ever synthesize such a broad transformation without losing the genius of ethnography: its ability to look closely at a small social space, to listen to the language, to pay attention to the social linkages and information exchanges, to notice the power relationships, and to pay attention to the cultural constructions of social life at play in everyday interactions? This is hard to pull off on a global stage.

In my efforts to study such a transnational phenomenon, I am following George Marcus's suggestion that anthropologists engage in multisited ethnography (1998: 79–104.) Although his term implies a comparison among sites, Marcus's model is not one of discrete comparisons. Instead, it is an ethnographic engagement with the fragments of a larger system that recognizes that the system is neither coherent nor fully graspable. I prefer the phrase "deterritorialized ethnography," which comes closer to the notion that this is a disembodied space of social life, one that exists in various spaces but is not grounded in any one of them. My focus is on a social world whose locations are diverse but whose words and practices sound and look the same, whether in Geneva, New York, Delhi, or Beijing. There are similar processes of document production, NGO and government conflict, political performances by diplomats, and NGO efforts to embarrass governments. The conference halls are inhabited by the same mobile actors who return to capitals and local programs to share their experiences. One could conceive of such people in terms of their relative mobility (see Gupta and Ferguson 1997 for other explorations of these issues).

As I began my deterritorialized ethnography, my first strategy was to focus on a single issue. In making this choice, I followed the lead of most NGOs, who categorize their work this way. NGOs focus on a single issue such as reproductive health, land mines, mental health, or aging. Violence against women is actually a huge collection of more specific issues, such as wife battering, trafficking, rape in wartime, prostitution, female genital mutilation, dowry murders, and sexual assault. Each of these problems has its own set of NGOs working on it. I had permission to attend UN meetings as a representative of an accredited NGO, the research center affiliated with Wellesley College. There is no provision for attending UN meetings as a scholar outside the NGO framework. I focused on a region, the Asia-Pacific, which although vast, has important internal linkages. And finally, I decided to foreground the international institutions of the United Nations, the central location for international deliberations and the construction of the human rights rhetoric, rather than regional bodies. I still had a great deal of space to cover, but it included issues I had already worked on: violence against women in the United States, contemporary legal pluralism, colonial systems of legal pluralism, the intersections of race, class, and gender, and colonial and postcolonial representations. I thought it might be possible to do an ethnographic study of how the global human rights system functions in a variety of particular social spaces.

I began this research, as any ethnographer must, by looking for a place to study. International institutions developing and enforcing human rights seemed the logical place, so I began to visit those UN agencies in New York and Geneva that dealt with violence against women. Some were commissions with annual meetings, such as the Commission on the Status of Women (CSW) and the Commission on Human Rights (CHR). Some were irregular global meetings, such as Beijing Plus Five, held in New York in June 2000. Some were monitoring bodies attached to UN conventions, such as the CEDAW Committee, which meets twice a year in New York. For three years I attended these meetings: the annual meetings of the CSW and the CHR, the twice-yearly meetings of the CEDAW Committee, and the Beijing Plus Five conference. At each meeting, I talked to NGO representatives, attended panels, participated in lobbying meetings, and watched government representatives talk to each other about document construction, both in large meetings and in smaller ones. I interviewed a few government representatives and regularly attended

US government briefings, but I participated more as an NGO representative than a government one. I attended several training sessions organized by NGOs to learn the UN process and how to lobby more effectively.

At each of these UN meetings, I discovered similar terms, procedures, and outcomes. It was common to hear talk of political will, capacity building, social capital, and national machineries. All followed similar rules of procedure for participating and expressing opinions and focused on producing documents that articulated a shared policy position. NGO and government representatives typically had a symbiotic but hostile relationship. These meetings were enormously international. UN rules demand equal representation from the various regions of the world in the membership of commissions and treaty bodies. NGO representatives also come from all over the world. Despite significant fractures based on region, religion, and wealth, this highly international and diverse group created a shared cultural world that agreed about the importance of the international domain, universal standards, and procedures of deliberation and decision-making. I came to think of this world as an instantiation of the culture of transnational modernity. This culture has a distinctly African, Asian, and Middle Eastern as well as European and American flavor. Its "other" is not the "Third World" but the poor and marginal members of urban as well as rural societies in all parts of the world.

My next question concerned the work of these groups: does it matter? Do the documents that are so arduously produced have an audience? Does anyone read them or pay attention to them? Do governments that ratify treaties such as CEDAW make any effort to follow them? Does the effort to define and prevent violence against women in different places around the world rely on these UN procedures? In order to answer these questions, I selected four locations in the Asia-Pacific region representing countries widely different in power and level of participation in the international community. I had already worked on violence against women interventions in the United States. In each location, I visited local activists working on violence against women. Although the human rights activists and the local gender violence groups typically cooperated and supported one another, these groups were quite different. The first adopted a lawyerly approach, the second a social service one.

As I talked to activists and scholars, I compared their activities and approaches to domestic violence initiatives I had studied in Hawai'i during the 1990s. I spent a decade studying local women's centers, courts, and judges and interviewed a large number of women who were battered and men who battered them in one small town. I also observed many women's support group meetings and men's violence control training sessions (Merry 1995a, 1995b, 2001a). There was a surprising lack of reference to human rights by advocates and activists working in Hawai'i in the 1990s even though this was the period of extraordinary global expansion of the idea that violence against women was a human rights violation. In Hilo, Hawai'i, women were encouraged to think of themselves as having rights but not human rights.

Fiji is a country similar in many ways to Hawai'i in size and economic relationships but also quite different in its ethnic composition and its history as a British colony (see Merry and Brenneis 2004). Human rights are far more important to the women's movement in Fiji than in Hawai'i. About half of the current population of Fiji is of Indian ancestry, resident in the islands since the nineteenth century, and half is ethnic Fijian. Like India and Hong Kong, it has a British colonial legal structure. It is a relatively small, poor, and economically dependent country that is more vulnerable to international pressure than larger and more affluent places. It rarely sends representatives to international conferences. At the same time, it is also a regional Pacific leader and the site of many regional governmental and nongovernmental organizations as well as the major university of the South Pacific. The Fiji Women's Crisis Centre, established in the mid 1980s, is a leader in setting up programs around Fiji and in other Pacific nations. The Fiji Women's Rights Movement (FWRM) has been working to disseminate human rights ideas since the 1980s and helped to persuade the country to ratify CEDAW (see Riles 2001). I visited Fiji in 2002, after observing the Fiji presentation to CEDAW in New York a month earlier and talking at length to Fiji NGO representatives. I made two more visits in 2003. A research assistant, Eleanor Kleiber, spent the summer of 2001 and the spring of 2003 doing research for me and working with the Fiji Women's Rights Movement.

India, in contrast, is a very large and powerful country with a long tradition of rights enshrined in its constitution. It is very active in global human rights forums and its representatives typically take leadership roles. Like Fiji, India is a former British colony and a regional leader. There is a long tradition of women's movements in India as in Fiji, and the Indian campaign against dowry deaths in the 1970s was one of the earliest efforts to address the problem of violence against women in the world. I spent three weeks in Delhi interviewing activists and scholars working in this field in 2001 and a month touring India meeting with grassroots activists and talking to women's leaders in 2000.

China is also a large and powerful country, but unlike India and Fiji has only recently begun to consider violence against women as a social problem. It has no long-standing commitment to a rights framework although its women's movement is long established and committed to the equality of men and women. The All-China Women's Federation is a mass organization committed to women's concerns, but China has very few NGOs. Its women's movement was galvanized by the World Conference for Women held in Beijing in 1995. In the last ten years, there has been a gradual recognition among scholars that there is a problem of violence against women in the country. I spent two weeks interviewing activists and scholars about their work on violence against women in 2001 and returned to the international conference sponsored by this group in the fall of 2002. The scholars and activists I talked to in Beijing were very interested in developing their capacity to deal with violence against women but were new to the problem and to the use of rights discourse. During my first visit, Ethan Michelson shared his knowledge of law in China and served as my interpreter. At the second visit, Wei-Ying Lin interpreted for me after spending the summer of 2002 translating Chinese documents on domestic violence.

Hong Kong is an intriguing comparative case since it shares language, culture, and kinship practices with China but was also shaped by a century of British colonial control. It did not experience the revolutionary upheavals of China. In Hong Kong as in China, scholars and activists insist that Chinese culture determines local understandings of domestic violence, but Hong Kong's historical relationship with Britain and its contemporary affluence as a global trading center make it a very different place from Beijing. It has a far more developed set of institutions for dealing with violence against women as well as a more extensive engagement with human rights. In the years following the Chinese crackdown at Tiananmen Square before the 1997 handover to China, there was a great deal of interest in human rights in Hong Kong. The comparison between Hong Kong and China highlights the impact of different colonial histories and rights traditions despite similarities in traditions of kinship and lineage. Rachel Stern worked as my research assistant for several months in 2002 and again in 2003, collecting background material, making contacts, conducting interviews, and setting up interviews for my visit in 2002, when I interviewed academics, activists, and political leaders in the domestic violence field.

Thus, in three of these four places I combined a relatively brief research trip with substantial help from a research assistant living in the area. I interviewed one hundred and ten people in these four locations and another 25 in the international forums, plus talking to many people more informally. Overall I spent about three and a half months in these four places while my research assistants spent another ten months. It is obviously not possible to know four such diverse places as Beijing, Hong Kong, Suva (Fiji), and Delhi in detail, but I was able to compare the way they used international human rights ideas to deal with violence against women. My study of Hilo, Hawai'i, was longer and more thorough and so provided a good basis for comparison. I found that knowing how a US community handles the problem of domestic violence enabled me to make valuable comparisons with the efforts in other countries.

In addition to studying the production and appropriation of human rights talk about violence against women in UN events and in different national settings, I also attended four international conferences on violence against women, places where ideas are exchanged and groups learn about other approaches. I attended a conference on Women in Palestine in Gaza in November 1999, the Color of Violence at the University of California, Santa Cruz, in April 2000, the Expanding Our Horizons Conference on domestic violence in the Asia-Pacific region held at the University of Sydney, Australia, in February 2002, and the International Conference on Violence against Women sponsored by the Wellesley Centers for Women in March 2003. Finally, I examined global flows by joining a series of electronic listserves and monitoring the conversations. There are many of these, but the most important are probably the UNIFEM-sponsored end-violence listserve that includes 2500 people in 130 countries and ran, more or less continuously, from 1998 until 2002; a six-month seminar sponsored by the UN training agency INSTRAW that focused on men's violence; the 16 Days discussion at Rutgers University, with about 620 members; and the cedaw4change listserve with 683 members. Although there is a great deal of interest in the way the Internet has increased the speed and breadth of knowledge exchange, I was impressed in my interviews by the significance of more conventional forms of academic training and exchange as well. Often, scholars in the countries I visited were aware of research and writing taking place in the United States and Europe, more than the people in the United States were aware of scholarly work elsewhere. But the Internet does increase accessibility of information. A scholar from Beijing told me that she regularly visits websites from US universities working on violence against women, for example. I became an agent of this transnational exchange myself as I told people I visited about American approaches to violence against women. The director of a counseling center in Beijing quizzed me about how to set up a shelter, for example, while others asked me how well men's treatment programs worked in the United States.

In each of these five sites I was able to rely on significant assistance from people who already knew the area to make contacts and provide me with background. I have also done background reading and research on each area, including perusal of the extensive "gray literature" produced by programs and government offices. For example, I have a copy of a major survey in India on domestic violence as well as similar surveys from Fiji and China. As an ethnographer with considerable experience in more place-based research, this transnational hopping from place to place was challenging, but essential to track the actors through the transnational world they inhabit. The rest of the book shows what I learned.

Creating Human Rights

The first time I went to a UN meeting, I was completely lost. It was the Beijing Plus Five Conference in New York in June 2000, and, walking through torrential rains to the conference, I joined thousands of other women navigating their way through a maze of hallways, conference rooms, lists of activities, and documents. I didn't understand the process of drafting documents, nor did I know how to find the documents under discussion. I was puzzled by the apparently tense relationship between NGOs and governments. And I was overwhelmed by all the acronyms — UNDP, WFP, WHO, UNIFEM, CEDAW, CRC, ICCPR, and many more — and the catch phrases, such as gender mainstreaming, capacity building, best practices, gender focal points, and political will, that I heard all around me. Everyone else seemed to know what was going on, how to find her way around, and what all those letters stood for. At one point, I was sitting in the large conference room for the early morning NGO briefing, and the chair, whose name and position I had not been told, said that if anyone had a problem, they should see Amina. There was no indication who Amina was, what her surname was, what her official position was, or where one might find her. I assumed everyone else knew, but I didn't have a clue. I have now been to several conferences and recognize that Amina Adam does indeed know a great many things about the NGO-UN relationship. She is chief of the Coordination and Outreach Unit of the Division for the Advancement of Women and works with NGOs to assist with their participation during the

CSW meetings (Commission on the Status of Women). And I realize that the way to gain information is simply to accost her in the hallway, conference room, or wherever she can be found.

It was confusing and exciting at the same time. During that first conference, I waited in lines snaking around the block to be registered and photographed in order to acquire the coveted identity card that gave me access to the vast network of corridors under the main UN buildings in New York. I attended as a representative of an NGO, the Wellesley Centers for Women, along with my research assistant, Justine Hanson. There were hundreds, probably thousands, of NGO and government representatives present from all over the world. About two thousand people registered for the conference representing about one thousand organizations. Most were women. The NGO representatives told fascinating stories of their efforts to improve the position of women in the places where they worked. An Indian woman described tracing trafficked women from Nepal to Mumbai and making a video of them and their abysmal working conditions. An Afghani woman demonstrated how the burkah turned a human being into something that looked like a piece of furniture. Women from Fiji talked about the recent coup in their country and the fact that the leaders of their government, which included a substantial number of women for the very first time, were still being held hostage in the Parliament Building in Suva. Overall, they were dynamic and fascinating people. They seemed to represent all the peoples of the globe. I felt that I was watching the creation of a new global legal order, with its rich cultural system of procedures, protocols, and practices of law-making. This chapter examines the process of *transnational consensus building* that produces the regime of human rights law (see also Riles 1998, 2001).

This is a transnational social space where actors come together simultaneously as locally embedded people and as participants in a transnational setting that has its own norms, values, and cultural practices. Representatives of countries and NGOs are concerned about the particular issues of the places they come from. They bring these into the global conversation. Their concerns range from the social status of gay and lesbians to the defense of wearing modest dress and veils. Yet each participant also inhabits local places in New York and Geneva: places defined by a transnational culture of modernity. This is an English-speaking, largely secular, universalistic, law-governed culture, organized around the formal equality of nations and their economic and political inequality. Participants in this transnational society live in two local places at the same time, navigating endlessly between them.

Creating Consensual Documents

Although the Beijing Plus Five Conference was my first engagement with the process of producing a consensual conference document, the document the delegates considered was the product of years of preparatory meetings. There had been meetings with experts, five regional meetings, and protracted negotiations by UN staff over previous drafts before the draft document was ready for consideration. Now, in the cavernous conference room, delegates from countries around the world sat behind curved rows of desks struggling to thrash out the final language of an outcome document for the world conference. Government representatives sat through interminable meetings trying to develop consensus on language in "working sessions" of the whole and smaller "contact groups," informal subcommittees that met in private to work out more intractable differences. The goal of the conference was to create a document that all the participating countries could agree upon. The delegates talked about this process as "cleaning up" competing language, "getting rid of brackets," and "taking out clutter."

The debates were time-consuming and opaque, often excruciatingly slow and seemingly irrelevant. Nevertheless, it was quite extraordinary that representatives from countries all over the world sat together and tried to come up with some shared way of talking about women's roles and rights. They even managed to produce an agreed text. Delegates meet at this and other conferences, talk to each other, develop new ideas and approaches, and reach some level of consensus. They sit for hours watching the text projected on a large screen in front of the delegates, seeking to negotiate their differences.

The discussion of a paragraph calling for the elimination of gender discriminatory legislation provides an example of this process. The representative from Sudan said that the proposed text, which called for eliminating this legislation by 2005, was not realistic and suggested replacing it with "as soon as possible." The NGO audience in the gallery collectively groaned and was hushed by the chair. The chair (from India) identified a general consensus on using the language "striving for" and the year 2005. Tunisia suggested replacing "striving for" with "with a view to eliminating by 2005." Iran advocated "striving for" without the date, arguing that countries have different paces of progress and different legal systems. Egypt said that "striving for" was weakening the text and that it was possible to accommodate those who worried about the pace of change and still keep the date and that Sudan should go along. At this point, the representative from Pakistan walked into the room and was told that they were about to reach consensus on the paragraph. The Pakistani delegate said that because of his great respect for the forum and a desire not to promise something that his country could not deliver, they should use "as soon as possible." In response to the chair's suggestion to say "as soon as possible, preferably by 2005," Namibia, speaking for a coalition of southern African countries, said that it wanted the 2005 included and would not accept "as soon as possible, preferably by 2005." Cuba agreed that this weakened the paragraph. Sudan countered that Namibia should not refuse to compromise, since "we are all sovereign states here." The chair complained that they were wasting too much time on this point. Pakistan countered that it was trying to compromise but that it already had other deadlines it had not met. Even though Pakistan planned to make the reforms before 2005, he said, the country did not want to make more promises that it could not carry through. JUSCANZ, a coalition of Japan, the United States, Canada, Australia, and New Zealand, supported Namibia's request for a firm date. Nevertheless, the chair accepted the phrase, "as soon as possible, preferably 2005." Namibia objected, saying there was not consensus and the chair had overridden them and given Pakistan its way.

The final document adopts Pakistan's more cautious wording about deadlines and the qualifying phrase "striving to." It states that governments should take action to "Create and maintain a non-discriminatory and gender-sensitive legal environment by reviewing legislation with a view to striving to remove discriminatory provisions as soon as possible, preferably by 2005, and eliminating legislative gaps that leave women and girls without protection of their rights and without effective recourse against gender-based discrimination" (A/RES/S-23/3: 21, par. 68 [b]).

This is a typical debate, in which the focus of discussion is particular phrases and the outcome is a long and turgid sentence, but important political issues lurk under the bland discussions about terminology. In this case it appeared to be about creating expectations to which governments might be held in the future. Government delegates speak for their countries and are called on by country name rather than personal name. Delegations typically include several people who caucus with one another about these changes. Most are appointed by their foreign office but increasingly include NGOs as well. The countries are organized into shifting coalitions, such as JUSCANZ and G-77, or Group of 77. Formed as a coalition of Third World nations at the UN after the Bandung Conference of 1955 (Rajagopal 2003: 74), by 2000 G-77 stood for a group of 134 nations from the developing world, including China and India. In 2001, it was referred to as G-77 plus China. Other regional negotiating factions were the EU (European Union), SLAC (Some Latin American Countries), and SADC (Southern African Development Community). These negotiating blocs differ significantly in voting power and in economic power. In 2000, the EU and JUSCANZ tended to work together, adding up to 21 countries (11% of all countries) that paid 87 percent of the UN budget. In contrast, the other major negotiating block, G-77, included 69 percent of all countries but paid only 8 percent of the UN budget (International Women's Tribune Center 2000: 6).

These codes were used to identify the coalition that had proposed wording in the document displayed on the large screen at the front of the room and were inserted in the brackets denoting alternative phrases. Although the wording debates seemed trivial, they revealed political differences in subtle ways. For example, JUSCANZ proposed changing the following sentence in a way that muted its critique of globalization: "29. The globalization process has [JUSCANZ delete: caused] [JUSCANZ: been characterized by] policy shifts in favour of more open trade and financial flows, privatization of state-owned enterprises [JUSCANZ delete: and lower public spending] [JUSCANZ insert: changing roles of the public sector.]" (p. 31). Not all JUSCANZ's proposals survived into the final document, but the final sentence is more qualified in its critique of globalization than the initial one: "The globalization process has, in some countries, resulted in policy shifts in favour of more open trade and financial flows, privatization of State-owned enterprises and in many cases lower public spending, particularly on social services" (A/RES/S-23/3: 14, par. 35). Despite its economic power, the JUSCANZ coalition could not impose its language completely.

Another debate concerned the list of forms of violence against women. In the proposed language, developed through a series of regional preparatory meetings and the work of the secretariat, there were no specific examples listed. G-77 suggested listing "rape, sexual abuse and exploitation, violence deriving from cultural prejudice, in particular the harmful effects of certain traditional or customary practices, violence resulting from racism, racial discrimination, xenophobia, pornography, ethnic cleansing, foreign occupation, religious and anti-religious extremism and terrorism." The Holy See, which has a seat in the UN even though it is not a country, listed "prostitution, pornography, trafficking, sexual and other forms of exploitation" (draft document pp. 48–49). The final document states: "Gender-based violence, such as battering and other domestic violence, sexual abuse, sexual slavery and exploitation, international trafficking in women and children, forced prostitution and sexual harassment, as well as violence against women resulting from cultural prejudice, racism and racial discrimination, xenophobia, pornography, ethnic cleansing, armed conflict, foreign occupation, religious and anti-religious extremism and terrorism are incompatible with the dignity and worth of the human person and must be combated and eliminated" (A/RES/S-23/3: 19, par. 59). As this example shows, most of the Holy See's suggestions were accepted. There is a tendency to cumulate alternative proposals, producing a comprehensive but somewhat unwieldy document.

An area of ongoing disagreement concerned the portrayal of women's role in the family. In a paragraph discussing the importance of women to the family, the Holy See proposed: "Women's contributions to the welfare of the family, the social significance of maternity, motherhood and the role of parents in the family and in the upbringing of children continue to be inadequately recognized. Despite repeated commitments to strengthen and support the family, family disintegration is still a major cause of the feminization of poverty and other social problems disproportionately affecting women and girls" (par. 51). The G-77 version begins, "The family is the basic unit of society and is a strong force of social cohesion and integration and its stability should be strengthened. It plays a key role providing social care. In different cultural, political and social systems, various forms of the family exist; the rights, capabilities and responsibilities of family members must be respected." The statement continues, "Women also continue to bear disproportionate burden in the household responsibilities. Such imbalance needs to be consistently addressed through appropriate policies and programmes, in particular those geared towards education and through legislation where appropriate" (p. 49). Here, the Holy See emphasizes family permanence and motherhood while the developing countries are more concerned with respect for cultural diversity and inequality in domestic responsibilities. (This language, but not its sponsor, appears in A/s-23/2/Add. 2 [Part IV]: pp. 4–5.)

In the final document, this paragraph begins, "Women play a critical role in the family. The family is the basic unit of society and is a strong force for social cohesion and integration and, as such, should be strengthened." The G-77 sentence about various forms of the family is retained along with a version of the Holy See's statement about the importance of motherhood, with fatherhood added. The paragraph refers to inequalities in domestic responsibilities and offers remedies: "Motherhood and fatherhood and the role of parents and legal guardians in the family and in the upbringing of children and the importance of all family members to the family's well-being are also acknowledged and must not be the basis for discrimination." The gender imbalance in family responsibilities should be addressed "through appropriate policies and programmes, in particular those geared towards education, and through legislation where appropriate. In order to achieve full partnership, both in public and private spheres, both women and men must be enabled to reconcile and share equally work responsibilities and family responsibilities" (A/RES/S-23/3: 20, par. 60). The sentence about the disintegration of the family has disappeared whereas the concern about unequal domestic responsibilities has been retained.

REACHING CONSENSUS

The final document at the Beijing Plus Five meeting was the product of compromise achieved through a relatively democratic process. Consensus occurred not when all agreed, but when no objections were heard. The language was not determined by the countries of the global North but often relied on suggestions from the global South. This process produced a document that was long, wordy, and mind-numbingly hard to read with occasional powerful sentences. Although there were often proposals to eliminate sections or to streamline language, there was a tendency to take an additive approach to resolving differences, producing very repetitive texts. Strong sentences were often qualified and lost their punch. Clear timelines for action and obligations on governments were shifted to vague normative recommendations. Code phrases, such as "as appropriate" or "as soon as possible," were used to diminish nations' responsibilities to accomplish goals. Statements urging ratification of a convention were diminished by asking nations "to consider" ratification. *Flame/ Flamme,* the African daily newspaper of the conference, felt that behind the G-77 reluctance to take strong positions was an unwillingness to make any move forward. For example, the EU proposed a number of additional implementation measures for violence against women, but the G-77 proposed only to review and revise "where appropriate" existing legislation on violence against women. The author of the news story concluded that "our" governments do not want to be pinned down to specifics and do not want to be held too accountable (Wambui 2000: 2). Indeed, North NGOs expressed concern that the global North governments were not working hard enough to resist conservative countries from the global South.

One of the drawbacks of the consensual decision-making process is that a small group of countries can exert its wishes in a way that it could not under majority voting. For example, at Beijing Plus Five, a few countries were able to block acceptance of some important issues, such as reproductive rights and recognition of diversity in sexual orientation. One of the key concerns of the NGO participants at the meeting was the erosion of women's rights, particularly reproductive rights and rights to protection from violence. There was widespread concern that the gains made at the 1995 Beijing conference were under attack by conservative religious groups. The Holy See led this effort, forming alliances with the global South and arguing that women's rights threatened family values. In recent years, the United States has sided with this faction as well. NGO representatives frequently talked about the need to fight a backlash against women's rights framed in terms of claims of culture and religion.

A common strategy in these wording debates was to import phrases, sentences, or even full paragraphs from other UN documents on which consensus had already been reached. Using "agreed upon language" meant that there was no need for further debate, nor was further debate even appropriate since global consensus already existed about this language. Thus, introducing sections from other documents was a common and popular strategy. Those with an extensive mastery of other UN documents are most influential as lobbyists since they can suggest "agreed upon language" to the delegates. Since some other UN body has already adopted the wording, it can readily be used in another document. There is no obligation to provide the original source. As Riles points out with her evocative analogy between document production and mat weaving, it simply becomes part of the whole (2001: 70–91). NGO representatives with long experience at international meetings and deep knowledge of relevant documents are clearly at an advantage in this situation. They often know more than the relatively young government delegates who do not necessarily have the same mastery. In a debate at the Beijing Plus Five Conference about how much "Beijing language" to use, some thought importing it stemmed the tendency to "water down" the Platform for Action, the outcome document from the Beijing conference, whereas others thought it was a mistake to repeat the same language.

The positioning of "agreed upon language" imported from another document can have a dramatic effect on the meaning of a text. For example, in the drafting of the resolution against violence against women at the Commission on Human Rights in 2002, Cuba's proposal to introduce a section from the Racism Conference of 2001 emphasized the impact of racism on violence against women even though the new language was simply juxtaposed to the old. The new language, inserted into the preamble text, read:

> Convinced that racism, racial discrimination, xenophobia and related intolerance reveal themselves in a differentiated manner for women and girls, and can be among the factors leading to a deterioration in their living conditions, poverty, violence, multiple forms of discrimination and the limitation or denial of their human rights, and recognizing the need to integrate a gender perspective into relevant policies, strategies and programmes of action, including effective implementation of national

legislation, against racism, racial discrimination, xenophobia and related intolerance in order to address multiple forms of discrimination against women. (WCAR Declaration, par. 69, in CHR resolution 2002/52 on Elimination of Violence against Women)

Those who know the documents better can often trump others in the language insertion game. In one debate in a drafting session at the Commission on Human Rights, someone suggested inserting agreed language from the Windhoek Declaration. Another representative protested that they should only use language from official UN documents. The first delegate triumphantly announced that Windhoek had been an official UN meeting and provided the website where the text was listed, thus simultaneously displaying his superior knowledge of texts and UN conferences and winning his case. Delegates often described new wording as "Beijing language," that is, phrases that had already been agreed on in Beijing.

These wording debates are all carried out in English. Although these meetings have simultaneous translation into the six official UN languages, the document itself is in English and the wording alternatives are presented in English. A person who has not mastered the language would have a great deal of difficulty assessing the implications and innuendos of different phrases and sentences. NGO caucuses are typically held in English only because they cannot afford translators. At Beijing Plus Five, some of the Spanish-speaking representatives complained about feeling excluded. Those who participated most actively in the debates were from countries in which English is the language of educated people; thus it tended to trace the boundaries of the former British Empire and its settler states.

CONTENTIOUS ISSUES

The role of religion in society is often the subject of debate. The Holy See and some Islamic nations were in constant conflict with the more secular states of Europe and North America at Beijing Plus Five. The latter countries were anxious to incorporate language about sexual rights, sexual orientation, and reproductive choice, while more religiously oriented countries saw this as an attack on the family. One debate illustrated these differences dramatically. The Holy See proposed the following language: "Encourage an appreciation for the central role that religion, spirituality and belief play in the lives of millions of women and men, in the way they live and in the aspirations they have for the future, and in this regard, protect and promote the right to freedom of thought, conscience and religion as inalienable rights which must be universally enjoyed" (preparatory document par. 132 [c]). One Latin American country suggested deleting the word "promote" because it was a secular nation. The United States suggested adding the word "may" before "play in the lives of millions of women and men." Sudan complained about protecting rights to freedom of conscience, thought, and religion but not reproductive health, and said that this shows that "we are not serious about women in poor areas." The Holy See countered that Article 18 of the Universal Declaration and Platform for Action, paragraph 24, already has this language. Nigeria wanted to include the reference to a "central" role and delete "may." Syria suggested deleting "millions." The final draft reflected much of the Holy See's language in 98 (c): "Promote respect for the right of women and men to the freedom of thought, conscience, and religion. Recognize the central role that religion, spirituality and belief play in the lives of millions of women and men" (A/RES/S-23/3: 38).

Developing countries, particularly in Africa, advocated references to poverty, armed conflict, and the problems caused by globalization and structural adjustment in the document while wealthier countries resisted this language. A proposal to establish a social fund to provide support for the effects of structural adjustment policies was very contentious. Europe was concerned about genetically modified foods. And many countries, most outspokenly Libya, Pakistan, and Cuba, sought to avoid mechanisms for international monitoring for compliance with the terms of the document, including by NGOs, and sought national control and sovereignty. Underlying all of these debates is the question of unequal resources and relatively poor countries' inability to afford new programs. While the global North encourages privatization, the global South insists on the need for more aid from the global North. For example, Libya resisted a sentence urging governments to achieve a 50 percent increase in adult literacy saying that this is not possible without international aid.

During the deliberations at Beijing Plus Five, which lasted for several days and often long into the night, a large body of NGO representatives sat silently in a balcony, excluded from any direct input into the process. When an agreement was forged among the government representatives that NGO representatives liked, a loud cheer sometimes erupted from the balcony, quickly hushed by the chair, who insisted on silence from the NGO audience. At other times, the group groaned at a decision. Charlotte Bunch, a very experienced NGO leader and the director of the Center for Women's Global Leadership, said that it is important for the NGOs to be present, since the delegates will look up and see if they are there even when the debate stretches far into the night. Meanwhile, in the hallways and coffee shops, individual NGO representatives energetically lobbied their government delegates to include particular language advocated by their organization in the document. One woman was overjoyed that she managed to have two references to women's mental health included in the document, for example. Some NGOs were pleased that honor killings were included in the list of "harmful customary or traditional practices," along with female genital mutilation and early and forced marriage (A/RES/S-23/3: 22, par. 69 [e]).

These groups vary significantly in their political views. Many of these NGOs are based on large established religions or are funded by transnational philanthropy or government grants. Although there are some radical NGOs, such as the Women's International League for Peace and Freedom, most are mainstream organizations, such as professional businesswomen's associations, the Girl Scouts, or the League of Women Voters. The left, progressive, social activist NGO seems to be the minority. The more conservative groups seem content to give such vulnerable groups as battered women a voice, while the more radical ones want to focus attention on economic and structural inequalities.

As I watched these proceedings, I was amazed by the energy devoted to crafting wording and by delegates' anxiety about failing to produce an agreed-upon document. I kept wondering why the wording mattered so much. I gradually realized that the struggles over wording were an effort to produce a document that could be adopted by consensus despite significant political differences. The debates about wording proceeded with virtually no discussion of the reasoning behind various positions or the evidence for or against them. Most of the time, delegates simply suggested wording changes. It is likely that substantive debates had already taken place during the deliberations before the final meeting. But there were still major differences of opinion in the room. For example, is globalization responsible for women's poverty around the world? Should women have the right to abort their unborn children? Are wealthy countries willing to pay for reforms in poorer countries? Is the basis for social order secular or religious? It seems unlikely that evidentiary arguments would produce agreement on these questions. Instead, the strategy of finding phrases that are vague and convoluted was a way to reach consensus. Wordsmithing produced a single document despite gaping disparities in views about women's place in society. The surface of the text papers over intractable differences. Indeed, this strategy of proposing alternative wording without substantive argument was common in all the drafting sessions I observed in international meetings.

Despite these enormous differences, there are some areas of commonality. At one point, a woman from India said, to a spate of applause, that the discussion should focus on common women's concerns, not government concerns. Most country delegates agreed on the importance of preventing violence against women, the benefits of development, and state responsibility for change. Most seemed to support nondiscrimination and gender equality. Approaches to change tend to be secular, focused on economic and political reforms rather than religious action. The notion that cultural diversity should be respected is awkwardly juxtaposed to the assumption that religion and culture are barriers to women's equality. I found myself deeply impressed by the fact that this conversation was taking place at all. I was watching people from countries all over the world trying to put together some words that every one of them could live with, despite their differences. In the process of negotiating, of working together toward common ground, some shared understandings about women's place in society emerged. As I attended subsequent meetings, I realized that many of these people had worked together before. Learning this cultural system takes time, and those with more experience obviously have an advantage. Many of the government delegates who were engaged in drafting documents and listening to debates were relatively young, in their thirties and forties, and often commented that they had to get approval from their superiors at home for documents and wording. It appeared that senior diplomats appeared only for special important events. This is clearly a kind of transnational community, with repeat actors, shared discourses and norms of dealing with conflicts and difference, and shared commitments to a vision of a universal form of justice. Where consensus was not possible, the only solution was to eliminate the paragraph.

Why was it necessary to reach consensus in drafting these documents? The process would have been far quicker if differences were resolved by vote. But the UN, as a collection of sovereign states, has very little power to coerce individual states. There is no international mechanism for punishing states that ignore or resist the policy recommendations of UN documents. States and coalitions of states can pressure other states, but a country's vulnerability to this pressure depends greatly on its economic and political power and its capacity to mobilize allies. While NGOs and other states often use shaming and social pressure against recalcitrant states, states vary greatly in their willingness to change in response to such pressures. Powerful states such as the United States and China are relatively impervious to this pressure. Consequently, decisions are more effective if they are reached by consensus. This global process of consensus building gives documents legitimacy as a tool for social reform by human rights activists. The documents articulate, often in an opaque way, a global set of ideas about women's human rights.

In this and other conferences and UN commission meetings, the process of

48

document negotiation, NGO and government interaction, lobbying, presenting NGO side events, and even the frequent use of stock phrases such as "political will," "capacity building," "the international community," "best practices," "lessons learned," and "gender mainstreaming" revealed a transnational culture of human rights activism. Those with more experience were more adept at speaking this language and using the detailed procedural rules and strategies for developing consensus. Although the process appears relatively open and participatory, it is also shaped by several important global inequalities. Differential national resources affect the size and experience of national delegations as well as a country's capacity to implement reforms. Small Pacific nations, for example, rarely send representatives at all, while wealthy nations send large delegations. National representatives differ in their ability to speak fluent English and their capacity to shape the document drafting process. The rest of this chapter explores the forms that human rights intervention takes in combating violence against women and the roles that NGOs play in this process.

Modes of Intervention

The UN human rights system deals with violence against women in three ways: (1) it sets policy; (2) it investigates complaints; and (3) it regulates compliance with treaties. Policies are set at major world conferences, such as the Fourth World Conference on Women held in Beijing in 1995 and its sequel, the UN General Assembly Special Session in 2000, called Beijing Plus Five. These global conferences produce major policy documents that reflect an international consensus and typically exert considerable moral force, although they are not legally binding. The principal documents defining violence against women as a human rights violation came out of the 1993 Vienna World Conference on Human Rights, the 1995 Fourth World Conference on Women held in Beijing, China (typically referred to as the Beijing Conference), and the 2000 five-year review of the Beijing Conference, Beijing Plus Five. Each of these conferences produced an important document, of which the Platform for Action of the Beijing Conference is the most significant. This document named violence against women as a serious global problem. The Beijing Plus Five Conference, designed to assess achievements in the five years after Beijing, resulted in an outcome document that reaffirmed the importance of this issue.

Policy on violence against women is also set in documents produced by UN permanent commissions, especially the Commission on the Status of Women (CSW), which meets annually in New York, and the High Commission on

Human Rights (CHR), which meets annually in Geneva. These are standing commissions of ECOSOC, the Economic and Social Council of the UN. Each is made up of representatives of governments. The CSW, with 45 member states, meets for two weeks a year, while the CHR, with 53 member states, meets for six weeks. Nongovernmental organizations send representatives to these meetings who play critical roles in educating government representatives about the issues, lobbying for words and sentences in the documents that reflect the issues they are concerned about, and holding panel discussions and lectures outside the formal meetings to inform NGOs and government representatives about initiatives taking place around the world. The documents produced at these conferences are not legally binding, but they constitute policies that governments commit themselves to follow.

Complaints are brought to the CHR and to a much lesser extent the CSW. CEDAW added a complaint procedure in 2000. The CHR procedure is more effective, since it has appointed an expert, or special rapporteur, whose tasks include investigating patterns of complaints through visits to particular countries. The rapporteur responds to complaints received by the CHR or requests from NGOs to travel to particular countries and investigate charges of abuse and writes reports that are presented to the Human Rights Commission and posted on the Internet. The special rapporteur on violence against women appointed by the CHR chairman in 1994, Radhika Coomaraswamy, was very effective in bringing more attention to the issue during her nine-year tenure. Coomaraswamy's work has helped to define violence against women as a human rights violation along with the duty of states to exercise "due diligence" in preventing violence against women in the family, the community, and the public space.

Regulation of treaty compliance takes place through hearings on country reports. This is the most legalistic part of the UN system. Conventions are ratified by individual states and are monitored by special committees, called treaty bodies. Each convention has a committee that monitors compliance through a system of periodic reporting. Although these committees lack the sanctioning power of state law, they bring international pressure to bear on recalcitrant states. Ideally, when a state ratifies a convention, its terms are incorporated into the state's domestic legal system.

The major convention governing violence against women is the Convention on the Elimination of All Forms of Discrimination against Women, or CEDAW. It regulates compliance with the treaty on a country-by-country basis. The convention was developed during the 1960s and 1970s, opened for signature in 1979, and put into force in 1981. By 2004 it had been ratified by

178 countries, indicating widespread global support. Its complaint procedure had been ratified by at least sixty countries. The convention is monitored by a system of periodic country reports required every four years from each ratifying state. Unlike the commissions, the CEDAW Committee is made up of experts who come from all regions of the world but do not represent their countries. Instead, they are chosen on the basis of their knowledge of the issues. This chapter discusses the policymaking and investigative activities of the commissions while the next chapter examines the treaty monitoring system.

NGO Participation

NGOs have several major roles in UN meetings. First, they develop issues. Many are regionally based, but their primary loyalty is typically to a specific issue such as trafficking, promoting breastfeeding, promoting women's role in development, advocating special cookers for water purification, and so forth. Outside the formal conference settings, NGOs usually sponsor a lively set of debates, panel presentations, and discussions focused on their issues. Here, NGO representatives talk about their programs, their work, and their countries to audiences that include other NGOs and sometimes the government delegates. These events take place alongside the regular deliberations of the government representatives and are typically referred to as side events. They are quite numerous. In 2001, there were 55 side events in the first week of the CSW. They often are panels discussing the same issue in a variety of countries. For example, a panel on women and poverty organized by the Asia Pacific Women's Watch featured eight speakers from Asian countries talking about the issue in Thailand, Kyrgyzstan, China, Japan, and Korea. Another panel explored trafficking and prostitution in several Asian countries with presentations by activists working on this problem in India and the Philippines. A CSW side event in 2001 was called Refugee Women: Perspectives on Racism and Discrimination, with speakers from the UN High Commission on Refugees (UNHCR) and the Refugee Women's Network in Atlanta, Georgia.

These sessions are generally well attended by audiences of between 30 and 50 people. NGOs must request space in advance for the events they intend to sponsor. Side events are generally either panels of experts or informal working groups, called caucuses, focused on developing language for the documents under discussion. Attendees also engage in networking and information sharing. The exchange of information and ideas about different local situations is critical for NGOs. In the conferences I attended, NGO representatives from around the world compared notes about raising funds, developing shelters for battered women, and promoting economic equality for women. Many commented on how much they learned at meetings. When they returned home they had a better idea of the issues of current concern internationally, helping them develop programs and frame funding proposals to international donors.

The second role for NGO representatives is making statements, called interventions. In general, NGOs may speak to UN commissions only for a very restricted time. Commissions are made up of governments, not NGOs. Although NGOs are increasingly recognized as important to the operation of these forums, they are often viewed suspiciously as irritants. Despite the frequent nostrums governments offer about the importance of civil society, they are thought to be sometimes irresponsible and inflammatory. In order to speak at Human Rights Commission meetings, an NGO has to prepare a statement a month in advance and submit it to the commission.[1] The length of the statement is determined by the status of the NGO: those of higher status (discussed later in this chapter) are allowed 2000 words; those in other statuses are entitled to 1500. NGOs are not allowed to read out the full text contained in their written statements when taking the floor of plenary meetings of the commission but must make shorter statements.[2] At the CSW, an accredited NGO can submit a written statement two months in advance and it will be distributed as a document. NGOs can make statements during question and answer sessions in which governments are participating, but they must submit these statements a day in advance and their length is restricted to five minutes.[3] This does provide an opportunity to present ideas to the commission, although of a very limited sort. As an experienced NGO representative said in a training session for NGOs, these statements must be relevant to the announced theme of the meeting, short and focused, and make their point clearly. There are debates about how much time NGOs are allowed to speak, dissatisfaction among NGOs, and current efforts to expand NGOs' speaking time.

The third role for NGO representatives is working with and lobbying governments concerning the text of documents. NGOs meet separately in caucuses, based either on regions or issues, and develop alternative ways of organizing sentences and ideas. They then take these texts, often produced by a regional caucus, such as the African Women's Caucus, or a theme group, such as one on the environment, and try to reach individual delegation members with their proposed language. Some delegates are known to be more sympathetic than others, while those in a region are clearly the focus of attention for regional caucuses. It is bad form for NGOs to lobby delegates in their seats. Instead, they try to reach them in the halls or coffee shop during breaks.

At Beijing Plus Five, NGOs formed two kinds of caucuses: issue caucuses and regional caucuses. Each held daily meetings and developed plans to pressure delegates about parts of the document of importance to them. For example, there was a Violence against Women Caucus that hammered out a statement it distributed informally to delegates. The caucus was open to any NGO representative, but a small core of NGO leaders working in organizations focused on violence against women did the final drafting. During caucus meetings, I witnessed the shaping of violence against women as an issue. A French-speaking participant from Africa wanted to include violence done in the name of culture and religion, such as polygamy. The chair of the meeting paused a moment, then replied, why not? Polygamy was included in the resolution produced by the Violence against Women Caucus. Internet discussions in 2004 have continued to develop this idea. Another woman spoke powerfully about the miseries of widowhood, and this issue was also added. Widowhood practices were emerging as a new issue in violence against women at the Beijing Plus Five meeting and attention to this issue has increased subsequently. The statement also included such contentious issues as marriage of girls and adolescents, honor killings, and violence against women and girls who are or are perceived to be lesbian, bisexual, or transgendered. These discussions were held in English and the leaders tended to be American and European. In order to generate more attention, the Violence against Women Caucus staged a demonstration protesting violence against women in a park across the street from the UN building during the conference.

Several regional caucuses also met regularly, although with mixed success. Some, such as the Asia-Pacific caucus, were well organized, whereas others met rarely or never. The regional caucuses were invited to report every morning at the NGO briefing, an hour-long event in the UN building normally attended by several hundred people.

The fourth role of NGOs is helping to disseminate the documents at home and pressuring their governments to abide by them. The documents offer a tool to use against recalcitrant governments and are more legitimate because they were created through international consensus. I will explore this process in more detail in chapter 5.

The sharp resource disparities between North and South radically limit the ability of poorer NGOs to participate in the process. In order for an NGO to participate in any of these events, it must receive consultative status from the UN. Only individuals representing such NGOs can acquire the identity badge necessary to gain access to the space where UN meetings are held and government representatives are available for lobbying. While this was a relatively easy process in the past, the number of applications has mushroomed and applicants are scrutinized more closely.[4] In order to gain consultative status, an NGO must apply through a complex procedure and describe in detail the nature of the organization, its mission, its membership, and its financial status. The decision can take over a year. As the number of NGOs has expanded, the difficulty of determining which groups should earn this status has grown as well. The committee that determines if an NGO is eligible, the UN Committee on Non-Governmental Organizations, requires that organizations carry out work relevant to ECOSOC, have a democratic decision-making process, exist for two years or more, and receive a major portion of their funding from contributions from national affiliates, individual members, or other non-governmental components (www.un.org/esa/coordination/ngo, March 2002). My observations of this committee suggest that a group's admission to consultative status depends on persuading the committee that it is promoting the goals of the UN, that it is not a profit-making organization, and that it is not a political organization. Conversations with some applicants suggested that they feel that achieving consultative status improves their ability to raise funds to support their projects. It is certainly essential for participating in these meetings, which provide information on donor agendas, current developments, and contacts with activists and government representatives around the world. The UN recognizes that the process for achieving consultative status is difficult, especially for organizations in developing countries, but despite efforts to make the process more accessible, it is still daunting.

Moreover, NGOs are not of equal consultative status. There are three categories of membership: general, special, and roster. The number of representatives who may attend and the opportunities for speaking depend on this status. Most NGOs are in *special* consultative status although some of the older and larger ones have the more privileged *general* consultative status and small newcomers are often given *roster* status. According to the UN website listing the NGOs in consultative status, as of November 2001 there were approximately 2000, of which about 130 were in general status, about 1000 in special, and 900 in roster (www.un.org/esa/coordination/ngo).[5]

Funding is a critical issue for all NGOs, although sources of support differ among organizations. Membership-based international organizations like Soroptimist International, Zonta International, Girl Scouts and Girl Guides, the YWCA, or the Women's International League for Peace and Freedom rely on dues. Member-supported groups also include established religions such as the Franciscans International (with one million members), Presbyterians, Lutherans, Anglicans, and the Baha'i International. Many service and advocacy NGOs are supported by donor funds. Groups relying on donor funds face ongoing challenges of fundraising to support their activities. Attending UN meetings is expensive, but it facilitates fundraising. Since funding comes primarily from the global North, both from private foundations and development aid, NGOs in consultative status that come to New York or Geneva have the opportunity to meet with funders, find out what the current hot topics are, learn the appropriate language in which to phrase funding proposals, and hear what other groups are doing. Some of the side events at UN meetings concern fundraising strategies or provide opportunities to meet with funders. As one funder said in a meeting at the CSW, "It is important for us to get to know you and your program in order to fund your activities." When I asked how NGO leaders in poorer countries who are unable to come to New York could do this, the speaker acknowledged the difficulty and suggested sending newsletters.

I interviewed three program officers in major private foundations about their funding strategies for women's NGOs. They pointed out that foundations face a dilemma. They are interested in supporting grassroots organizations but at the same time they need to be accountable to their donors. This means that they need to achieve something that they can report back to their donors and avoid embarrassing the foundation by misuse of funds, the failure of the project, or negative publicity. Consequently, there is a tendency to fund the same organizations for many years. Program officers differ in their knowledge about various parts of the world and therefore in their willingness to take risks on unknown organizations. Major funders are more reluctant to take risks with their funding than smaller foundations, but an unknown organization that has not established trust with a foundation and its program officers will have difficulty getting funding from anyone. Foundations are governed by boards that may or may not be interested in risky funding for projects in unknown regions. As a result, established organizations with reputations for reliable services and fiscal responsibility do far better. Achieving ECOSOC accredited status probably aids fundraising, although I have no statistics to show that this is the case. It is difficult to see how the funding process, which advantages inside players and those with connections to the global North, can be changed without increasing the riskiness of funding decisions. As any activist NGO knows, this is not a problem that will be fixed until it is clearly identified and labeled as such. And, as these NGOs also know, naming and shaping a problem for intervention is a major political task that requires funding, staff, and political support.

It is obviously expensive and difficult for global South NGO members or social movement leaders to attend UN meetings in Europe or the United States. Many who do come are working in projects with international donors, but they can usually come only while the project lasts. One of the recurring complaints of international NGOs is that they can only get funding for a short period, such as three to five years, and this is not enough time to set up a program and show that it works. NGO representatives who can go to commission meetings year after year develop the expertise in personnel, lobbying strategy, and documents essential to making an impact on the document drafting process. NGO representatives who know the language used in past documents are much more influential in lobbying than those who lack this expertise, given the preference for agreed-upon language. Consequently, the leading NGO representatives tend to be experienced heads of major US, Canadian, and European organizations. I heard little complaint about this situation by developing countries' NGO representatives, however. Instead, there is generally a sense of camaraderie and support as well as openness to learning from one another. Nevertheless, the hurdles for NGO participation from poorer parts of the world are substantial.

The Commission on Human Rights

The Commission on Human Rights is one of the specialized commissions under the Economic and Social Council and through it, the General Assembly. It has evolved since its first meeting in 1947 into the single most important UN organ in the human rights field (Alston 1992: 126). The commission meets for six weeks annually in Geneva in a vast conference center overlooking the lake. Its 53 member states are elected for three-year terms and are regionally distributed. The CHR also has a substantial number of delegates from non-member states that cannot vote but can participate in discussions and document-drafting sessions. There is an NGO gallery with roughly 40–50 people present on average. In sharp contrast to the government representatives at the Beijing Plus Five meeting and the Commission on the Status of Women, the body is largely male. The commission produces resolutions, receives complaints of human rights violations from around the world, and responds to these complaints in many ways, including by sponsoring independent investigators who explore patterns of complaints by making country investigations and reporting back to the commission. Only since 1979 has the CHR made a serious effort to develop mechanisms to respond to an ever widening range of types of human rights violations (Alston 1992: 139).

The core concerns are civil and political rights including protection from torture, freedom of expression, and religious intolerance. However, there is increasing focus on economic, social, and cultural rights, women's rights, and indigenous peoples' rights. Like other parts of the UN human rights system, the commission is constantly evolving, developing new mechanisms and new conceptions of rights. It responds to contemporary political struggles, whether the US effort to sanction China for its human rights violations (see Foot 2000) or the Palestinian effort to sanction Israel for its treatment of Palestinian people. Like the rest of the human rights system, the CHR is changing, fragmentary, and sometimes inconsistent, a creature of high moral standards and pragmatic political pressures. It operates within a structure of sovereign nations even as the concept of human rights itself is premised on the necessity for international intervention that transcends sovereignty.

Much of the ongoing work of the commission is carried out by the Sub-Commission on the Prevention of Discrimination and Protection of Minorities, a committee of 26 independent experts elected by the commission which meets four weeks a year and provides analysis and advice to the commission (Eide 1992: 211–30). It allows considerable input from NGOs and functions through a set of semipermanent working groups. The subcommission reviews the complaints and passes them on to the commission, which spends some of its meeting time discussing them. By the late 1980s, the commission was receiving up to 300,000 complaints annually. Between 1978 and 1991, the commission subjected 39 countries to scrutiny (Alston 1992: 147–48). NGOs play an important role in developing and presenting complaints. The subcommission establishes separate working groups made up of members with regional diversity to deal with particular issues, such as the Working Group on the Rights of Indigenous Populations formed in 1982 or the Working Group on Enforced or Involuntary Disappearances set up in 1980 in response to developments in Argentina and Chile (Alston 1992: 174; Eide 1992: 235).

Special rapporteurs are appointed in response to particular crises and have become an important part of the work of the commission over the last two decades. As one special rapporteur put it, they are the "eyes and ears" of the commission. Some of the roughly thirty rapporteurs focus on particular countries and others on thematic issues. For example, there are special rapporteurs on torture, on extrajudicial, summary, or arbitrary executions, on religious intolerance (established in 1982), and on the sale of children, child prostitution, and child pornography as well as on Burma and Afghanistan. The administrative support for the CHR is provided by a secretariat in Geneva and the High Commissioner on Human Rights. Rapporteurs receive expenses but are not paid for their work. In the process of creating a new issue, the establishment of a special rapporteur, a special representative of the secretary-general, or a working group of the subcommission is a critical step.

The development of this special investigative wing of the Human Rights Commission is relatively recent, dating from the 1980s. The first rapporteurs were diplomats who were not too intrusive in their work, but some of the more recent appointments are from NGO backgrounds and are more willing to criticize governments. As of the early 1990s, there were only four special rapporteurs with a thematic mandate, but the number is expanding. The 2000 meeting of the Commission on Human Rights appointed special rapporteurs on the right to adequate housing and the right to food. The task of special rapporteurs includes collecting information about violations of specific rights, receiving and forwarding to governments communications received from individuals or organizations alleging violations of the rights that fall within the relevant mandate, reporting on the extent and practice of the violations of the relevant rights, formulating policy recommendations, and, in some cases, visiting individual countries at the invitation of those countries. The report of each rapporteur to the Human Rights Commission is a public document that contains summaries of communications and of replies from governments, as well as more general material. "The Rapporteurs do not adjudicate on the accuracy of the allegations contained in material which they receive from individuals and organizations or from Governments in reply" (UN Doc E/CN.6/1991/pars. 133, 134, cited in Byrnes 1994: 206–7). The Commission on the Status of Women has not appointed special rapporteurs, although it has discussed doing so.

As with other UN commissions, NGOs play an important role. NGOs are allowed to address the CHR after submitting written statements, ranging from 1500 to 2000 words depending on the status of the NGO. These were due before the beginning of February for a conference that begins in mid-March in order to have them translated and distributed. NGOs are not allowed to read out the full text of their statement when they take the floor at the plenary meetings of the commission but are given much more limited time.[6] Forty-six intergovernmental and nongovernmental groups addressed the plenary on the subject of violence against women in 2001. Some of these speeches are more general while some focus on local problems, sometimes describing a particular egregious situation such as Iran's High Court's approval of the sentence of stoning for three women or the arrest and whipping of twelve women for being badly veiled. In 2001, the All-China Women's Federation branded the Falung Gong an "evil cult," a Native American group asked to have a special rapporteur established for indigenous peoples, a representative from the World Muslim Congress reported a problem with torture in occupied Kashmir, and a representative from the Women's International League for Peace and Freedom (WILPF) argued that honor killings should be stopped along with all laws, customs, and practices that support them and that states are complicit when they give light sentences for the offense. WILPF asked the CHR to prepare a working paper on this topic through the subcommission. Other NGOs raised issues such as violence against women in military conflicts in Aceh and the Moluccas and trafficking of women from Burma to Thailand.

Governments have the right to reply to NGO statements, many of which are accusations of government misconduct. For example, Malaysia complained that one NGO, instead of talking about general issues, used this forum for political mileage. Yemen complained that the International Law Group had used erroneous sources. Iran wished to refute the "baseless allegations" of two NGOs that are well funded and based in a neighboring country. The spokesman asserted the need for a renewal of the traditional outlook that emphasizes the superiority of men.

Outside the formal meeting room a plethora of special events organized by NGOs and special rapporteurs bring developments around the world to the attention of government delegates and NGO representatives. Sessions offer the opportunity to hear more details about the work of special rapporteurs, to hear about new NGO initiatives such as protecting the rights of sexual minorities, and to hear about the work of UN agencies such as UNIFEM and UNICEF from prominent members of their staffs. At the same time, a large coffee bar area with a sweeping view of the lake and the mountains beyond is the locus of intense lobbying by NGOs and informal meetings among government delegates. I attended some informal planning sessions as NGOs strategized about which delegates were most sympathetic to their issues and how they should be approached and by whom. For example, on the issue of honor killings, the NGO group decided that it would be far better to have a spokesperson from an Islamic country than a non-Islamic one. As in the New York meetings, however, access to the hallways and lobbying spaces as well as to the formal meetings and informal negotiations about resolutions is open only to government delegates, UN personnel, and NGO representatives with ECOSOC consultative status. Those who are allowed in, however, have full access to the documentation provided to government delegations and the simultaneous translation system that makes UN proceedings available in the six official languages: English, French, Spanish, Russian, Arabic, and Chinese.

DRAFTING RESOLUTIONS

Much of the time at CHR meetings is devoted to drafting and approving resolutions and decisions. Behind the formal proceedings, smaller groups of country representatives meet to hammer out the language of these resolutions.[7] Most of these resolutions are drafted by member states and the large number of observer states that also attend. Although the primary women's rights issue during the 2001 and 2002 sessions was violence against women, only about three of the one hundred resolutions dealt with women's issues. One was on violence against women, one on trafficking, and one on gender mainstreaming. The CHR has passed a resolution concerning violence against women every year since 1994 and has regularly produced a resolution against trafficking.

A number of countries collectively develop and sponsor resolutions. The sponsors organize a series of meetings, usually lasting for two hours at a time over a period of one or two weeks, open to any country delegates concerned about the resolution. These informal meetings offer the opportunity to argue over the language in a manner reminiscent of the Beijing Plus Five process. Because of this process, in most cases when a resolution comes to the floor of the CHR, it is accepted by consensus instead of by a vote. According to Alston, 77 percent of the 97 resolutions reached in 1990 were the result of consensus (1992: 197). Delegates to the CHR told me that resolutions reached by consensus had much more credibility than those passed by vote. Thus, sponsors of a resolution invest a great deal of effort in negotiating the language of resolutions informally in order to deal with objections and avoid a vote. Consensus does not mean that all are enthusiastic about the resolution, only that those who care enough to protest have been satisfied. These resolutions are not legally binding but are made widely available and posted on the website.

I observed the process of drafting the violence against women and trafficking resolutions in both 2001 and 2002. In 2001, there were 75 co-sponsors to the violence against women resolution. In both years, about 20 government representatives attended each drafting session, with five or six NGOs present as well. Governments that send larger delegations are clearly better able to participate in such informal discussions. In the official list of attendees in 2001, for example, India sent 8, Vietnam 12, Pakistan 17, the UK 17, Canada 20, China 21, Germany 27, Russia 28, and US 38, and among nonmember states, Bhutan sent 5, Myanmar 6, Finland 16, Equatorial Guinea 19, Congo 20, and Sweden 40. Fiji sent none (E/CN.4/2001/MISC.2/6 April 2001). In one drafting session on the violence resolution, for example, Canada chaired and country representatives came from Libya, Pakistan, Thailand, Korea, New Zealand, Australia, Netherlands, Sweden, Russia, Cuba, Japan, Germany, India, US, Malaysia, and Italy. The discussions were always done in English without simultaneous translation.

As I watched the drafting process in 2001 and 2002 and read the texts of earlier resolutions, I saw that new forms of violence against women were added over time. In 2000 the resolution referred for the first time to "crimes committed in the name of honour, crimes committed in the name of passion" to the list of forms of violence against women (par. 3). The definition of violence against women was expanded in 2002 to include trafficking and "early and forced" rather than only "forced" marriages. In 2002, there was discussion about incorporating the violence that women experience as a result of their sexual orientation and about whether to list widows as particularly vulnerable to violence. Several representatives from South Asian countries objected to the latter change. Including sexual orientation evoked far more resistance, including a cameo appearance from a representative of Saudi Arabia who stopped by to say that his government did not support recognizing sexual orientation and then walked out. After considerable debate, the representative from Pakistan said she would accept widows if sexual orientation were deleted, and the issue was settled. The demand that governments not invoke "custom, tradition or practices in the name of religion to avoid their obligations to eliminate such violence" (2001: 10 [b]) was expanded in 2002 to add "in the name of religion or culture" (2002: 14 [c]), paralleling a deepening critique of culture as an obstacle to women's human rights. At the same time, proposed language to take the next step and urge governments "to prevent, eliminate and prosecute crimes against women committed in the name of honour" was not adopted in 2002. The 1999 version referred to "traditional or customary practices affecting the health of women and girls" (preamble paragraph), while the subsequent drafts simply referred to "traditional practices harmful to women" (2000: par. 3), deleting the reference to health.

As in other UN document-drafting sessions, these discussions took place without much substantive information about the extent to which, for example, widowhood or sexual orientation did or did not render women more vulnerable to violence. This is a deeply ideological debate but is also shaped by political pragmatism and the need to reach some agreement. Many of the participants in the 2002 drafting group were the same as those in 2001, suggesting that they work together over time. A small number of NGOs attended these sessions, but they were not allowed to speak. Sponsors of some resolutions even prohibited NGO attendance. It is possible that as government representatives work together to produce a document that must be consensual, a shared commitment emerges and perhaps some areas of agreement.

Document drafting is a process of cultural creation. In this transnational discursive process, an epistemic community emerges through ongoing dialogue among middle-level foreign service representatives, speaking both as representatives of nations and for themselves as raced and gendered persons.

The similarity of the document production process at Beijing Plus Five, the CSW, and the CHR facilitates negotiating a global consensus. The language may be vacuous and tortured, but it is the product of a group of people from all over the world trying to reach some agreement about how to describe women's position and how to imagine a more just arrangement.

THE SPECIAL RAPPORTEUR ON VIOLENCE AGAINST WOMEN

Since the position was created in 1994, the special rapporteur on violence against women has produced a series of highly influential reports that have defined the problem of violence against women and explored its forms and prevalence in many countries (see Thomas and Levi 1999). Radhika Coomaraswamy held this post from its inception until 2003. She has produced both general reports that define the issues and special reports that describe her investigatory field missions to particular countries. Activists and government officials often use the definitions of violence against women developed in these reports. Her investigative reports are usually based on a two to three week trip in which she interviews victims, government officials, and NGO representatives. For example, between 28 October and 15 November 2000, she visited Bangladesh, Nepal, and India investigating trafficking in women and girls. Her report (E/CN.4/2001/73/add/2) describes her findings and recommends that the international community take a proactive role in preventing trafficking in the South Asian region, along with national governments, and that governments should develop regulations that do not violate the rights of women or restrict their free movement under the guise of fighting trafficking (UN Press Release HR/CN/01/40, 9 April 2001:3). These visits are encouraged by NGOs who hope to use the international visibility of the rapporteur to expose their issues. For example, in 2001, a Saudi requested investigation of Saudi Arabia's refusal to allow women identity cards or the right to drive. An American suggested investigating cultural practices that control women's sexuality such as sending women to mental hospitals, kidnapping, and other efforts to "reeducate" lesbians taking place in the United States. But governments must be willing to invite the rapporteur for her to investigate. Some governments resist by refusing to guarantee her safety.

The special rapporteur presents a short verbal report to the plenary commission every year and holds several longer briefing sessions during the approximately two days of the six-week session devoted to women's rights. Countries object to special rapporteurs' reports in the plenary session, arguing that the criticisms are unjustified and describing their efforts to deal with the problem.

For example, after the 2001 report on the study of trafficking in South Asia (India, Nepal, and Bangladesh), Bangladesh said it had signed and ratified the Optional Protocol to CEDAW, withdrawn two of its reservations to CEDAW, and made more efforts to arrest offenders than the report recognizes. India described its efforts to end trafficking and expressed regret at the special rapporteur's reliance on "unsubstantiated sweeping reports based on NGO reports from an area of wartime conflict" (April 9, 2001). Apparently countries care about the criticisms the rapporteur makes and wish to defend themselves.

The written reports are highly visible and widely available as UN documents on the Internet. I discussed Radhika Coomaraswamy's work with her several times in Boston and Geneva and heard her give several talks at UN conferences. In contrast to many of the rapporteurs of the past who were diplomats (Alston 1992: 167), she comes from an academic and NGO background and, like other rapporteurs with such backgrounds, is more willing to challenge governments. The work she does is similar to that pioneered by the Women's Rights Project of Human Rights Watch in investigating particular abuses of women all over the world (Thomas and Levi 1999).

At the 2002 meeting of the High Commission on Human Rights, the special rapporteur on violence against women presented her annual report, which focused on what she described as a sensitive topic: cultural practices in the family that are violent to women. She described it as "an important issue that would define the international human rights debate over the next decade" (HR/CN/ 02/32: 10 April 2002, UN Press Release). It moved into a new domain of behavior, that of sexuality and its regulation, and challenged cultural practices considered acceptable by at least some members of many societies.[8] The report discussed a variety of practices in the family that are violent toward women and harmful to their health. It covered practices such as female genital mutilation, honor killings, pledging of daughters to temples at an early age to be sex workers or handmaidens of gods (the *devadasi* system in India and similar systems in Nepal, Benin, Nigeria, Togo, and Ghana), witch hunting (found mainly in Asia and Africa), caste-based discrimination and violence, early and forced marriage, marital rape, discriminatory laws, son preference, restrictive practices such as foot binding and veiling, and images of beauty that emphasize thinness, a widespread problem in the West. The report argues that these cultural practices harmful to women's human rights to bodily integrity and expression have avoided national and international scrutiny "because they are seen as cultural practices that deserve tolerance and respect." "Cultural relativism," she asserts, "is often used as an excuse to permit inhumane and discriminatory practices against women in the community despite clear provisions in many human rights instruments, including the Convention on the Elimination of All Forms of Discrimination against Women, in accordance with which States parties shall take all appropriate measures to modify the social and cultural patterns of conduct of men and women, with a view to achieving the elimination of prejudices and customary and all other practices which are based on the idea of the inferiority or the superiority of either of the sexes or on stereotyped roles for men and women" (E/CN.4/2002/83 [art. 5]: p. 3). Coomaraswamy asserts that all cultures have such practices and that many focus on the regulation of female sexuality and masculinity and violence. Despite an effort in this report to be inclusive and refer to a range of countries engaging in these practices, most of those discussed are found in Asia and Africa.

The report seeks to navigate between blaming culture and protecting cultural diversity. It condemns cultural practices violent to women, not cultures as wholes, and includes language supportive of cultural diversity. "The Special Rapporteur recommends that women from the various communities should be listened to and assisted to transform harmful practices without destroying the rich cultural tapestry of their societies which makes up their identity" (p. 3). Paralleling the general international women's rights perspective, she urges states "not to invoke any custom, tradition, or religious consideration to avoid their obligation to eradicate violence against women and the girl child in the family." She recommends that states adopt penal sanctions to eradicate these practices as well as engaging in education to modify social and cultural patterns of conduct that foster these cultural practices (p. 4). The report shifts from the older labels "traditional practices" or "harmful traditional practices" to "cultural practices in the family that are violent to women," expanding the spectrum of cultural practices under scrutiny.

This report evoked far more resistance from governments than others the special rapporteur has done, particularly from South Asian countries. Many governments expressed considerable displeasure with the report, and some, such as Pakistan, were quite hostile. The discussion of honor killings was particularly contentious. The regulation of women's sexuality is a fundamental feature of social life in many societies, urban as well as rural, and it is inextricably linked to maintaining family, communal, and even national honor. Killing a woman who has violated sexual modesty rules preserves the family's honor. The report challenged the authority of men to kill women in their families to protect their honor, claiming that the international community had the right to decide that it was not justified. In one meeting at the CHR, a representative from Pakistan objected to the report's portrayal of the dress code of Muslim women, early marriage, and practices restricting women's mobility and freedom as violence against women. (The text referred to dress codes that "restrict women's movement and their right to expression" [p. 28].) One government delegate said, "If the Special Rapporteur continues to criticize religions and cultures as part of her mandate, we have a problem with that." In the drafting sessions for the resolution against violence against women, the Pakistani representative objected to the shift from the term "harmful traditional practices" to "cultural practices harmful to women and girls, that constitute, or lead to, violence against women" (par. 22). She worried about this language because, she said, "We are all proud of our cultures." Delegates from New Zealand and Mexico countered that this was "Beijing language" from paragraph 118. The language from the Beijing Platform for Action says, "Violence against women throughout the life cycle derives essentially from cultural patterns, in particular the harmful effects of certain traditional or customary practices and all acts of extremism linked to race, sex, language or religion that perpetuate the lower status accorded to women in the family, the workplace, the community and society." As a result of these struggles, the final text of the violence against women resolution in 2002 refers to "traditional or customary practices harmful to women and girls" (par. 24) rather than "cultural practices harmful to women and girls."

Perhaps one reason this report drew such fire is that it evoked the idea of culture as national identity rather than culture as tradition. The phrase "traditional or customary" practices is positioned differently within the politics of culture than "cultural practices in the family." The former, and older, phrase targets practices acceptable among those groups considered traditional in Africa and Asia — usually the uneducated, rural poor. The latter, newer one implies national practices. The older term allowed transnational elite activists to locate themselves within modernity and far away from tradition and its criticized practices. In contrast, the more encompassing label targets the entire country, not just its "backward" members. Instead of attacking culture in the sense of tradition, this criticism attacked culture in the sense of national identity.

In contrast, Special Rapporteur on Extrajudicial, Summary, or Arbitrary Executions Asma Jahangir, a lawyer and human rights activist from Pakistan, criticized honor killings not as a part of culture, which she said includes music, art, and dance, or religion, but as custom. "Culture is not custom," she said in a talk at the CHR. Thus, she sought to unlink honor killings from religion and culture. By calling honor killing a custom, she located it in the domain of traditional harmful practice. She says it worked to proceed this way in Pakistan, where she was able to get support from some religious leaders. Many women's groups in Pakistan are mobilized against the practice and General Musharaff, of Pakistan, spoke out against honor killings in 2000 even though these efforts have not been supported by much government effort at implementation. Rhetorically separating honor killing from national culture and locating it within custom may provoke less nationalist resistance.

I wondered if this resistance occurred partly because the critiques resonated with colonial critiques of family and gender practices, ranging from assaults on *sati* to child marriage. At a side event panel on cultural practices against women in Asia, I asked if anyone was concerned about the parallels between these cultural critiques of the family and imperialist efforts at social reform. The chair, a woman from India, replied that these critiques were different because the initiative came from national and grassroots movements rather than foreign ones. It was the men who resisted. An audience member from the Philippines told me rather testily that human rights are not just Western; "they are ours too." An activist from Thailand commented that the cultural relativism position harms human rights. A feminist leader from Korea noted that most who advocate cultural relativism are men, sometimes promoting Confucian ideals of "strong families." It is, she said, important to examine whose rights cultural relativism protects and whose position it strengthens. A woman from Malaysia commented that it is important to have rights, not Asian values, and that the assertion of Asian values is government talk. These global South activists insisted that human rights belong to them and are not being imposed on them by the global North. They tangle with governments that use claims to culture to resist their reform efforts. Not surprisingly, they view resistance to women's rights in the name of protecting a national culture as self-serving and illegitimate.

The Commission on the Status of Women

The Commission on the Status of Women is one of the so-called functional commissions of the Economic and Social Council of the United Nations, set up in 1946 to focus on questions concerning the position of women. Its original mandate was to prepare recommendations and reports to the council on promoting women's rights in political, economic, social, and educational fields (E/CN.6/2001/8: 2). It also makes recommendations to the council on urgent problems concerning women's rights and the equality of rights between men and women, as well as developing proposals to carry out these recommendations. In 1987, its mandate was expanded to include promoting the objectives of equality, development, and peace, monitoring the implementation of measures for the advancement of women, and reviewing and appraising progress made at subregional, regional, and global levels (E/CN.6/2001/8: 2). The CSW has energetically promoted gender mainstreaming, particularly since the mid 1990s. Gender mainstreaming usually means thinking about all policies and programs in terms of their implications for women, so that questions of gender difference become fundamental to all policy planning. ECOSOC resolution 2001/41 declared that the CSW "has a catalytic role with respect to ensuring the integration of a gender perspective in United Nations activities" (E/CH.6/2002/11: p. 10).

Although the CSW is the major policy-making body for women's issues in the UN system, there is some concern that it is less powerful and effective than other major UN commissions. The commission organized and promoted a series of worldwide conferences on women, beginning in Mexico City in 1975, Copenhagen in 1980, Nairobi in 1985, and Beijing in 1995. In an interesting geographical fixing of these events, they are now referred to by place rather than by subject or date. This kind of insider talk marks those who know how to play the game and those who do not. Since the Beijing meeting, the commission has focused on monitoring the implementation of the Platform for Action. The CSW planned a ten-year evaluation of the Platform for Action at its regular meeting in 2005, called Beijing Plus Ten.

Commission members are elected by the Economic and Social Council of the UN for four-year terms. Like all UN organs, membership is regionally distributed. The CSW has 13 African members, 11 Asian, 4 Eastern European, 9 Latin American and Caribbean, and 8 Western European and other states. A government representative told me that many governments are eager to serve on the commission. Although there is usually a lively meeting of NGOs accompanying the CSW, its government members are not particularly receptive to their views and opinions. Indeed, the endemic relationship of distrust and symbiotic dependence between states and NGOs runs through the CSW as it does through the CHR and the world conferences.

The CSW meeting in New York has the sense of excitement and exchange found in the larger world conferences. Like the Human Rights Commission, the CSW is a setting for the lawlike construction of texts and debates over wording, yet is also at the center of a rich flow of information and analysis from people from all over the world. Nineteen hundred NGOs registered for the 2001 meeting, for example, and organized 105 side events. At large gatherings, some NGOs bring statements that they distribute themselves, leaving piles of variously colored paper announcements of events and brochures about various programs all over the world displayed on tables outside the conference rooms and posted in front of meeting rooms. NGOs frequently graze through these papers, picking up information about events and programs all over the world, a pattern found in major UN conferences as well.

The CSW handles a small number of complaints. Although the commission receives some complaints directly and others indirectly from the CHR, this activity is far less important than it is for the High Commission for Human Rights. At the 2002 meeting, there was discussion about developing a complaint procedure and appointing special rapporteurs. Member states of the CSW did not feel, however, that they had the resources to take on these tasks and were generally unenthusiastic about adding them. Hearing specific complaints often requires legal expertise and considerable staffing to follow up on the process.[9]

Since the Beijing Conference, the CSW has focused on two specific issues each year that serve as the basis for its policy documents. In 2001, these were AIDS and racism and in 2002 a gender perspective on natural disaster and eradicating poverty (E/CN.6/2002/9). In 2003, the themes were access for women to information technology and the elimination of all forms of violence against women and girls. The CSW holds panel discussions on each topic under the guidance of a group of experts, organized by the Bureau of the Commission, a subgroup of five members selected for two-year terms on a regional basis (E/CN.6/2001/8: 2). The commission then draws up policy documents expressing the consensus of the members about each topic. The panel discussions are often exciting and innovative while the process of fine-tuning the policy document is tedious to an extreme. Each topic leads to an "agreed conclusion" adopted by consensus of the entire commission. The secretariat, the Division for the Advancement of Women, and the Bureau of the Commission provide the initial draft and the full commission discusses it line by line. It includes the same negotiating factions—the Group of 77 plus China, JUSCANZ, the EU, SADC, and GRULAC (Group of Latin American and Caribbean Countries).

The CSW also produces resolutions, documents initiated by particular countries that develop a proposal and then work with other interested countries to produce a text. The text is adopted by the whole body, either by consensus or by vote. Resolutions are generally more focused and shorter than agreed conclusions. Many delegates feel that resolutions are the most authoritative format and that the drafting process is superior. One government representative to both commissions thought that resolutions are more rigorous. Nevertheless, the CSW has shifted from resolutions to agreed conclusions as its major policy documents. The Legal Affairs Office of the UN says they carry the same authority as resolutions (E/CN.6/2001/8: 5). In my interviews with government representatives, some expressed concern that agreed conclusions

68

required a painstaking process of consensus building that produced long, repetitive, and complex documents in order to get all groups to agree. Some worry about how time-consuming the editorial process is and about how unwieldy the texts are after endless negotiations about wording. Because they incorporate a wide range of views, they are not as "conclusive or action-oriented as the Commission might wish" (E/CN.6/2001/8: 6). In contrast, resolutions depend on collective drafting by smaller groups of interested countries and simple acquiescence by the larger group rather than detailed participation of all member states in the drafting process, the working method I have already described for the CHR. At the 2002 CSW meeting, there were two agreed conclusions, one on poverty alleviation and one on disaster mitigation, as well as five resolutions. These conclusions and resolutions are made generally available through governments and have in recent years been posted on the UN website.

Although not enforceable, these documents articulate general principles of policy and action for the global community. Like other policy statements, they set standards that those who wish to be members of the "civilized" international community must recognize (Foot 2000). These standards are important for prestige and for enhancing trade and aid relations. For example, at a March 2002 meeting of the National Assembly of Nigeria, the chairman, Chief Phillip Ume, said that the subject of human rights has become so important all over the world that "it is now the benchmark for the assessment of good governance and good governments, as well as being the pre-qualification and pre-condition for the grant of aids by international donor agencies."[10] The status of women has become a measure of "civilization," although whether civilization is manifested by gender equality or by keeping women modest and protected is a point of global contestation. At the beginning of the CSW meeting, all member governments take the floor to trumpet their achievements in promoting the status of women, emphasizing the number of treaties they have ratified, commissions formed, laws passed, and innovative programs developed. Pakistan, for example, pointed out in the 2001 meeting that it is committed to equality of women, that this is included in its constitution, and although it still has a long way to go, it has made progress in educating women. Japan noted that it had passed eleven new measures in December 2000 to promote gender equality and sees this as a high priority for the next century. Croatia announced that it had recently ratified the Optional Protocol to CEDAW and that gender equality is of the highest order of importance in the constitution. Thus, countries take this opportunity to assert their "civilized" status in terms of their alleged progress in protecting women's rights.

The Ambivalent NGO Position

I was puzzled about the role of civil society in the deliberations among government delegates at the Beijing Plus Five meeting as well as at the Commission
on the Status of Women and the Commission on Human Rights. Despite the
celebrated interdependence of civil society and the international system of law,
the relationship between states and NGOs is fraught with tension and ambivalence. While some governments welcome NGO participation, others resist. Some do not want NGOs to be involved in the process at all and insist that
the UN is a body of governments. NGO representatives were typically seated
behind a railing and enjoined to be quiet, making clear their second-class status. They were virtually excluded from speaking and occasionally were told to
leave the room during confidential deliberations, much to their annoyance.
Many governments wish to restrict NGO speaking time and to know in advance what they are going to say. The attention of the government delegates
is typically less during NGO interventions, with more talking and walking
around than in other deliberations.

There is a great deal of irony in the participation of NGOs in these global
conferences. Despite constant references to the importance of civil society by
government delegates, there is reluctance to allow NGOs to participate extensively in the meetings. Most observers of the process agree that it is the NGOs
that raise new issues, do the research to develop them, generate public support,
and reach the media. Their attention to issues pressures governments to act
and produces the political visibility of these issues. Their expertise often con-
tributes to drafting new documents, particularly in the language of previous
documents. Yet, many governments are very skeptical about NGOs and worried that they will embarrass them or bring up difficult issues. Some governments accuse NGOs of speaking largely for themselves or a very small group, a
phenomenon described as having "my own NGO." They may retaliate against
the NGOs when they get back home. One NGO representative from Africa
said that some governments even threaten treason trials against outspoken
NGO representatives. The United States also resists criticisms by NGOs. At a
March 2002 US briefing to NGOs, a representative from the Women's International League for Peace and Freedom pointed out that discussions of gender
and poverty need to take into account the way US economic polices are producing global poverty. The US team was annoyed by this comment and accused
the NGO representative of being unpatriotic.

NGOs are often more radical than government representatives, who focus
on putting the best face on what their governments have done. At the 2002

CSW meeting, for example, the Asia Pacific Forum on Women, Law, and Development, a Thailand-based organization on roster status and therefore not entitled to present a statement, printed a flyer on two sides of bright yellow paper which argued that development did not inevitably improve employment and promote progress, but instead exploited the lands and resources of the marginalized, indigenous, ethnic, and caste groups and led to increasing feminization of poverty and environmental degradation. The group urged attention to the human causes of environmental degradation and disaster, arguing that "disasters occur in areas where large-scale commercial and development projects are implemented. More often than not, these are projects of transnational companies and international finance institutions." The statement points out that women and girls are made more vulnerable by these disasters and are increasingly exposed to the risk of violence. Thus, this statement addresses the theme of the meeting, a gender perspective on environmental disasters, but unlike the official documents, places responsibility on transnational resource extraction and questions the human activities that produce these disasters. It is more critical than the document produced by the commission itself.

There is also tension between the UN process, shaped by diplomatic conventions and the legalistic niceties of producing texts through wordsmithing, and the NGO process. NGOs work to develop clear and simple issues based on gripping personal stories capable of generating outrage at a perpetrator, either an individual or the state. Those who succeed best in mobilizing outrage receive more media attention, more funding, and more supporters at home and internationally. This approach is likely to antagonize the government held responsible. It is not surprising that there is conflict.

As in so many other areas of UN human rights activity, the role of NGOs is a developing and changing one. NGOs are gradually gaining more acceptance and a stronger voice, but still face considerable resistance to their participation. Their role has expanded greatly in the last twenty years. At the Beijing Plus Five meeting, NGOs prepared at least 112 alternative reports assessing their countries' compliance with the Platform for Action (International Women's Tribune Center 2000, 4: 2). They now have a parallel organization, CONGO, the Conference of Non-Governmental Organizations in Consultative Relationship with the United Nations, based in New York, Vienna, and Geneva. CONGO holds training sessions for NGOs before and during the CSW and CEDAW meetings. At the CSW meetings, this group organized two all-day sessions and several shorter meetings that provided guidance about the UN system and advice on lobbying. Despite government discomfort, the human rights system depends on NGO activities. Human rights documents create the legal categories and legal norms for controlling violence against women, but the dissemination of these norms and categories depends on NGOs seizing this language and using it to generate public support or governmental discomfort. This is a fragile and haphazard process, very vulnerable to existing inequalities among nations and the availability of donors, but the NGO role is essential and increasing.

Gender Violence and the CEDAW Process

The most lawlike of the human rights mechanisms is the system of treaties ratified by member states. Committees, called treaty bodies, monitor the compliance of signatory nations. But the committee charged with monitoring compliance with CEDAW, like those monitoring the other major UN treaties, has limited power to compel states to comply (see Foot 2000: 269–70). Treaty bodies work within the global structure of sovereignty and cannot impose sanctions on noncompliant states. Many legal scholars, activists, and NGOs are concerned about the lack of enforcement mechanisms within this legal process (see, e.g., Byrnes and Connors 1996: 679; Afsharipour 1999; Ulrich 2000: 637; Bayefsky 2001; Resnik 2001: 678).[1] A recent major study of all six treaty bodies concludes "the gap between universal right and remedy has become inescapable and inexcusable, threatening the integrity of the international human rights legal regime. There are overwhelming numbers of overdue reports, untenable backlogs, minimal individual complaints from vast numbers of potential victims, and widespread refusal of states to provide remedies when violations of individual rights are found" (Bayefsky 2001: xiii).

CEDAW is law without sanctions. But a close examination of the way the CEDAW process operates suggests that although it does not have the power to punish, it does important cultural work. It articulates principles of gender equality and state responsibility and demonstrates how they apply to the countries under scrutiny. The process of ratification, preparing reports, and presenting and discussing reports fosters new cultural understandings of gender and violence. The hearings clarify how the convention applies to a particular country. This is a cultural system whose coin is admission into the international community of human-rights-compliant states. Since the end of the cold war, the idea that legitimate sovereignty rests on democratic governance and humane treatment of citizens has grown, so that the new international "standard of civilization" includes acceptance of human rights (Foot 2000: 11). These ideas resonate with colonial era conceptions of what it means to be a "civilized" nation and a respected member of the international community. Countries all over the world endeavor to present themselves as human-rights compliant, cooperative with the international regime of treaty law.

Moreover, other governments sometimes press countries to comply. For example, a prominent CEDAW expert said that for Eastern Europe, pressure from the European Union provides 90 percent of the effect of the treaty. Indeed, Keck and Sikkink argue that transnational NGOs work through the boomerang principle, in which the NGOs in one country persuade transnational NGO networks in another country to convince their country to put pressure on the first country (1998). I saw relatively little direct pressure by one country on another in order to enforce women's rights except when there were other strategic interests at stake, but membership in the world of human rights nations is important to many participating countries.

After presenting the content of the convention and its monitoring process, I analyze the way culture is conceptualized and discussed within the CEDAW process. I use the country reports of Guinea and Egypt to the CEDAW Committee that I observed in 2001 as examples. The next chapter explores the tensions between the application of global standards and local political contexts through a discussion of the hearings of India and Fiji. I interviewed nine committee members, several of them at length, observed hearings at five sessions between 2001 and 2003, talked to many participants from national and international NGOs, and spoke to several government representatives about their reaction to the hearing process. Each session lasted three weeks and considered reports from about eight countries. I also talked to local activists and government representatives from Fiji, India, and Hong Kong after they returned home from attending CEDAW hearings.

The Convention

CEDAW is one of six UN conventions that have been widely ratified and monitored by a committee, referred to as a treaty body. The six conventions of the

UN system form the legal core of the human rights system. Conventions enter into force through national ratification. The other treaties are the Covenant on Economic, Cultural, and Social Rights, the Covenant on Civil and Political Rights, the Covenant against Racial Discrimination, the Convention against Torture, and the Convention on the Rights of the Child (see Bayefsky 2001: 2; Jacobson 1994). CEDAW incorporates features of the Universal Declaration of Human Rights (1948), the Covenant on Civil and Political Rights and the Covenant on Economic, Cultural, and Social Rights, and International Labor Organization (ILO) conventions. CEDAW has been described as an international bill of rights for women. It focuses on eliminating discrimination against women that violates the principle of equality of rights and respect for human dignity (Division for the Advancement of Women 2000: 5). It emphasizes equal rights for men and women and explicitly prohibits discrimination on the basis of sex. Like other human rights discourses and instruments, it is committed to universalism: to the idea that there are minimal standards of human dignity that must be protected in all societies (An-Naʿim 1992b; Schuler 1992; Wilson 1996; Ignatieff 2001). Universal gender equality requires eliminating those laws and institutional practices that treat women in discriminatory ways.

The convention is based on ideas about women's status developed during the 1950s, 1960s, and 1970s. A 1950s and 1960s equal rights orientation is supplemented by 1970s concerns with political and economic development (Reanda 1992: 289–90). It emphasizes the principle of nondiscrimination and legal equality, focusing only on discrimination against women rather than on all discrimination on the basis of sex (Jacobson 1992: 446). It endeavors to remove barriers that prevent women from being the same as men. Its origins are in conventions on the political rights of women and the nationality of married women developed in the 1950s. Between 1965 and 1967 the Commission on the Status of Women expanded it into a declaration (Division for the Advancement of Women 2000: 4; see also Jacobson 1992). In 1979 it was adopted as a convention by the General Assembly and opened for ratification. It achieved a sufficient number of ratifications to go into force by 1981.

The convention covers substantive as well as formal equality. Many articles address economic and political inequalities between men and women while others talk about educational disparities, which generally produce economic inequalities. The thirty articles to the convention cover a broad array of social issues such as political participation, education, employment, health, and the special difficulties faced by rural women. States parties are required to eliminate discrimination in the exercise of civil, political, economic, social, and cultural rights both in the public domain and in the family (Division for the

Advancement of Women 2000: 5). CEDAW not only proscribes discrimination but also advocates positive steps such as the elimination of sex-role stereotypes in the media and educational materials and the creation of "temporary special measures" to benefit women, measures which are not forms of discrimination but efforts to overcome past disabilities. The convention focuses on laws that selectively disempower women such as regulations requiring women to have their husband's permission to acquire a passport. It assumes that producing equal rights for women requires the transformation of marriage laws, access to education and employment, and gender images within the media.

CEDAW explicitly calls for cultural changes in gender roles. Article 2f, the core of the convention, requires states parties "To take all appropriate measures, including legislation, to modify or abolish existing laws, regulations, customs and practices which constitute discrimination against women" (Division for the Advancement of Women 2000: 14). Article 5a on sex roles and stereotyping calls on states parties to take all appropriate measures: "To modify the social and cultural patterns of conduct of men and women, with a view to achieving the elimination of prejudices and customary and all other practices which are based on the idea of the inferiority or the superiority of either of the sexes or on stereotyped roles for men and women" (Division for the Advancement of Women 2000: 18). In 1987, after considering 34 country reports, the CEDAW Committee produced General Recommendation 3 noting "the existence of stereotyped conceptions of women, owing to socio-cultural factors, that perpetuate discrimination based on sex and hinder the implementation of article 5 of the convention, Urges all States parties effectively to adopt education and public information programmes, which will help eliminate prejudices and current practices that hinder the full operation of the principle of the social equality of women" (Division for the Advancement of Women 2000: 56).

In 2001, one expert observed to me that she found it striking that in all the countries they had considered, including the apparently most progressive Scandinavian ones, gender stereotypes had proved extremely resistant to change. While there was clearly greater equality in some countries than others, stereotypes about men and women persisted, particularly those that focused on women as caretakers.

The committee has developed several General Recommendations interpreting the convention on issues that go beyond the discrimination framework and focus more on social and economic development. CEDAW General Recommendations are not legally binding in the same way as the terms of CEDAW, but they are designed to show states their obligations when they are not mentioned or not sufficiently explained in the convention itself.

Although the convention does not refer to violence against women explicitly, probably because of the era in which it was drafted, its monitoring committee has subsequently prepared two general recommendations on that topic. In 1989 the committee adopted General Recommendation 12 urging consideration of the issue and requiring statistics on gender violence. General Recommendation 19 from 1992 developed the issue further, defining gender-based violence as a form of discrimination "that seriously inhibits women's ability to enjoy rights and freedoms on a basis of equality with men" (Division for the Advancement of Women 2000: 63). The recommendation discussed the ways that violence against women was relevant to each of the articles of the convention. For example, it pointed out that "traditional attitudes by which women are regarded as subordinate to men or as having stereotyped roles" justify and perpetuate forms of gender-based violence such as family violence, forced marriage, dowry deaths, and female circumcision and that these forms of violence help to maintain women in subordinate positions and contribute to their low level of political participation, education, and work opportunities (par. 11, General Recommendation 19). This recommendation became the basis for the UN General Assembly Declaration on Violence against Women in 1993 (GA Res 48/104(1994), UN Doc A/48/49, at 217). A former CEDAW member, Desiree Bernard, of Guyana, considers this declaration one of the most significant efforts to combat violence against women (1996: 81). It urges states to condemn violence against women and not to invoke any custom, tradition, or religious consideration to avoid their obligations toward its elimination. Although this declaration is a policy statement without binding force, it carries significant international legitimacy as an expression of the collective body of member nations of the UN.

Violence against women is now discussed extensively in country reports and during hearings. At least eight articles bear indirectly on violence against women, including those on gender stereotypes, trafficking in women, prostitution, disruptions of employment through sexual harassment, women's health in rural areas as well as urban, and women's position in the family (Bernard 1996: 80). Committee members frequently ask questions about the extent of violence and the strategies a government has taken to reduce it. The committee encourages reporting states to recognize the close relationships among discrimination against women, gender-based violence, and violations of human rights and fundamental freedoms and to take positive measures to eliminate all forms of violence against women (General Recommendation 19: 4). Thus, the committee grounds its concern about gender-based violence in the overarching framework of discrimination. Gender-based violence is defined as "violence that is directed against a woman because she is a woman or that affects women disproportionately. It includes acts that inflict physical, mental or sexual harm or suffering, threats of such acts, coercion and any other deprivations of liberty" (General Recommendation 19). The recommendation specifies all the rights and freedoms that gender-based violence infringes, such as the right to equality in the family and the right to equal protection under the law.

The convention and its statements on violence emphasize individual autonomy and physical safety over the sacredness and permanence of the family. The underlying theory is that improving women's status with relation to men will reduce their vulnerability to violence.[2] There are other approaches to protecting women from violence, of course. For example, although some Islamic states insist that women and men are not equal, it is nevertheless possible within this religious tradition to critique violence against women (Hajjar 2004). At a conference on Women in Palestine that I attended in Gaza in 1999, many of the Palestinian women argued for a reinterpretation of Islam that would provide them more choice and safety, but they did not ask for gender equality nor did they reject Islam. Similarly, some conservative Christian groups in the United States emphasize the inequality of man and woman in marriage while stressing the duty of husbands to honor their wives (see Merry 2001a). Gender equality as a way of dealing with women's vulnerability to violence is only one approach to the problem, one promoted by feminists in many parts of the world as well as by CEDAW. Although it is the most promising approach, it has not succeeded in eliminating gender violence.

No country has come close to achieving gender equality, but even those that have achieved relative equality still experience violence against women. In the country reports of both Norway and Luxembourg to CEDAW in 2003, for example, governments described their extensive programs for gender equality along with persisting wage differentials and patterns of violence against women. The transition to a modern, industrialized society with somewhat greater gender equality can exacerbate rather than diminish violence, as it has with the rapid modernization of China, according to a report from Human Rights in China (1995). As Jane Collier argues on the basis of her long-term research in Spain, the transition to a modern family system does not necessarily produce greater autonomy and power for women (1997). In the modern system, marriage is less secure: wives are viewed as spending family resources and must maintain their attractiveness in order to preserve the marriage. In the earlier system their status as wives was guaranteed by the church and by their productive role in the family. Consequently, the impact of modernity has been to make women more rather than less vulnerable to violence.

In the decades since the drafting of CEDAW, feminist scholars have queried whether an approach that uses similarity to males as a standard can achieve substantive equality for men and women (e.g., MacKinnon 1989; Charlesworth 1994; Fineman 1995). Many feminists advocate some attempt to recognize women's difference as the basis for justice. Some have advocated interpreting discrimination not as difference but as disadvantage, powerlessness, and exclusion (Cook 1994: 11–12). Others note the very limited sphere of women's lives that is governed by the law and that can be improved through the law and the state (Charlesworth 1994; Coomaraswamy 1994). Some argue that since law is a patriarchal institution—emphasizing rationality, objectivity, and abstraction and opposing emotion, subjectivity, and contextualized thinking—it may be of little value in transforming women's subordinate status (Charlesworth 1994: 65). In India, where law itself is to some extent gendered and oppressive, feminists note the limitations on its capacity to promote equality for women (Kapur and Cossman 1996: 24–27). In South Asia in general, the law has relatively little autonomy with relationship to the state and is often viewed with suspicion as a consequence of the colonial past (Coomaraswamy 1994: 46–47). Feminists in the United States have long emphasized the limitations of a rights-based framework for eliminating violence against women (see Schneider 2000: 41–42). They argue that gender violence is a problem that reveals acutely the limitations of the gender-neutral approach to equality and the need for special treatment—such as the creation of shelters—rather than formal equality (Cook 1994a: 20). The ongoing jurisprudence surrounding the convention, including the general recommendations, update the convention and bring it closer to contemporary feminist thinking.

The Monitoring Process

Treaty bodies monitor compliance with ratified treaties by requiring countries to write periodic reports detailing their efforts to put the treaty into force.[3] The committee reads and comments on the report. Many of these treaty bodies have developed an optional protocol, which allows individuals to file complaints directly to the committee.[4] CEDAW's Optional Protocol entered into force by late 2000. It allows individual women or groups to submit claims of violations of rights protected under the convention to the CEDAW Committee, but only after all domestic remedies have been exhausted and only in countries that have ratified it. The protocol also creates a procedure by which the committee can inquire into situations of grave or systemic violations of women's rights (Division for the Advancement of Women 2000: 7). As the Optional Protocol comes into force more widely, there will be a new system of sanctioning in place, but it only applies to those countries that have ratified it. At the July 2001 meeting, CEDAW experts encouraged national delegations to ratify the Optional Protocol and urged NGOs to bring complaints forward under the new procedure.

The reasons why a nation would choose to ratify CEDAW and subject itself to periodic reporting and examination are not obvious. There are, however, important political and economic dividends. Compliance with human rights instruments is important for participation in the international community and for benefits such as aid, trade relations, and foreign investment (see Foot 2000). Country representatives often emphasize the number of conventions and treaties they have ratified, sometimes indirectly linking this to their openness to foreign investment. An expert from Europe noted that European companies look at the standards of a country as well as potential profits when they invest, so that improving the status of women attracts business. EU aid is also facilitated by commitment to human rights. Another expert said that ratification helps with bilateral aid and aid from UN agencies. Bayefsky notes that states may consider ratification an end in itself and, given the relatively innocuous monitoring procedure, are not seriously concerned about the national consequences (2001: 7). States frequently refer to the conventions they have ratified in statements they deliver to UN bodies and in country reports. In her study of human rights treaty compliance, Hathaway argues that there is an expressive dimension to human rights treaty ratification (2002). In sum, it appears that participating in the international human rights regime allows countries to claim civilized status in the present international order, much as ideas of civilization provided the standard for colonized countries during the imperial era. Fanon's famous afterword to *Wretched of the Earth* (1963) testifies to the power of this idea as he urged decolonizing nations to look to other definitions of moral virtue than the ideas of the rights of man established by Europe.

By the end of 2004, the convention had been ratified by 179 nation states and the Optional Protocol by 68. By that time, the committee had received three complaints under the new protocol. The United States has not ratified CEDAW, along with Somalia and about eight other states. The convention has been under consideration by the Senate since the early 1980s and, according to a spokesman from the US delegation to the UN, was voted out of committee with a set of reservations and declarations in 1994. The Senate Committee on Foreign Relations again considered it in 2002 and sent it to the full Senate for ratification (Schneider 2004: 717–19). Again, however, it was not ratified. Harold Koh, a prominent international law professor, argues that the United

States' double standards approach to international human rights undermines US credibility and weakens the system as a whole (2003: 1499–1500). In her study of human rights in China, Foot also observes that the United States' failure to ratify many important human rights conventions has undermined its credibility as a promoter of international human rights (2000). There has been considerable discussion of the United States' failure to ratify this and several other core human rights conventions. Explanations range from the lack of domestic political support by a constituency that feels its rights are already adequately protected to the nation's system of popular sovereignty, which means that ratification requires a legislative vote rather than an executive order, to ideas of American exceptionalism (see Ignatieff 2002). Neoconservatives in the Bush administration argue that ratification threatens the sovereignty of the United States and the security of the Constitution (see Spiro 2000; Greenberg 2003: 1816–17). These conservative scholars claim that while multilateral agreements may be reasonable for middle-level powers such as European states or Canada, for the United States superpower they limit it unnecessarily by tying it down with international agreements (see Ignatieff 2002: 8).

States that ratify CEDAW are obliged to incorporate it into their domestic legislation (see Cook 1994c). According to Hanna Beate Schöpp-Schilling, a member of the CEDAW Committee for 12 years, "States Parties are obliged to undertake all legislative and other appropriate measures to eliminate discrimination against women without delay" (2000). She notes that this contrasts with other conventions, such as the International Covenant on Economic, Social, and Cultural Rights, which obliges states to take steps "progressively" to achieve the full realization of rights. Nevertheless, she notes that states often hide behind financial shortfalls and other difficulties to avoid initiating reforms. Indeed, in the hearing on the Burundi country report in 2001, there was widespread recognition by CEDAW Committee members that in a largely rural country undergoing a protracted civil war, relatively little could be anticipated in the way of reforms to benefit women. It is common for states of the global South to complain that they need more financial help from the global North in order to make the desired changes.

States may ratify CEDAW with reservations to particular items of the convention by declaring that certain parts of the treaty do not bind the state. The committee discourages this and endeavors to persuade ratifying states to remove their reservations. In the past, this convention had more reservations to it than any other (Division for the Advancement of Women 2000: 6; see also Cook 1990). A recent study shows that CEDAW is not the most reserved convention, yet it still has 123 reservations, declarations, and interpretive statements, which are in effect reservations. Three quarters of these (76%) refer to the substance of the text itself rather than to its procedures (Bayefsky 2001: 66). Forty-nine states parties, or 30 percent of those that have ratified CEDAW, have entered reservations. In comparison, the Convention on Civil and Political Rights has 181, 88 percent of which are normative, representing 35 percent of states parties. The Convention on the Rights of the Child has 204, 99.5 percent of which are normative, from 32 percent of states parties. Thus, like CEDAW, these conventions are heavily circumscribed by reservations. Some of the reservations are to core portions of the convention, such that they undermine the purpose of the convention itself. Egypt, for example, entered a general reservation on Article 2, explaining that it is "willing to comply with the content of this article provided that such compliance does not run counter to the Islamic Shari'a" (Egyptian Non-Governmental Organizations Coalition 2000:5). Yet Article 2 embodies the core of the convention, stating: "States Parties condemn discrimination against women in all its forms, agree to pursue by all appropriate means and without delay, a policy of eliminating discrimination against women" and lists a variety of constitutional, legal, and legislative measures to eliminate this discrimination. Bayefsky notes that Article 2 has five general reservations, another eight normative general declarations and interpretive statements, and twelve more specific reservations, while there are 25 reservations to article 16, the article that requires equality in marriage and family law (2001: 66, 717–18).[5] The CEDAW Committee is concerned that reserving on Article 2 constitutes failure to adopt the spirit of the convention. On the other hand, as Schöpp-Schilling notes, even states with significant reservations present reports and engage in dialogue with the committee's experts, a potentially constructive experience.

THE COMMITTEE HEARINGS

The CEDAW reporting process is intended to monitor compliance with the convention by signatory countries. It consists of questions and answers between the experts and high-level country representatives but does not lead to penalties or fines for noncompliance. Its power lies in exposure and shaming, not force. Although CEDAW hearings are legal in form, like other human rights mechanisms the process is fundamentally political. A key feature of this process is its capacity to create a cultural category such as violence against women, to mobilize support against it, and to articulate for a wide variety of countries how they might go about taking responsibility for reducing it. The CEDAW process provides global legitimacy for a more egalitarian model of gender relations, presses governments to improve services for women, and provides a mechanism for sharing ideas globally.

The dialogue between a country and the committee occurs during the regular meetings of the CEDAW Committee. At these hearings, the committee of 23 reads the report and meets with a delegation from the country, often a high-ranking minister for women's affairs. The committee members, called experts because of their knowledge and experience in the field, ask questions about discrepancies between the actions of the country and the obligations it assumed when it ratified the convention. The experts are expected to act independently and not to speak for their national governments.

These experts are nominated by their national governments and elected for four-year terms by the state signatories to the convention. Although membership on this committee was not viewed as important in the early years of the 1980s, by 2003 there was considerable interest among governments in having their candidates elected and extensive lobbying by governments on behalf of their candidates. According to one expert, she was selected because the NGOs in her country encouraged her government to nominate her and her government then negotiated with other governments to get its candidate elected. Her primary base of support was the NGO community. Another expert described how her government lobbied for her, holding social events and exchanging votes with other UN country missions. In general, experts serve in addition to holding regular jobs and devote considerable time to their responsibilities, for which they receive expenses but little remuneration.[6] They have impressive credentials in terms of scholarship and publication, NGO activism, extensive government service, senior diplomatic posts, and international experience. Most have a strong background in women's issues.

Experts are elected by region, to insure equal representation from Latin America and the Caribbean, Africa, Asia, Western Europe, and Eastern Europe. A member of each region is elected as vice-chair and serves on the bureau, while the chair of the committee rotates through the regions. In general, the experts from the same region as the reporting country take the lead in asking questions. Experts are lawyers, diplomats, government bureaucrats, scholars, judges, medical doctors, and educators (Schöpp-Schilling 2000). Based on the biographies they provided to the UN as candidates for election to CEDAW, of 32 who served during 2002 and 2003, almost 60 percent (19) have NGO and/or academic backgrounds. Two of these were also in elected political positions and one recently joined her government after an NGO career. Six are professors, from Israel, Sri Lanka, Sweden, Netherlands, Hungary, and Turkey. The academics bring considerable scholarly expertise and independence to the process. The other 40 percent (13) of the experts are employees of their national governments in the foreign service or women's ministries. Some are ambassadors or other government employees even though the UN prefers that experts not be civil servants. This is a highly educated and transnationally active group of people. The experts are often educated in other countries. Of the 32, 24 studied at some point in Europe or North America. They generally have considerable previous exposure to UN activities, with 24 saying they attended other UN meetings and conferences (CEDAW/SP/1996/3, CEDAW/SP/1998/3, CEDAW/SP/2000/6, CEDAW/SP/2002/3/Add. 1, CEDAW/SP/2002/3). Since CEDAW hearings began in 1983, all but three of the experts have been women. There is some circulation between CEDAW service and high government positions at home. One CEDAW expert became a supreme court justice, one the secretary-general of the National Council of Women, and one a governor. This means that some country delegations have previous connections with the committee. For example, the chair of the Egyptian delegation was a former member of CEDAW. She said that things had really changed since the early days when the committee was thought of as a group of women pestering governments.

The experts present a united front in these hearings, although they differ on some issues such as abortion and the value of separate legal systems for different religious communities within a country. Those more closely connected to NGO or academic communities tend to challenge governments more than those employed by their national governments. The latter tend to be less confrontational and more inclined to praise a country's efforts than to condemn its shortfalls. Despite these differences, the hearings give a sense of unanimity among the experts as they pose questions to government representatives.

The CEDAW Committee was originally restricted to meeting once a year for two weeks. In 1995 it expanded to three weeks a year and in 1997 three weeks twice a year. In 2002, it held an exceptional third meeting to catch up with the backlog of reports. According to a long-standing member of the committee, country reports were initially only two to three pages but now routinely run to 60 and occasionally up to 150 pages. By 2001, it was common practice to hear two or even three periodic reports from the same country at once. By January 2004, CEDAW had considered 124 initial reports, 96 second reports, 76 third reports, 50 fourth reports, 23 fifth reports, and one sixth report (UN Press Release WOM/1421 8 January 2004). However, a substantial number of ratifying states have failed to file a report at all or have fallen behind. By mid-2001, forty-nine states had not filed an initial report, 65 were late in filing their second periodic report, 42 the third periodic report, 52 the fourth, and 41 were late in their fifth periodic report. Several states that ratified in the early 1980s have never filed a report and thus appear in all of these lists, such as Brazil, Bhutan, Congo, Costa Rica, and Togo (Secretary-General Report 2001: CEDAW/C/2001/II/2). States are catching up by filing multiple reports at once. For example, in January 2003, El Salvador filed its third, fourth, fifth, and sixth periodic reports stretching back to 1987.

The focus of the CEDAW Committee's work is reading the periodic reports of signatory countries, asking questions, and writing concluding comments. Every ratifying country is obligated to provide an initial report within one year of ratification on the legislative, judicial, and administrative measures it has adopted to comply with the convention and obstacles it has encountered and to prepare subsequent reports every four years. For initial reports, the committee uses a two-stage process. First, the national delegation presents its report and the committee members, sitting in a large conference room at the UN building in New York, go through it carefully and ask questions, request clarification, and note contrasts with other countries' experiences with these particular reforms. After 48 hours, the national delegation returns to the committee and provides answers to these questions. Some answers are brief and inconclusive and some issues are not addressed, but the committee can do little under these circumstances. For subsequent reports, a subcommittee consisting of a representative from each of the UN geographical regions meets at the end of the previous session to read the report and pose questions to which the national representatives provide written responses within 40 days. At the next meeting of CEDAW six months later, government representatives present an updated overview statement of perhaps one hour and are asked further questions by the experts to which they reply immediately. This process is thorough: Egypt noted that it had received 64 additional questions from the presessional working group from the previous meeting. The questions and the replies, as well as the country reports, are available to all the members of the committee.

The goal of the reporting process is to promote change in the government by forcing it to review domestic law, policy, and practice and to assess to what extent it is complying with the standards of the convention. According to the secretariat, the Division for the Advancement of Women, "Strengths and weaknesses are submitted to public scrutiny, while consideration of the report by CEDAW provides a forum for discussion with a wholly independent body whose brief is to provide constructive assistance so that States meet their treaty obligations" (Division for the Advancement of Women 2000: 8). Questions by experts frequently point out the need for more information, particularly disaggregated by sex, in order to assess the relative participation of women in school, government, and the workplace, for example. Their questions show how the convention applies to the country giving the report, pinpointing areas where there is noncompliance, and provide comparative information about how other countries have handled these issues. The tenor is unfailingly courteous, although questions are sometimes pointed. The experts I have talked to emphasize that their goal is to be constructive as well as critical. Rarely are criticisms explicit. More often, experts speak of "concerns" or of the need for more information. Privately, some experts commented to me how frustrated they felt about one or another country's report, such as its abysmal gender-based statistics or failure to implement policies, but they did not level such accusations against governments in the hearings. If a country acknowledges that it has had difficulty in implementing CEDAW, the experts tend to be more supportive than if a country tries to cover up its failures. Their sternest criticisms are reserved for countries that fail to send delegations or those with the resources who nevertheless fail to produce a thorough and competent report. One expert said that this was a political process, and if a country chooses to ignore it, there is nothing the committee can do. A member of the secretariat noted, for example, that India paid very little attention to the CEDAW process even though there were NGOs present. Other governments work hard on the reports, such as Finland and the Netherlands.

Some governmental representatives find the experience of reporting helpful. A government representative from Guyana said although she did not get any new ideas from the process, the attention and concern of the international community energized her and supported her work at home. A delegate from Finland said that it is good for the government ministers to come to the hearings to hear the questions and the praise the experts give to countries such as her own that have made significant progress toward gender equality. This provides valuable feedback about Finland's place and image in the world as a leader in women's human rights. In her concluding comments, the minister from the Maldives said that she knows that the experts are all very committed people anxious to improve conditions of women and that the questions they have asked are in the best interest of the women of her country. A government representative from the Maldives told me that the opinions of international experts are very important in her country and have greater credibility than the views of local experts. A CEDAW expert with long experience said that it was important to have government ministers come so that they can take the committee's arguments back to their governments.

After hearing these reports, the committee meets in closed session to develop its "Concluding Comments" for each country, which praise or express concern about efforts to comply with the convention and make recommendations to be considered at the next review four years hence. These comments are publicly available and posted on the Internet. The committee urges governments to make these comments public. Governments differ in the extent to which they make these comments public, but NGOs publicize them in an effort to shame their government into action.

In recent years, NGOs have begun to offer important support for this process (see Afsharipour 1999: 157). Although their input was described as minimal in the 1980s, the situation is changing (Jacobson 1992: 467). NGOs are encouraged to write "shadow reports," which provide their version of the status of women in their countries, and are often offered training in producing these reports by UN agencies such as UNIFEM or UNDP (see, e.g., Afsharipour 1999: 165; Economic and Social Commission for Asia and the Pacific 2000). Some representatives of NGOs appear at the committee meetings in New York, where they are not allowed to speak but can sit in the conference room and informally lobby the experts, suggesting questions to ask. Their shadow reports are available to the committee. Committee members also receive reports from UN agencies such as FAO, UNICEF, UNIFEM, and the ILO on the status of women in a particular country. Representatives of international NGOs such as Equality Now and International Women's Rights Action Watch as well as national NGOs usually attend the hearings. The audience ranges from about 10 to 40. The results of these hearings are made available to other UN agencies such as the Commission on the Status of Women, ECOSOC, and the General Assembly and are available online as press releases. However, it does not appear that they are considered extensively by these bodies, based both on my own observations of CSW meetings and comments by Jacobson (1992: 463–65).

A US-based NGO, the International Women's Rights Action Watch (IWRAW) and its Asia-Pacific office based in Malaysia have trained NGO representatives and regularly produced shadow reports on the countries under examination (see, eg., Afsharipour 1999: 165). IWRAW began as a channel for NGOs to get information to committee members, initially summarizing information and presenting it to committee members in the 1980s (Jacobson 1992: 467). In the last few years, IWRAW's Asia-Pacific branch has focused on bringing national NGOs to the CEDAW hearings in New York and encouraging them to write their own shadow reports. IWRAW works to arrange funding from UNIFEM or other sources and provides training and support to NGO representatives in New York.

I interviewed Shanthi Dairiam, the head of IWRAW-AP in 2002, who said that since 1997 she has focused on bringing NGO representatives to the CEDAW hearings in New York and providing them information on the hearing process. It is difficult to raise funds for this activity, since funders want to focus on specific issues such as health, population, or violence against women rather than developing a broad human rights framework. Dairiam has had funding from UNIFEM, the Ford Foundation, and the Netherlands. IWRAW-AP recently held a meeting in Delhi and brought three CEDAW members to meet with NGOs and talk about the process, with funding from UNIFEM. She finds that NGOs get very involved in preparing for the meeting, writing the shadow report, and coming to the meeting, but are less effective in following up with the concluding comments. They work hard on the shadow report and lobbying with the experts, but then run out of steam when they get home. Nevertheless, she and others agree that NGO support for CEDAW activities is of critical importance for the success of the process. She was elected as a member of CEDAW in 2004.

The CEDAW Committee sets aside an afternoon to hear NGO presentations at the beginning of each session. Government delegations are not present. For example, at the January 2002 meeting, 18 of the 23 experts were present to hear NGO representatives make their oral statements. Committee members listened attentively to the issues the NGOs raised and asked the government representatives many of the questions the NGOs suggested. Moreover, NGOs can organize a special closed meeting to talk with the experts, as Canadian NGOs did in 2003. The CEDAW Committee is far more supportive of NGO input than the government-based UN bodies such as the Commission on the Status of Women or the High Commission on Human Rights. Many of the members of the CEDAW Committee are quite positive toward NGOs and make an effort to listen to them informally and come to the NGO briefing. Those experts who have NGO backgrounds are particularly receptive to NGO representatives. The effectiveness of CEDAW depends on the extent to which NGOs use the concluding comments to pressure their governments. Thus, the NGO presence at CEDAW meetings is critically important and is increasingly recognized by the experts.

ESCAPING SURVEILLANCE

There are a variety of ways for countries to escape scrutiny. One is to fail to write a report or to do so only after a long delay. The list of countries that are derelict in their reports is very long. By January 1, 2000, there were 242 overdue reports to CEDAW from 165 states parties. Fifty-three states had initial overdue reports. Overall, 78 percent of all states parties had overdue reports, although the average for all treaty bodies is an equally high 71 percent (Bayefsky 2001: 471). The second is to write a superficial or partial report. Sometimes reports just recite the provisions of the constitution or other legislation or are very brief and do not offer candid self-evaluations of a state's compliance with its treaty obligations (Jacobson 1992; Bayefsky 2001: 21). The third is to send low-level government representatives instead of high-level delegations of ministers or assistant ministers. In 2002, Uruguay, complaining that it was financially strapped, asked its UN mission in New York to report and sent no one from the country, much to the displeasure of the CEDAW Committee. The UN mission is not as informed about national issues as leaders of women's ministries. A fourth way to escape scrutiny is to evade direct answers to questions. A fifth is to promise changes that do not in fact take place. A sixth is to reserve on important articles on the grounds that they conflict with basic cultural, legal, or religious tenets of the country. A seventh is to refuse to present a report orally even after it has been submitted (Bayefsky 2001: 23).

Although the NGO community is present at CEDAW hearings to help publicize the discussions and conclusions, treaty body meetings are quite different from the major world conferences or commission meetings. NGO participation is far smaller at CEDAW hearings. Moreover, participation varies significantly depending on the country and its NGO population. During the discussion of Egypt's report in January 2001, a large audience of NGO representatives attended, perhaps 30 people. Egypt has a large NGO community. Burundi and Kazakhstan had smaller audiences, and relatively few NGOs attended. Discussions with very small countries with few NGOs, such as Andorra, generated very few observers. About fifteen to twenty came to hear the reports of Vietnam, Nicaragua, and Guyana. Despite these small numbers, NGOs make a critical contribution to the process. Based on her detailed survey of all six treaty bodies, Bayefsky concludes "The treaty bodies have been heavily dependent on information from NGOs in preparing for the dialogue with states parties. State reports are self-serving documents that rarely knowingly disclose violations of treaty rights" (2001: 42).

Clearly, governments can escape this system, but they face internal pressure from national NGOs, which may be supported by international donors and therefore active even if the country does not have enough wealth to support them. In theory, they face pressure from other countries as well via their NGOs, but I saw little evidence of pressure by other nations. Instead, it was primarily domestic NGOs that used the hearings to exert pressure on their governments to comply. Countries are concerned about their reputations in the international community, but they clearly differ in their vulnerability to international pressure depending on their size, wealth, form of government, and dependence on the international community for trade, aid, and other symbolic and material forms of exchange. Countries that are economically and politically dominant, such as the United States, may resist the system by failing to ratify at all.

CEDAW AS LAW

Does the convention matter? Unlike the documents discussed in the previous chapter, at least in theory CEDAW becomes the law of the land after ratification. Documents such as the outcome document from Beijing Plus Five and the Platform for Action of the 1995 Beijing Conference are of an entirely different character. They represent an effort to achieve a global consensus, but they are not legally binding. The documents articulate desirable behavior and aspirations with the legitimacy of international consensus. As they define problems and frame social issues in the language of human rights and freedom from discrimination and gender equality, they provide a language of argument that resonates with the values of a secular global modernity. Similarly, a critical feature of the CEDAW process is its cultural and educational role: its capacity to coalesce and express a particular cultural understanding of gender. Like more conventional legal processes, its significance lies in its capacity to shape cultural understandings and to articulate and expand a vision of rights. This is a form of global legality that depends deeply on its texts, not for enforcement but for the production of cultural meanings associated with modernity and the international. It is ultimately dependant on generating political pressure on states from the CEDAW Committee, from sympathetic leaders within a country, and from international and national nongovernmental organizations. There are clearly ways to slip through this grid of surveillance, including the US strategy of failing to ratify CEDAW at all.

This perspective on CEDAW underscores its culturally constitutive role, a phenomenon that others have argued is characteristic of law within nation-states (see Merry 1990; Sarat and Kearns 1993; Ewick and Silbey 1998). Indeed, international human rights law is like nation-state law in its focus on the cultural production of norms. In both forms of legality, law operates more in the routines of everyday life than in moments of trouble. Compliance depends on the extent to which legal concepts and norms are embedded in consciousness and cultural practice. Legal documents in both situations name problems, specify solutions, and articulate goals. Both state law and international human rights treaty law influence cultural meanings and practices beyond the reach of their sanctions. CEDAW monitoring is a powerful site of cultural production. A document produced by a body of sovereign states that names problems, articulates areas of global consensus, and offers moral visions of the good society is applied to specific countries in a formal process. The process takes place in a transnational community that shares ideals of a secular society based on gender equality and women's safety. This is an instance of transnational consensus building.

The Meanings of Culture in the CEDAW Process

How is culture discussed in CEDAW hearings? As we have seen, demands for cultural change are a fundamental part of the convention. Experts' questions often focus on the need to change gender stereotypes and to eliminate harmful cultural practices and customs. Many countries respond that they are unable to achieve progressive change because of the persistence of patriarchal culture, tradition, customs, or ancient ways. One expert from an African country commented that in her country, cultural factors contributed to male resistance to vasectomy, as it does in other countries "where culture also plays a very big role." This comment implies that "culture" is more important in some countries than in others. Those countries are often the poor countries of the global South. The experts tend to see culture as a barrier to women's human rights. For example, one expert, concerned about honor killings, warned that NGOs working in the global North countries with minority populations from the global South are often not the best representatives for their ethnic minorities since these NGOs try to protect the minorities' culture and therefore do not adequately protect their human rights.

The human rights regime articulates a particular cultural system, one rooted in secular transnational modernity. Indeed, its strength as a mode of social change is its cultural specificity and link to the international. In order to change the meaning of gendered violence in intimate relationships from natural acts to crimes, it is necessary to radically reframe the meaning of the violence and to legitimate this new understanding. The human rights system, rooted in mechanisms of international consensus building, is valuable precisely because it differs from many prevailing practices and it is internationally legitimate. Thus, it often challenges religious, customary, and national conceptions. CEDAW, like the rest of the human rights regime, assumes that culture, custom, or religion should not condone violations of human rights. The committee members of CEDAW often present a united front against recalcitrant or evasive government representatives. They uniformly condemn injurious cultural practices that discriminate against women, a position which is clearly articulated in the text of the convention.

This universalizing approach is structured by the convention itself. The committee's mandate is to apply it to all countries equally. Countries that ratify it assume the burden of conforming to its requirements, regardless of their specific cultural attributes. This is the mission that the committee adopts. Thus, the committee is not explicitly promoting transnational modernity but is pressing governments to conform to the terms of a convention that embodies many of the ideals of that modernity. The convention is the product of global negotiation and consensus building by government representatives within several UN deliberative bodies such as the Commission on the Status of Women and the General Assembly (Jacobson 1992: 445–46). It offers a universal vision of a fair society in which local differences do not justify continuing discrimination against women. In other words, claims to culture do not justify deviation from the culture of transnational modernity. Cultural differences are respected, but only within limits. The human rights approach resists seeing claims to cultural difference as a valid justification for practices harmful to women, children, or other vulnerable populations.

When committee members or the convention invoke culture in CEDAW proceedings, it is more often as an obstacle to change than as a resource or a mode of transformation. The convention and the questions of the experts suggest that certain features of cultural belief and institutional arrangements, such as patterns of marriage, divorce, and inheritance, can serve as barriers to women's progress. At CEDAW hearings, governments sometimes blame their failure to achieve gender equality on intractable patriarchal culture, presenting this as an apparently fixed and homogenous cultural space that seems beyond intervention and change. These arguments justify noncompliant national policies such as discrimination against women in access to schooling or divorce.

On the other hand, committee members and NGO representatives recognize the importance of building on national and local cultural practices to promote transformations of marriage and family patterns and gender stereotypes. They argue that reforms need to be rooted in existing practices and religious systems if they are to be accepted (see An-Naʿim 1992b, 2002). Thus, alongside the portrayal of culture as an unchanging and intransigent obstacle lies another more fluid conception of culture as a process of continually creating new meanings and practices that are products of power relationships and open to contestation among members of the group and by outsiders. In CEDAW discussions, when culture is raised as a problem, it is usually culture defined as tradition or as national essence. The first is, of course, the way the term is used in the convention itself, which explicitly condemns cultural practices that discriminate against women in Articles 2 and 5 (see below). When culture is discussed as a resource, or when there is recognition that the goal of the CEDAW process is cultural reformulation, a far more fluid and contested idea is implied. Needless to say, the coexistence of these quite different understandings of culture in the same forum is confusing. It obscures the creative cultural work that the CEDAW process accomplishes.

CULTURE IN COUNTRY REPORTS

Although the theme of culture as static and resistant to change appeared in many country reports, it occupied a particularly prominent role in the Republic of Guinea's report, heard in the July 2001 CEDAW meetings. Guinea's report demonstrated the discrepancy between a legal system promoting formal equality between men and women and the practices of everyday life. It shows how the concept of culture is used to explain and justify that discrepancy. This was Guinea's initial report as well as its second and third periodic reports since it had not filed any reports since ratifying the convention in 1982. In the opening speech and in the country report, the delegation from Guinea emphasized the extent of gender equality in its constitution and its laws. The country has equal rights to work, to unionize, to strike, to own land, to freedom from discrimination at work, and to be elected to political office. The penal code is equal for all. All work for the same task is to be paid equally. Moreover, the government representatives argued that Guinea has carried out huge efforts to implement the convention, despite wars and a heavy burden of foreign debt. It is now drawing up a plan for the country for the next 10 years, endeavoring to strengthen civil society to benefit women, to encourage the private sector, to develop a national program for youth and for population management, and to support programs for village communities. The government is working on a document to reduce poverty and holding workshops that will develop a poverty-alleviation initiative. This initiative will include gender studies and attention to women in the informal sector. Thus, both the delegation and the report present Guinea as a modern country engaging in planning and fully committed to the principle of gender equality.

Yet the report also says, "Both in general terms and within the home, Guinean women remain in a subordinate position to men who exercise power in virtually all areas of life. Guinean women live in a society and culture that is traditionally androcratic and where marriage is often polygamous" (Initial Reports of States Parties: Guinea 2001: 31). The drafters of the report asserted a vision of human rights in terms of autonomy and liberty as opposed to traditional culture. For example, the report included several customary practices in its definition of violence against women. It listed: beating, repudiation, levirate, sororate, early and forced marriage, and sexual mutilation. Even beating was described as a traditional right for a man, although reprehensible. The report continues: "The persistence of cultural traditions and customary law perpetuates certain prejudices which sanction violence against women. On the other hand, there is no sex-based discrimination in the law and most acts of violence are subject to legal penalties" (Initial Reports of States Parties: Guinea 2001: 32). Violence is attributed to customary practices, while law opposes it. The government and NGOs have carried out public awareness campaigns about violence against women, including "the eradication of traditional practices that are harmful to mothers and children, the control of sexually-transmitted diseases and AIDS and the elimination of the practice of forced and early marriage." But the report acknowledges that various forms of violence against women including the levirate and female excision are still widely practiced, particularly in rural areas. Although there are no discriminatory laws, in practice the family is patriarchal, the man controls the domicile, and children by the age of seven are under his control. Women are assigned a narrow range of tasks and their lives seem governed by fears that they will become pregnant before marriage. For example, with reference to education, the report says: "There are many parents who still believe that education is not indispensable, or even necessary, for girls. They bring their daughters up to find a 'good husband' before it is too late. Their priority is to prepare their daughters to become ideal, or model wives, by which they mean submissive wives. For them, it would be unwise to allow girls to go to school with boys. Even if a girl managed to avoid all the 'traps' at school and were to graduate and join the Civil Service, she would, according to this thesis, have too much freedom. This would undermine the authority of her husband, who, it should be remembered, is seen as the bridge between a bride and God" (2001: 49).

Although this report portrays the problems for women as rooted in a traditional culture that will not change, women's levels of health, education, and employment are strikingly low. The rate of female illiteracy was 85 percent; outside the capital city, it was 93 to 96 percent (Initial Reports of States Parties: Guinea 2001: 61, 66). Only 11 percent of students in higher education are women (2001: 21). Although a 1992 study found that the cohort fertility rate was seven children per woman, only 2–3 percent use birth control (2001: 4, 21). There is a high rate of infant mortality and maternal mortality (666 per

100,000 live births) and a life expectancy of 53 (2001: 4.) The median age for women at marriage is 16. Women do most of the subsistence agricultural work, producing 80 percent of all food (2001: 22). Thus, the report locates responsibility for the widespread violence women suffer in an intractable traditional culture rather than in the government's failure to provide schools, health clinics, and jobs for women. The government offers women legal rights but not the means to assert them. The explanation it offers for this disparity, however, is culture. The report concludes: "Generally speaking, however, while women in the Republic of Guinea are accorded the same legal rights as men, these gains are powerfully diluted in their daily lives by the coexistence of modern law with customs and traditional and religious practices" (2001: 123). This conclusion was followed by a long list of international conventions that the government of Guinea has signed and ratified.

The experts praised the delegation for its political will and commitment to women's equality but noted that there were serious gaps in its accomplishment of that goal. They questioned the low level of education and health care, whether an Islamic or customary legal system operated alongside the egalitarian national law enforcing gender inequality, and the disparity between the progressive laws and the lack of efforts to implement them. They noted the contradictions between the laws promoting gender equality and those giving power over the domicile, marriage, and children to men. Several stressed the importance of more education for women as well as for men (62% illiterate) and encouraged more work on female genital cutting, still a widespread practice. One expert noted the contradiction between acknowledging problems of gender discrimination due to social and cultural customs and traditions and a lack of positive action to eliminate those customs. For example, polygamy is illegal but still prevalent. The tenor of questions was praise for the political will of the delegation but skepticism about the extent of equality on the ground and an insistence that the government invest more resources in women, especially women's education. Criticisms were framed as concerns. It was clear, however, that the experts were not persuaded by the argument that Guinea had done all it could despite its claims about the intractable nature of its "traditional culture."

The report was presented by a large delegation of twelve government ministers, lawyers, doctors, and professors, about evenly divided between men and women. The men were dressed in dark Western suits, the women in elaborate West African gowns. All spoke French to one another as they waited in the elegant lounge outside the conference room in New York. Thus, as the national elites participate in this international forum and construct a modern legal system, they juxtapose their urban and educated world, in touch with the international community, to that of the apparently ancient and unchanging traditional culture of the rural areas, riddled with patriarchal culture. There is clear resonance with the colonial past. The use of this framework is driven by economic necessity. Guinea describes itself as eager to pursue democratization based on a liberal development model and as a country with vast mineral resources dependent on foreign partnerships (Initial Reports of States Parties: Guinea 2001: 6–7). Appearing to promote the human rights of women is critical to economic development since it marks the nation as modern and suitable for foreign investment. Culture provides a good excuse for failure. Yet the analysis in this report fails to consider the way culture itself is constituted by the systems of law, government, education, and politics within which groups of people live.

Egypt's country report, presented in January 2001, both denigrated culture as backward tradition and asserted the value of Egypt's cultural distinctness as national identity. The introduction to the report defended Egypt's reservations to CEDAW and other international human rights instruments "which have the purpose of ensuring their implementation while at the same time preserving the national particularities of Egyptian society along with those of its historical and cultural customs, characteristics and creeds that do not conflict with or infringe upon the instruments but are decidedly within the scope of the protection they provide to rights and freedoms" (CEDAW/C/EGY/4–5, 30 March 2000: 3).

Egypt was one of the earliest countries to ratify CEDAW, doing so in 1981, and in 2001 was presenting a combined fourth and fifth periodic report. The report asserted Egypt's respect for the full and effective implementation of international human rights treaties and conventions but also said it respects the diversity of societies in the country and the "heritage, cultural characteristics and prevailing values stemming from their historical development" (CEDAW/C/EGY/4–5, 30 March 2000: 3). The introduction concludes with the optimistic, if unrealistic, statement that these cultural characteristics should not conflict with the values the international community protects by means of these instruments, as stressed in the 1993 Vienna Conference. Thus, Egypt declared its commitment to universalism at the same time that it insisted on preserving its national particularities of culture and custom.

Much of the text of the report describes Egypt's efforts "to overcome all the obstacles created by the negative aspects of some prevailing customs and concepts" (CEDAW/C/EGY/4–5, 30 March 2000: 32). The report notes progress in eliminating "many harmful customs and practices, particularly in the fields of health care and family planning," and describes female circumcision as "a practice that continues in some remote areas" which the government has been energetically trying to eliminate (CEDAW/C/EGY/4–5, 30 March 2000: 42–43). When the delegation listed the problems in Egypt, they mentioned illiteracy among women, violence in the family, few women in Parliament or the judiciary, and "backward traditions affecting women." The delegation, chaired by the Secretary-General of the National Council for Women, noted that cultural constraints and conditions sometimes impeded change and obstructed the implementation of the law.

In its oral report, the delegation emphasized the importance of making reforms within the national culture and religion, using indigenous formulations rooted in Egyptian and Islamic culture. They argued that Islam was not against equality for women but that Shari'a specifies equality for women and that it is "our culture" that made it patriarchal. One speaker described how Egypt passed a new law in 2000 that allowed women the right to a unilateral divorce by repudiation without the need to prove damage. Under this new law, a wife could repudiate her husband because of incompatibility. A judge has three months to try to conciliate the marriage, and then the woman is allowed to divorce, without the right of appeal. Thus, women are allowed to divorce at their own discretion on the basis of incompatibility. They argued that this law could be passed only because it was based on the past traditions of the country. Although the right of repudiation in Shari'a is generally thought to exist only for men, the women's movement in Egypt found that "true Shari'a" gives men the unilateral right to divorce and women the unilateral right to repudiate. They argued that it was a practice already followed in rural areas. To promote this law, they found support for gender equality in religious texts, showing that Islam promotes gender equality, and argued that it is patriarchal culture that has transformed everyday practices. This enabled them to counter the arguments of many — particularly Islamic law professors in religious universities — that allowing women to divorce was opposed to Islam. They had many fights in promoting this new law because many feared that all women would want to end their marriages. But the support of the First Lady, Mrs. Mubarak, and the National Committee for Women (replaced by the National Council for Women in 2000), enabled passage of the new law. (Some members of the National Committee attended the Beijing Conference in 1995, showing the influence of transnational human rights ideas and conferences on national policy-making.) In this example, the activists within and outside the government saw culture as a resource for legitimating innovations.

The country report describes the new law in optimistic terms, saying that this is a measure to alleviate the suffering of women by speeding up litigation to allow divorced women to receive the maintenance that has been awarded to them, to protect them from violence from their husbands, and to require the Nasser Bank to pay women in distress their maintenance, raising taxes to provide them with this support (CEDAW/C/EGY/4–5, 30 March 2000: 32, 44, 89). The version of the law that was passed, however, was a watered down one that allowed a woman to divorce without proof if she refunded her dower to the husband and forfeited all financial rights and claims from the marriage (Hajjar 2004). According to the shadow report of Egyptian NGOs prepared in December 2000, the new law allows divorce if the wife pays monetary compensation to her husband, giving back the dowry and waiving all her legal rights. According to Shari'a, in divorce only the original dowry must be returned but not any interest she has accrued from it, but in practice the woman usually spends her dowry furnishing the marital home rather than investing it so she has no interest to keep (Egyptian Non-Governmental Organizations Coalition 2000: 50–51). Thus, this option is open only to relatively affluent women.

At the hearing, some of the CEDAW experts challenged the claim that religion does not undermine women's rights in Egypt and questioned whether it could really serve as the basis for reform. Some experts noted the flaws in the new law that gave women a divorce without maintenance and queried whether the new divorce law meant that the woman loses support and rights to her children. One pointed out that promoting the rights of women is fundamental to any modern society and that the rights of women in Arab and/or Muslim countries are fragile. Another asked why it was necessary to give women the unilateral right to divorce if it was already in the religious texts of Islam. She noted that it is not enough to create laws, but that they must be applied if they are to be progressive and promote the development of modern society. An expert from Turkey said she was pleased to have an analysis of problems based on prejudicial, patriarchal mentalities rather than Islam and recognized the value of working within a religion, but warned that this is a slow road to follow. She suggested working within a culture of human rights instead. She pointed out that in this form of divorce, a woman forgoes all claims on property that she may have built up or acquired during her marriage and wondered how it was to be enforced given a "backward, patriarchal culture." Thus, Egypt's new divorce law exemplifies the strategy of legitimating reforms within existing religious and cultural practices but reveals its limitations. The CEDAW experts are skeptical about this approach to change.

In their concluding comments, the CEDAW Committee noted that the introduction of this legal reform was a positive development but expressed concern over the fact that it requires women to forgo their right to financial provision, including the dower, and recommended a revision of the law to elim-inate this financial discrimination against women (pars. 328, 329, p. 35, UN General Assembly 2001 A/56/38). The committee observed that, although the Constitution guarantees equality of men and women and the convention pre-vails over national legislation, the persistence of cultural stereotypes and patri-archal attitudes with respect to the role of women and men in the family and society limit the full implementation of the convention (par. 325, p. 34, UN General Assembly 2001 A/56/38). They note with concern that the Egyptian Constitution states that the state shall enable a woman to reconcile her duties towards her family with her work in society and guarantee her equality with men in the sphere of political, social, cultural and economic life, which appears to entrench a woman's primary role as mother and homemaker (par. 332, p. 35, UN General Assembly 2001 A/56/38).

Thus, the CEDAW experts argued that embedding women's reforms within existing religious and social structures that were patriarchal was a slow and rel-atively ineffectual strategy. They advocated adopting a human rights perspec-tive instead. Like other transnational actors, they stressed the value of global abstract principles rather than working within the cultural practices of partic-ular situations. They maintained their position that culture is an obstacle to women's rights and interpreted Egypt's claims to cultural distinctiveness as an excuse for failing to protect women's human rights.

COUNTRY COMPARISONS

An examination of country reports and CEDAW discussions from the 2001/2002 sessions indicates significant differences in the way countries talk about the role of culture. Some use culture as an excuse for their failure to achieve greater progress in women's rights. Others talk about efforts to overcome gen-der stereotypes or prejudices that affect women's access to education, work, political position, and increase their vulnerability to violence. Some celebrate their cultural distinctiveness. Those that describe culture as an obstacle are also those whose governments are doing less for women's equality and for whom the disparity between the convention and the situation of women is greatest. Those with greater government investment in preventing discrimina-tion against women are far less likely to blame a lack of progress on traditional culture, although they may discuss efforts to overcome gender stereotypes.

For example, in neither the country report nor the CEDAW discussion was there reference to cultural obstacles by Finland, Denmark, the Netherlands, Kazakhstan, Guyana, or Andorra. Russia blamed persistent "old traditions" and gender stereotypes for violence in the home, while Estonia discussed gender stereotypes and prejudices. The Netherlands mentioned cultural barriers with reference to its immigrant population that continues to practice female genital cutting. Denmark described its commitment to gender equality and the many government programs promoting it, but not as a struggle against culture. Men's failure to take advantage of extended parental leave was attributed in part to "attitudes and traditions," but this led the government to engage in public education and to develop more flexible leave schemes rather than to see the problem as intractable (CEDAW/C/TTO/1–3, 6 February 2001: 45).

On the other hand, Egypt, Fiji, Trinidad and Tobago, the Maldives, Nicaragua, Uruguay, and Vietnam referred more broadly to difficulties with culture. Nicaragua bemoaned its machismo culture. Trinidad and Tobago said, "Patriarchal ideologies and notions of male dominance still persist and are proving difficult to change" (CEDAW/C/TTO/1–3, 6 February 2001: 43). An expert noted that the patriarchal ideology of Trinidad was very deeply rooted. Vietnam focused on the traditional culture of minorities living in rural and mountainous areas. For example, when asked about the penalty for forced marriages in highland areas and among minority ethnic groups, and the measures taken to prevent forced marriages, the government replied: "The 2000 Law on Marriage and the Family acknowledges the principle to respect and develop the traditions and customs imbued with national identity in marriage and family relations which do not contradict other principles of the Law. However, in reality, due to some persistent backward customary belief and practices, compounded by limited understanding of the law, forced marriages and marriages between children remain very popular in many mountainous and ethnic minority areas. Besides measures taken to enhance the legal understanding of ethnic minorities and to mobilize elders and heads of villages in encouraging villages to change their outdated thinking, violations are dealt with in accordance with laws and regulations" (CEDAW/PSWG/2001/II/CRP.2/Add. 3, dated 5 June 2001: 23).

Thus, national culture is something to be valued while culture in the rural villages or among immigrant minorities needs to change. In Vietnam, the coasts and deltas have national culture while the people in mountainous and remote areas and the minorities are backward. European countries seek to change the cultural practices of immigrant communities. When the leaders of a major initiative to develop domestic violence materials in China planned their curriculum, they thought that the minorities would need culturally different materials but that a single set for the Han majority group was sufficient. They thought of the dominant, majority group as similar despite major urban-rural, regional, and class differences. Only the minorities had diverse cultures. When educated urban elites in postcolonial countries as well as those of the global North call for reform, they have a tendency to define the national culture as desirable and that of remote and rural peoples as deficient.

Yet, both the culture of the center and the culture of the margins exist on the same terrain, although clearly unequal in power. A theory of culture as contested, historically produced, and continually defined and redefined in a variety of settings (see Lazarus-Black and Hirsch 1994; Lazarus-Black 1994), an idea that rarely appears in country reports, would enhance understanding the human rights monitoring process as promoting gradual cultural transformation rather than as law without sanctions confronting intractable cultural difference.

It is clear that human rights language is a powerful discourse to promote women's status, yet a critique of culture that marginalizes poor and rural peoples or immigrants risks replicating colonial discourses. A more nuanced critique of particular practices or gender stereotypes is less likely to evoke nationalist defenses and justifications and more likely to build on local movements of resistance and contestation. Moreover, viewing problems as caused by poverty, warfare, displacement, and governmental crises instead of cultural beliefs and practices suggests different avenues for intervention.

Conclusions: The Space of Transnational Modernity

Human rights processes such as CEDAW monitoring take place in the space of transnational modernity. This space incorporates postcolonial elites as well as elites from the global North. It is not an exclusively Western space but a transnational one within which people from all over the world participate to produce a social reformist, fundamentally neoliberal vision of modernity governed by concepts of human rights. Its participants — government representatives, NGO representatives, and staff — are, of course, products of particular localities, but within global human rights settings, they have developed a distinctive cultural repertoire of procedures for dealing with difference, conceptions of how change takes place, and strategies for implementing change. They spend considerable effort drafting and editing documents that express the norms of this culture.

The international campaign to deal with violence against women was created by this culture of transnational modern society. Although it is influenced by the West, this culture is shaped by cosmopolitan elites from around the world who participate in international institutions such as the United Nations and international NGOs. The principles of this international campaign are, first, that universal standards cannot be compromised by claims to cultural or religious difference and, second, that gender equality is the optimum approach to protecting women from violence. The transnational leaders who are forging this new normative system support the first point even though they value cultural diversity. Although there is far from global consensus on the second point, with many societies advocating gender inequality and complementarity as their ideal, transnational human rights reformers generally agree that gender equality is the best route to safety for women. Underlying these basic principles are cultural assumptions about the value of the autonomous self, the capacity to make choices among alternative cultural paths, the protection of physical autonomy, and the possession of rights.

This is a reformist space in which vulnerable people such as women and children or victims of state violence deserve protection. The opponent of reform is often culture, defined in a very specific way as unchanging, irrational, patriarchal, and justifying the oppression that women face in families, in society, and by the state. Culture is described as a set of ideas that determine behavior, such that people have no alternative but to conform to cultural expectations. This conception of the relationship between beliefs and actions is inherently opposed to the culture of the transnational modern that emphasizes the value of informed choice. The central actors in this system are transnational cosmopolitan elites: people who have studied and lived in different countries, are «uent in more than one language, travel often, attend international meetings, and understand their own sociocultural world within the context of a transnational society. These are the kinds of people who serve as experts on the CEDAW Committee, who work for international NGOs, who attend UN conferences and meetings, and who construct the documents that serve as the blueprint for transnational modernity. These people come from particular cultural traditions but are not exclusively rooted in them. Instead, they see alternative ways of doing things. Mastery of English is important to participating in this world.

There is some cultural consensus to this world. The possession of human rights by every individual and resistance to hierarchies based on race and gender are fundamental. It tends to be neoliberal rather than socialist, although there is considerable variation. It values people's freedom to make choices about their situations. There is deep commitment to the rule of law and the need for accountability for state actors who violate human rights. Protection of the individual from violence is a central value. The discursive world created in these forums juxtaposes culture to the law. For many transnational elites, culture is far away. It is mostly located "out there"—in villages, mountains, deserts, deep forests, or among minority communities. These areas are sometimes referred to as "traditional societies," implying that they have a static and timeless social system. This usage distances societies that are not represented at the global conference tables. Here there is law, with culture hiding from view, buried in the everyday practices of modernity. The appeal of global modernity is reminiscent of the appeal of civilization during the era of empire. In the post-colonial era, the glamour of the modern is still juxtaposed to backward others, but now it includes those who are "developing" but still burdened by culture. Transnational legal settings are producing culture, but it is a culture that relegates culture to the margins. The fight against "culture" is a deeply cultural one.

Disjunctures between Global Law and Local Justice

As a legal system, human rights law endeavors to apply universal principles to all situations uniformly. It does not tailor its interventions to specific political and social situations, even when these might suggest different approaches to social justice. Local context is ignored in order to establish global principles. Moreover, human rights interventions are framed within a particular vision of social justice based on a neoliberal privileging of choice rather than alternatives that could be more community-based or focused on socialist or religious conceptions of justice.[1] These gaps between global visions of justice and specific visions in local contexts create a fundamental dilemma for human rights practice. There is a struggle between the generalizing strategies of transnational actors and the particularistic techniques of activists working within local contexts. How to negotiate this divide is a key human rights problem. This chapter describes these tensions while the next two chapters examine the processes of transplantation and translation that bridge them. —*purpose*

The CEDAW Committee is one of the human rights mechanisms that confront the challenge of applying general principles to specific situations. The CEDAW monitoring process is committed to using CEDAW norms for all situations and resists excuses for noncompliance based on the particularities of local situations. The reliance on legal rationality further diminishes the incentive to take local context into account. Nor does the structure of international regulation provide the time or resources to examine local political, social, and historical conditions. Faced with the frequent use of local culture as an excuse for failure, CEDAW members, along with most transnational women's human rights activists, reject claims to culture that justify practices detrimental to women's human rights. In practice, human rights standards are powerful because of this resolute commitment to norms that transcend particular situations. Such tenacity makes them more valuable resources for local activists. When these activists challenge the acceptability of domestic violence, for example, they find the transnational prohibition that rejects all cultural justifications very helpful.

Yet, the reified conception of culture that underlies this rejection impedes transnational activists' ability to work with local situations. It denies alternative conceptions of social justice and obscures ways that local arrangements can promote human rights and social justice. This tension between transnational principles and the importance of local context is inevitable. National and local NGOs tend to take local contexts more seriously. It is these groups that navigate the divide between the local and the global, translating global approaches into local terms and seeking to give local groups voice in global settings. The NGOs who work at this interface typically recognize the contested and shifting nature of culture and rarely describe culture as an obstacle or a thing.

The disjuncture between global norms and local contexts emerged dramatically when the CEDAW Committee considered the country reports of India and Fiji. In both cases, the CEDAW Committee criticized certain national and local practices as oppressive to women. It chastised India for retaining its system of distinct personal laws for different religious communities and complained about Fiji's use of a traditional reconciliation procedure for rape. In both situations, the committee did not consider the local political context. Feminist activists in each country, who pay greater attention to local conditions, took a somewhat different approach from the CEDAW Committee. The committee's lack of attention to local situations impedes productive collaboration with grassroots activists despite the desire of the CEDAW Committee to promote this collaboration and the shared commitment of both transnational and local activists to improving the situation of women. These two case studies reveal the underlying tension between a transnational perspective on reform and one grounded in local particularities. They show how a reified conception of culture as tradition exacerbates this tension.

The Reform of Personal Laws in India

In the presentation of the initial report from India in January 2000, which I did not observe, CEDAW experts complained about India's use of separate religious laws for family relations and marriage. They felt that these separate laws undermined women's status. India has long had separate personal laws for different religious communities: Hindu, Muslim, Christian, Jewish, and Parsi. Personal laws govern family relationships such as marriage, divorce, inheritance, maintenance, guardianship, succession, and custody. Although various religious communities have their own family laws, the current arrangement of separate systems of personal law is not an ancient practice but a legacy of the British colonial era. The colonial state ensured uniform application of the civil law but left women's position in the family to be governed by the customary laws and practices of different communities (Agnes 1996a: 106, 1996b: 72; see also Cohn 1996). A regionally diverse set of local laws was reformulated into four uniform systems, one for each major religious community. Since independence, the government of India has maintained a policy of noninterference in the personal laws of minority religious communities, despite the directive in the Indian Constitution to develop a uniform secular personal law (Singh 1994: 378). When India ratified CEDAW in 1993, the government of India filed a declaratory statement (in effect a reservation) on Article 16 (1) that calls for nondiscrimination in marriage and family relations because of its policy of "non-interference with the personal affairs of any community without its initiative and consent' (India Report to CEDAW 1999, CEDAW/C/IND/1, 10 March 1999: 2), reaffirming the statement India made when it signed CEDAW in 1980 (Byrnes 1996: 52–53).

The women's movement in India has long pressed for a uniform secular code for personal laws, often bemoaning the state's lack of effort in developing such a code (Singh 1994: 378–80). However, with the rise of a Hindu right social movement and a Hindu nationalist political party in the 1980s, the demand for a uniform civil code took on a new political complexion. For Hindu nationalists, demanding a uniform secular code was a way to criticize Muslim law with regard to women's status. The Hindu right seems less concerned about women's rights than about attacking minorities, particularly Muslims (Basu 1995; Kapur and Cossman 1996: 156). The rise to political power of the Hindu right has been accompanied by a resurgence of ethnic violence against minority religious communities, particularly Muslims (Hossain 1994; Singh 1994; Agnes 1995, 1996b; Basu 1995: 161, 141–46; Sarkar and Butalia 1995; Chowdhury, Kannabiran, and Kannabiran 1996; Kapur and Cossman 1996: 234; Sarkar 2001). There were serious riots in 1992 and again in 2002 (see International Initiative for Justice in Gujarat 2003).

Consequently, by the 1990s the women's movement found itself in an uncomfortable alignment with the Hindu right and backed away from demanding a uniform civil code. By 2000, the year India reported to CEDAW, the issue of a uniform civil code pitted women's rights groups against minority rights groups. Although a uniform system of personal laws had been a key demand of the women's movement for at least fifty years, at this point this reform fanned the flames of communal hostilities. Promoting a uniform code of personal law was an important part of the antiminority propaganda of the Hindu right. It enabled them to focus on the inadequacies of Muslim law, ignoring gender biases of Hindu law which lead to murders, suicide, and female feticide. "A myth created by the media is that the 'enlightened' Hindus are governed by an ideal gender-just law and this law now needs to be extended to Muslims in order to liberate Muslim women" (Agnes 1996a: 107). Opposition to the uniform civil code came from minority communities fearful of the Hinduization of civil law (Chowdhury, Kannabiran, and Kannabiran 1996: 99). Many women's groups dropped their support for a uniform civil code, worried that this issue was being used to promote communal tensions between Hindus and Muslims (Basu 1999). A prominent Indian feminist argues that reforms are necessary, but that it is important to avoid placing fuel in the hands of antiminority forces (Agnes 1996a: 111). Leaders of the women's movement whom I interviewed in Delhi in 2001 agreed that the women's movement has withdrawn from the campaign to promote a uniform civil code. They now seek gender justice and women's rights rather than uniformity of personal laws across religious communities (Hasan 1999: 86–87).

Muslim-Hindu tensions surrounding personal laws erupted in the 1980s in the aftermath of a celebrated case concerning maintenance for a divorced Muslim woman. In 1985, Shah Bano, a seventy-five-year-old woman who was abandoned by her husband, filed for maintenance under the criminal code. Under neither Muslim nor Hindu law does a woman have the right to alimony. Muslim law entitles her to the return of the engagement gift and Hindu law to the gifts she brought with her to the marriage (stridhan). Concerned about the large number of destitute windows in India, the British colonial government passed a law under the Criminal Procedure Code (Section 125) that entitled destitute women to maintenance by their husbands. Shah Bano filed for maintenance under the criminal code, which applies to all religious communities. Although the Congress Party defended retaining an unreformed separate Muslim law (Hasan 1999: 73), the Indian Supreme Court upheld Shah Bano's right to permanent maintenance from her husband and asserted that the criminal law transcended personal law. Moreover, it criticized law that subjected women to unjust treatment, citing both Hindu and Muslim religious lawmakers, and urged the government to frame a common civil code (Kumar 1999: 77).

The leaders of the Muslim minority community protested vigorously against this intrusion into Muslim personal law and argued that the judgment violated the principles of Islam. Large demonstrations against the judgment took place in Bombay and Bhopal. On the other side, some cast Muslims as "archaic, obscurantist, and anti-national" (Hasan 1999: 79). During this period, the Hindu right escalated agitation against the Babri Masjid, a Muslim mosque in the city of Ayodhya, claiming that it was built on the site of a Hindu temple. These issues became linked in a communal assault on the Muslims (Kumar 1999: 78). In 1986 the government of India acceded to the demands of Muslim leaders and passed the Muslim Women's (Protection of Rights on Divorce) Act, perhaps reflecting the importance of Muslim voters to the Congress Party (Hasan 1999: 82). This law excluded Muslim women from the protections of the criminal statute providing for maintenance of divorced women (Singh 1994: 376). It required maintenance of the wife only for the *iddat* period, 3 months and 10 days after the divorce (Hameed n.d.: 32). A report by a member of the National Commission of Women on Muslim women's perspectives says, "A section of the progressive Muslim opinion declared this enactment to be the most retrograde step for all Muslims" (Hameed n.d.: 32). Shah Bano herself faced such pressure that she gave up the right she had fought for. As Kumar notes, it was one of a series of incidents that showed Indian feminists how easily their issues could be exploited by groups with other political agendas (1999: 78–79). Thus, women's rights fell victim to communalism, with women's rights claims buried by ethnic politics.[2]

The Hindu right, including its political party Bharatiya Janata (BJP), a paramilitary organization Rashtra Swayamsevak Sangh, and a religious organization Vishva Hindu Parishad, gained substantial power during the 1990s. The BJP was the governing party of India from 1999 until 2004. The origins of the Hindu right movement lie in the nationalist movements of the nineteenth century, but in the 1920s it took on its distinctive form as a movement of Hindus against Muslims.[3] Since the 1960s, the movement has expanded, promoting references to "Muslim domination," "appeasement of minorities," and "Hindu pride." It argues that the policy of giving Muslims and other religious minorities separate treatment has perpetuated the oppression of Hindus and caused the political malaise allegedly widespread in society. As a solution, the movement urges converting India into a Hindu state (Kapur and Cossman 1996). While the BJP is in most respects deeply patriarchal, it sometimes promotes women's rights as a way of isolating and attacking the Muslim community (Basu 1995: 170). Basu observes that Hindu nationalists bemoan the degraded status of Muslim women to demonstrate their own superiority in a manner reminiscent of British colonial discourses about degraded Indian women (1955b: 176).

Support for a uniform civil code is the most important BJP stance concerning women (Basu 1995: 172).[4] It allows the BJP to emphasize its support for women and at the same time talk about the repressive aspects of Muslim law. The Hindu right argues that Hinduism is the only religion with tolerance and therefore the only basis for a secular country. The movement's goal is to assimilate minorities into the broader, more tolerant fabric of Hinduism (Kapur and Cossman 1996: 239–40). There is an assumption that the code the BJP promotes would be based primarily on Hindu norms and practices (Kapur and Cossman 1996: 261). Yet, despite claims that Hindu law is less discriminatory toward women than the law of other religions, there are many features of Hindu law that subordinate women and define them as dependent wives within joint families (see also Agnes 1996b). In Hindu law, as well as in the law of other religious communities, succession and property rights discriminate against women and reflect the assumptions of a patrilineal/patrilocal family system.[5] For example, the provision of dowry and the subsequent battles over it are a consequence of the failure to provide inheritance rights to women other than dowry (Kapur and Cossman 1996: 127–29). The case law on dowry deaths relies on the idea that women are weak, passive, and in need of protection as they are transplanted from one family to another (Kapur and Cossman 1996: 129). There are similar assumptions about women's economic dependency in all of the personal laws. Wives and sometimes daughters are not entitled to the same inheritance as husbands and sons (Kapur and Cossman 1996: 137). One scholar notes that all the personal laws are antiwoman, antiliberal, and antihuman (Singh 1994: 379). In fact, Sarkar points out that, as the BJP becomes more patriarchal, its earlier pride in a reformed Hindu law that was used to assert superiority over Muslims seems to have declined. "It seems that Hindu patriarchy, uncontaminated by western influence, has once again emerged as the embodiment of preferred values. And once again, women must forget about gender rights to ensure community supremacy" (1995: 212).

Moreover, feminists argue that the most significant barrier to women's rights in India is a hostile state uninterested in giving women rights or in implementing the laws that exist. Despite the amendment of rape and dowry laws during the 1980s, for example, these laws have not been enforced or implemented. The problem of dowry murders continues (Singh 1994: 376). There is also a pervasive gender bias in the judiciary. Organizations such as Sakshi in Delhi have reported very conservative views among the judiciary in surveys and have worked to train judges in new ways of thinking about gender. In the early 1990s, Sakshi studied judicial attitudes toward women and violence against women in India by interviewing 109 judges in a project supported by the Canadian International Development Agency (Sakshi 1996). They found widespread gender bias among judges with reference to how they viewed marriage and domestic violence. Three quarters thought that they should preserve the family even if there was violence in the marriage (74%). Half of the judges thought that women who stay with men who abuse them are partly to blame and just about half thought that there were certain occasions when a man was justified in slapping his wife (Sakshi 1996: 5–6). Over three quarters (78%) had never heard of CEDAW and the other 22 percent knew nothing of its contents or its General Recommendation 19 on violence. The head of Sakshi told me in a 2001 interview that when they showed this study to the judges, they were shocked.

Feminists in India recognize the difficulty of locating CEDAW and a uniform civil code in this political context. Flavia Agnes, a pioneer feminist activist in India, observes: "While the Women's Convention stipulates equality for spouses within the marriage, this provision needs to be contextualised within national and regional politics and plurality of cultures. Resisting homogenization of communities through uniform legislation has become an important agenda of human rights, and women's rights need to be situated within this context" (Agnes 1996a: 111). The demand for a uniform civil code places minority women in an especially difficult dilemma: they have loyalties both to their religious community and to their gender and confront the constant imposition of the majority over the minority. To argue for a secular law is to oppose one's own community (Agnes 1996b: 90). There are currently efforts by Muslim women to reform Muslim family law, but many Muslim women's activists do not want a uniform law, such as a proposed ban on polygamy, that would drive a further wedge between communities without strengthening the position of Muslim women (Agnes 1996a: 110). The All-India Muslim Women's Association would like to see reforms in the Muslim personal law but not a uniform civil code (Kapur and Cossman 1996: 258).

THE COLONIAL LEGACY

Even though the retention of religion-based personal laws is defended in the name of culture and tradition, the personal law system is a British colonial legacy. The colonial state focused on uniform application of the civil law but left women's position in the family to be governed by the customary laws and practices of different communities. This was a common British colonial policy intended to minimize resistance to imperial rule. In the past, the regulation of family relationships had fallen to religious heads or local caste or community bodies, producing a great diversity of cultural practices (Agnes 1996a: 106). Gradually, however, the British intervened in some aspects of family relationships, such as the regulation of *sati* (widow immolation) and child marriage. Moreover, they relied heavily on ancient texts and the interpretations of religious pundits and *ulama* to determine the laws for Hindus and Muslims (Singh 1994: 380). The creation of personal law systems for religious groups united a highly disparate system of regional and caste-based legal systems. This had the added effect of strengthening the sense of commonality within religious communities. At the same time, the British approach ignored the way customary indigenous systems were flexible and open to change. They rendered the law more certain, rigid, and uniform. As a result, personal laws remained static as society changed (Agnes 1996b: 72; see also Cohn 1996).

During the 1930s and 1940s, separate personal laws were increasingly linked to distinct communal identities. The creation of a common Muslim law in the 1930s had the hidden agenda of joining disparate Muslim communities together, much as the postindependence reform of Hindu personal laws had the goal of unifying the nation through uniformity in law and establishing the supremacy of the state over religious institutions (Agnes 1996b: 76, 78). During the communal conflict in India at the time of partition in 1947, Muslim leaders came to see personal laws as a symbol of their cultural identity. They resisted state interference in personal laws. Reform of Hindu family laws was also linked to communal politics. There were efforts to reform the Hindu laws in the 1940s and 1950s, but Hindu fundamentalists opposed them (Kapur and Cossman 1996: 56–57). Women gained the right to divorce and acquired more property rights but not equal rights of inheritance. Thus, the communal politics of partition and its aftermath gave new political significance to separate personal laws.[6]

Colonial rule contributed to the crystallization of personal law and, in the case of the Muslim law of inheritance, even its retrogression (Hossain 1994: 475–76). Although the system of personal laws is largely the product of British colonial policy, it is defended in the name of culture. In the new Hindu nationalism, the defense of ancient Hindu culture takes on great significance and is opposed to a secular feminism based on human rights. The opposition to women's human rights is again framed in the language of culture, both culture as national identity and culture as tradition.

THE CEDAW HEARINGS

The government's report to the CEDAW Committee stressed its commitment to a policy of noninterference in personal laws, noting that there have been reforms in Hindu, Parsi, and Christian laws (CEDAW/C/IND/1, 10 March 1999: 3). It also noted that the Supreme Court has recently asserted the need for a uniform civil code for all women regardless of religion, in accordance with the Directive Principles of the Constitution (pp. 5, 21). The report indicates that the Christian community is working to reform its archaic personal laws dating from 1869 (which was accomplished in 2001) and that there have been reforms in Parsi laws (pp. 99–100). It notes, however, that "Recent fundamentalist assertions of a specific view of culture by both religious and ethnic groups have . . . posed new threats to gender" (p. 28).

At the CEDAW hearings, the experts were critical of India's stance of not intervening. One commented that the state's principle of nonintervention was impeding progress in guaranteeing women's rights. The committee insisted that the government be charged to change the personal laws of the distinct religious communities. It was firm that there needed to be a single, nondiscriminatory system and pressed India to adopt a uniform code for all its religious communities and to eliminate separate personal laws on the grounds that they were discriminatory. The experts noted that ethnic and religious groups tended to maintain patriarchal traditions and that perpetuating the personal laws of these ethnic and religious communities was incompatible with women's rights and was a breach of the convention (UN Press Release WOM/1161, 24 January 2000 and UN Press Release WOM/1162 453rd Meeting (PM) 24 January 2000). One expert said that it was necessary to change social and cultural values often perpetuated by religious and ethnic communities to eliminate existing discrimination. The expert added that India needed to reinterpret its values governing religious and cultural norms. She observed further that ethnic and religious groups were often responsible for patriarchal traditions that discriminated against women and that the state had the obligation to enact legislation to counteract those values. "Perpetuating the personal laws of ethnic and religious communities was incompatible with women's rights and a breach of the Convention. Unless a creative way was found to deal with the country's position, the many specific advances in India's policies on education, health and other areas could be nullified." The expert concluded her comments by asking what active steps would be taken to induce a nondiscriminatory mindset (UN Press Release WOM/1161: 5). Another expert asked if there could be one comprehensive code to ensure equality of women in all aspects of Indian life regardless of religion or culture (UN Press Release WOM/1161: 5).

The government representatives apparently ignored this issue in their response. The UN press release did not indicate any statements by the delegation chair—the Secretary of the Department of Women and Child Development of

India—on the issue of separate personal laws for religious and ethnic communities (UN Press Release WOM/1171, 31 January 2000: 2–3). The committee chairperson, Aida Gonzalez Martinez of Mexico, reiterated in her reply to the government that the committee was concerned about the question of amendments to personal and family laws, and that rather than waiting for the religious communities to amend their personal and family laws themselves it was important to encourage them to change (UN Press Release WOM/1171, 31 January 2000: 4). She noted that separate legal codes for religious communities violates the presumption of CEDAW that women should be treated equally. Moreover, at least some and probably all of the systems of personal law violate some of the nondiscrimination provisions of the convention.

In its extensive concluding comments, the committee praised India for its constitutional guarantee of fundamental human rights and the recognition of a fundamental right to gender equality and nondiscrimination, as well as for its affirmative action program, which has reserved 33 percent of seats in local government bodies for women (UN General Assembly 2000: 9). But it worried that there had not been steps taken to reform the personal laws of different ethnic and religious groups in order to conform to the convention and that the policy of nonintervention perpetuates sexual stereotypes, son preference and discrimination against women (UN General Assembly 2000: 10). The committee urged India to adopt a secular universalism in its laws governing the family, a significant cultural break from past practice. Further, the committee expressed concern about the high rate of gender-based violence against women, "which takes even more extreme forms because of customary practices, such as dowry, sati and the devadasi system. Discrimination against women who belong to particular castes or ethnic or religious groups is also manifest in extreme forms of physical and sexual violence and harassment" (UN General Assembly 2000: 11). The committee recognized that there is legislation against these practices but encouraged the government to implement this legislation. While applauding the equal gender rights provided in national-level government documents and noting the existence of laws against dowry, discrimination against Dalits, and sex-selective abortions, the committee worried about the lack of implementation of laws and the inadequate allocation of resources for women's development in the social sector, which they saw as serious impediments to the realization of women's human rights in India (UN General Assembly 2000: 10).[7]

In my conversations with experts after this hearing, most agreed that the government should reform these separate personal laws. One expert said women should not have to live under patriarchal laws. Another said that it was the government's responsibility to reform personal laws rather than leaving it to the leaders of minority communities, who are often religious leaders opposed to change. A third member of the committee thought a uniform secular code was neither necessary nor possible in India, but she was overruled by others who strongly advocated a secular state with a uniform legal code. The CEDAW Committee, following the mandate of the convention, interpreted the situation entirely in terms of gender. An intersectional approach that looks simultaneously at gender, ethnicity/race, and class would have provided a better analysis, but this is not part of CEDAW. Moreover, the brief, formal exchanges at CEDAW hearings do not lend themselves to discussions of complex intersectionality.

Ironically, the committee's concern about the discriminatory provisions in these personal laws could strengthen the positions of Hindu nationalists *and* Islamic religious leaders. When transnational activists criticized India for failure to reform personal laws or eliminate them altogether, they provided ammunition for Hindu nationalists trying to demonize Muslims and their personal laws. At the same time, they might encourage Islamic leaders to resist this pressure by defining women's subordinate status in Islam as foundational to an Islamic communal identity.

The CEDAW hearing did not navigate this complex conjuncture of feminism and communalism. Instead, the committee juxtaposed the secular modernity of uniform civil law to a religion-based and oppressive set of family laws and sought to support the former and undermine the latter. They saw the persistence of separate religious laws as oppressive to women. However, it was the colonial ossification of marriage laws and the very contemporary politicization of culture that confronted the CEDAW Committee, not a tenacious ancient culture. The system of personal laws is not simply rooted in the past but created by contemporary political struggles in which women's subordinate status has been ethnicized: redefined as fundamental to the maintenance of an ethnic identity and communal political group. Viewing personal laws as a cultural problem underemphasizes this political context.

Bulubulu and Transnational Modernity

The debate over a Fijian customary practice called *bulubulu* at the January 2002 CEDAW hearings demonstrated dramatically the challenges of communicating between the transnational human rights community and the specificities of local and national situations.[8] In bulubulu, a person apologizes for an offense and offers a whale's tooth (*tabua*) and a gift and asks for forgiveness. The offended person is under some pressure to accept the apology and make peace. The Fiji country report complained about the use of bulubulu for rape cases in court, but committee members objected to using the custom at all. The Fiji government representative told me later that bulubulu was central to Fijian village life and that she was frustrated and annoyed that she did not have enough time to explain the situation in Fiji to the committee. This example shows the difficulty transnational experts face in locating cultural practices in context. It also reveals the power of the interpretive lens that envisions many nonstate customs as harmful traditional practices.

The January 2002 hearing was Fiji's first report to the CEDAW Committee. The assistant minister for women presented the report and I observed the proceedings. Two other representatives from the government attended, along with three from NGOs. The government's official report criticized the courts' failure to intervene firmly in sexual assault and violence cases. It objected to the use of bulubulu to escape legal penalties.

> The prevalent attitudes about gender-based violence are reflected in the relatively lenient penalties imposed on offenders. For example, rape is a form of violence that is particularly directed against women. Despite the serious nature of this crime, Fiji's courts tend to treat rape and indecent assault as reconcilable in the same way as common assault and it is currently the only form of serious crime that can be reconciled. Furthermore, the Fijian custom of bulubulu (apology and recompense/reconciliation) is accepted by the courts as a reason not to impose a charge or custodial sentence on a convicted rapist. In some cases, the victim's father accepts the apology and the victim has little say in the outcome. This situation is changing, largely as a result of active lobbying by women's organizations. This is evident from a recent judgment by a magistrate for the award of the maximum sentence. The magistrate commented: "Women are your equal and therefore must not be discriminated on the basis of gender. Men should be aware of the provisions of the CEDAW, which our country [has] ratified. Under the Convention the State shall ensure that all forms of discrimination against women must be eliminated at all costs. The courts shall be the watch-dog with the obligation. The old school of thought, that women were inferior to men, or part of your personal property, that can be discarded or treated unfairly at will, is now obsolete and no longer accepted by our society. I hope that this sentence imposed on you, shall be a deterrent to all those who are still practicing this outmoded evil and cruel behaviour (from *Fiji Daily Post,* Jan 20, 2000)." Offenses against property

are likely to attract lengthier custodial sentences than rape, even though rape is a felony for which the maximum sentence is life imprisonment. (CEDAW/C/Fiji/1, 14 March 2000: 11)

Thus, the country report criticizes the legal system's ineffectiveness in dealing with rape and blames bulubulu for contributing to the problem. In the questions they posed to the Fiji government, however, the CEDAW Committee challenged the custom itself. I took detailed notes on the questions, which are also available as press releases. One expert said that it sounded like bulubulu was a very old and very patriarchal custom and asked, "Have you provided to eliminate that custom? What has your ministry done to abolish this practice?" Another said it provided an escape route for people who commit crimes against women to avoid punishment. At least two experts asked, "When will this practice be made illegal?" One said, "While acknowledging the importance of cultural practices, and even the importance of reconciliation, we think it is important that the requirements of the convention be attended to, especially in the case of sexual violence. Thus it is important to the committee that you increase awareness of practices such as bulubulu, and of rape, because sometimes the impact of rape comes years after negotiation takes place" (quotations based on my notes). According to the UN press release (January 16, 2002), "A question was asked about the custom of 'bulu-bulu,' which imposed only a custodial sentence on the convicted rapists. The victim's father had a right to accept an apology from him, and the victim herself had no say in that situation. What was being done to abolish such practices?" These questions reveal the slippage between condemning the use of bulubulu for rape in court proceedings and condemning the practice altogether.

The Fiji government objected to this critique of bulubulu. In its official reply to the CEDAW Committee delivered in New York in January 2002, Assistant Minister Losena Salabula, of Fiji's Ministry for Women, Social Welfare, and Poverty Alleviation, said:

> "Bulu-bulu" is a vital custom of the indigenous Fijian community for reconciliation and cementing kinship ties. The Government was addressing its recurrent abuse in relation to modern court processes and the legal system in handling sexual offences such as rape. The acceptance of "bulu-bulu" often led women victims not to report crimes. Offenders were discharged and sentences mitigated. Improved awareness of the practice had allowed the law to take its course on sexual offences. In some cases, families had declined the offer of "bulu-bulu." In other cases, families had

accepted "bulu-bulu" but had agreed that the law should take its course. The reform of the sentencing law, which was at an advanced phase, was aimed at codifying sentencing options and guidelines. (UN Press Release 22/01/2002)

In response to this report, the committee's chairperson, Charlotte Abaka, of Ghana, said that while acknowledging the importance of national traditions, especially the practice of reconciliation, it was important to do away with traditions discriminating against women, especially in the case of domestic violence. The country should pay more attention to such negative aspects of the problem as the practice of bulubulu, she said. Measures were needed to increase public awareness of the issues involved. It was also disturbing that some cases of violence were referred to as "family discipline" in Fiji (UN Press Release January 22, 2002).

The committee's Concluding Comments criticized bulubulu for providing legitimacy to rape. After stating the committee's concern about the high incidence of ethnic and gender-based violence in civil unrest and about domestic violence and sexual abuse of girls and women, the Concluding Comments say, "The Committee is also concerned that the social customs on the husband's right of chastisement, and '*bulu bulu*', give social legitimacy to violence" (par. 58). It requests the state party to strengthen its initiatives against gender-based violence and to adopt proposed laws on domestic violence and sexual offenses. "In particular, it calls on the State party to reinforce its 'no drop' policy by prohibiting the reconciliation of cases of rape and sexual assault on the basis of the '*bulu bulu*' custom (par. 59)" (A/57/38 [Part I]: 12).

When I interviewed the assistant minister for women a few weeks later in Suva, the capital of Fiji, she said that the CEDAW Committee didn't understand bulubulu and how important it is, and she noted that there had already been legal decisions that defined it as inappropriate for rape. I talked to her again in 2003. Again she said that the committee did not give her time to explain. The CEDAW hearing was so formal there was no time to talk. The custom of bulubulu, she said, is to encourage people not to hold grudges. Eliminating bulubulu was impossible since it was the basis of village life. The custom was used for a wide range of conflicts and disputes as well as for arranging marriages. Without it, the village could not function. She said that the people who wrote the report did not know Fijian custom. "The Fijian people won't let this go, this custom. If they don't have it, society will fall apart." Changing bulubulu, she said "is very contradictory with our culture. When the family wants a girl, they will plant crops for her for three or four years and present things to her.

It is an investment. But now, with women's rights, you can marry anyone you want, and forget about this custom." Elopement is increasingly used instead of the protracted gifts of food and goods by the boy's family to finalize a marriage. It is typically followed by a bulubulu ceremony in which the groom's family apologizes and gives gifts to the bride's family. When I talked to the assistant minister in 2003, she bemoaned the impact of women's rights, which have persuaded women that they can do whatever they want, including dressing and acting without sexual modesty. These ideas have contributed to the breakdown of the family. There is little bulubulu now in the villages, even after elopement. Those who do bulubulu to get out of court are the "smart" people. She said that Fiji feminists told her she was old-fashioned and not promoting women's rights when she expressed these views.

In response to the critique of bulubulu as well as criticism of racial policies and affirmative action for Fijians from this and other UN treaty bodies, she said that if the international community did not like what Fiji did, Fiji would go its own way.[9] Her comments reflect contemporary politics: a nationalist ethnic Fijian movement is asserting the centrality of Fijian village life to the nation. As Fijian village custom has become a politicized aspect of Fijian nationalism, attacks on Fijian village custom are seen as assaults on the Fijian nation. The women's minister did not defend the use of bulubulu for rape, but she did insist on the importance of bulubulu for village conflict resolution. At the end of our meeting, the minister gave an impassioned plea for Fijian tradition. She said that the individualist human rights system is disrupting this tradition and that the Fijian culture and its conditions were not understood. The "expert" label of the CEDAW Committee members sounded intimidating, but they did not appreciate the particularities and specific features of Fiji.[10] When I spoke with the NGO representatives from Fiji, they also thought that the committee had misunderstood bulubulu.

How did this discussion go wrong? Both the Fiji government representatives and the CEDAW experts shared a concern about overly lenient treatment for rape. Yet, they seem to have spoken past each other, annoying the Fiji government representative even though she was also concerned about using bulubulu for rape cases in court. It certainly seemed to me that using village reconciliation for rape could fail to protect a victim, but it was also clear that the courts were not working effectively either. Perhaps it depended on how bulubulu actually functioned in different contexts.

In order to answer this question, I scoured the anthropological literature for descriptions of bulubulu and returned to Fiji to interview the activists in the antirape movement who had complained about the practice as well as

118

magistrates, police, and religious leaders who worked on rape and questions of Fijian custom. In the spring of 2003, a research assistant, Eleanor Kleiber, spent three months investigating the question of bulubulu and rape. I joined her for an additional nine days of interviewing. Altogether we interviewed 42 people during this period and two additional weeks of research in Fiji. The story we uncovered differed in important respects from the view that the experts — and I — had gleaned from the CEDAW hearing.

Two critically important points emerged. First, the way bulubulu functions depends a great deal on the social context in which it takes place. As Fijians shift from a predominantly rural village life to a more educated, urban style of life, the custom itself is being redefined. In some cases, it has become a shallow and meaningless exercise, while in others it is being reshaped to emphasize offender accountability and victim support. Second, the real grievance of the women's groups was not the use of bulubulu for rape cases but the use of bulubulu to persuade prosecutors to drop charges and magistrates to mitigate sentences. They were worried about the way a modern and relatively superficial use of the custom was used to undermine the legal process. Indeed, as punishments for rape increased in severity in the late 1980s, the use of bulubulu shot up and feminists became concerned about the way it was being used to escape legal penalties.

Why did the CEDAW Committee miss these important points? The nature of transnational legal processes and the conceptions of culture shared by CEDAW experts through which they interpreted the meaning of bulubulu both contributed. It is, of course, impossible to understand the complexities of the operation of a particular custom when a committee is dealing with eight different countries in two weeks. One cannot expect committee members to spend a month reading the anthropological literature and two weeks interviewing Fijians in order to determine the meaning of a custom. As I discovered, bulubulu is a complicated and changing practice.

BULUBULU IN THE VILLAGE AND THE CITY

A foray into the ethnographic literature on the process reveals something of the complexity of this custom and its changing meaning over time. Bulubulu is an instance of *soro,* sometimes considered another name for the same process or a more informal version of it (Arno 1976: 49, 53, personal communication 2002; Geraghty personal communication 2002). Ethnographic studies from the 1970s and 1980s describe soro as a formal ceremony of apology in which the offender offers gifts such as a whale's tooth and kerosene along with an apology and seeks reconciliation with the victim (Hickson 1975; Arno 1976, 1980, 1993; Aucoin 1990). It provides reconciliation between equals or when an inferior has offended a superior (Hickson 1975; Arno 1976, 1980, 1993; Aucoin 1990; Toren 1994; Brison 2001). In the 1970s, it was used by villagers throughout Fiji as a form of surrender or submission and a request for forgiveness (Arno 1976: 49). Arno and Hickson describe its use by both men and women for a variety of forms of personal insult and conflict as well as rape and marriage transgressions. Soro was suggested (but not carried out) when a cow broke into a neighbor's garden and ate the produce and was used when a man became drunk and insulted his father (Arno 1993: 19, 95). Hickson reports the use of soro among women when a child becomes sick and the angry person needs to make peace in order to restore good relations and therefore heal the child (1975). Arno asked many heads of households in the remote island village where he worked what they remembered as its common uses. The most common was making peace between families after an elopement (1976: 55). Before the period of British colonialism, abducting women caused intervillage raiding and warfare, so ritual apology may have been a way to avert this kind of warfare. Hickson also reports the use of soro in the past when there was considerable intervillage fighting and a village might make an unconditional surrender and accept a subordinate role in order to prevent attack (1975: 105–6). If a man's sister is sexually assaulted, he has an obligation to beat up the offender (Geraghty, personal communication, 2002). Bulubulu replaces vengeance.

More recent studies report that it is still frequently used to negotiate a peaceful relationship between kin groups after a marriage by elopement (Brison 2001; Geraghty 2002). The boy's family approaches the girl's family after the elopement and offers gifts and an apology, seeking bulubulu, which means literally to bury the bad feeling between the two groups. Although its primary use is to manage conflicts among kin groups in a Fijian village, ritual apologies can also take place at the level of the nation. Arno reports, for example, that the nonchiefly Fijian who carried out the 1987 political coup in Fiji used soro to apologize to the chiefs for overriding them in his actions (1993: 131).

Bulubulu is a practice of renegotiating relationships of inequality. Fijian villages are organized into patrilineal households that are aggregated into larger patrilineal subclans, called *mataqali* (Hickson 1975; Kaplan 2004). Households are the groups engaged in everyday economic cooperation and intimate family life while the mataqali are the corporate landholding units (Arno 1980: 344, 1993: 9). Individuals trace their membership in lineages and clans by descent through males, but they also have important kin ties with the mother's patrilineage. Marriage is exogamous and residence after marriage is virilocal: the bride typically goes to live with her husband's kin group. Hierarchy is fundamental to the system. Within the village, households within a mataqali are ranked by birth order. Rank also depends on whether a mataqali, or household group, is chiefly or of the land (Arno 1993: 53, 54–56). However, villages also have important relations of equality. Relations within households are hierarchical as are relations between chiefly lines and subordinate lines, while relations across households are relatively egalitarian. These more equal relationships are marked by balanced reciprocal exchange. Cross-cousins and affines tend to have more equal relationships (Toren 1994). Marriage takes place between cross-cousins, who are relative equals, and wedding rituals express the relationship of equality between the groups involved (Arno 1993: 70).

This juxtaposition of hierarchical and egalitarian relationships means that villages are constantly negotiating the relative status of individuals and kin groups (Toren 1994). Ceremonies of apology and reconciliation take place between these kin groups and are an important way of renegotiating these relationships (Arno 1976, 1980, 1993; Brison 2001). The person seeking an apology brings a gift and subordinates himself to the person he or she wishes to make peace with. The penitent remains silent and looks down, acting and dressing in a conservative and nonassertive way while a spokesman presents the *yaqona* (kava, a beverage) or whale's tooth he or she has brought. There is no substantive discussion of the problem during the soro, but it restores normal relationships after a breach (Arno 1993: 98, 132). The relative merits of both sides are typically thrashed out in village gossip. Within the pervasive inequalities that characterize Fijian village life, soro is a way for subordinates to escape punishments from their superiors when they have offended them (Hickson 1975: 106–7). Within the situation of pervasive inequality that Hickson observed in the early 1970s, the soro exaggerates the inequality, since the subordinate surrenders to the superior, but at the same time by capitulating to the superior in anticipation of the exercise of his power, the subordinate may avoid legal sanctions, such as court, supernatural sanctions, such as illness, or other social sanctions, such as severing a relationship (1975: 106–7).

This use of soro to escape punishment by subordinates is not recent. A missionary writing in 1859 describes the practice as a failure of justice, since it is used by the guilty as well as the innocent to escape punishment (Hickson 1975: 107). However, Hickson argues that since the ceremony occurs in situations of status inequality in which the weaker surrenders and thus forces the superior to accept the apology out of pride, it minimizes the punishment for an inferior. Within a system of pervasive inequalities of rank and power, it serves to mitigate the control of higher-ranked individuals over lower-ranked ones (1975: 188; Kaplan 2004).

When bulubulu is embedded in the village kinship system, it holds a perpe- trator responsible for his actions. The offender experiences sustained gossip and is shamed, along with his close patrilineal relatives. Chiefs and senior men lecture and correct juniors who are a source of shame and embarrassment to the family (Hickson 1975: 54–55). Offenders may receive a tongue-lashing or beating not only for hurting a girl from another clan but also for wronging the spirits. Offenses may lead to illnesses and other supernatural sanctions. If the offender leaves his village, he may be accepted back if he stays away for five or six years. While a person can leave his village and settle in another one if rela- tionships sour, he will always be viewed as an outsider and is ultimately better off to stay in his own village (Hickson 1975: 32).

Thus, the process of apology and reconciliation sanctions the offender, par- ticularly if senior kin view the offense as important and the offender wishes to stay on good terms in the village. Within interdependent, face-to-face commu- nities, bulubulu works along with other forms of social pressure to exert some control over offenders. In the past, when villages were more isolated and the control exercised by seniors over juniors was greater, bulubulu was a powerful process that could reintegrate a raped woman into the community. She might be married to the offender. Under village conditions, a bulubulu carried out by powerful, respected leaders with the support of an outraged village could pro- vide better punishment and deterrence than the police. One Fijian leader I in- terviewed said that an offender's family might give the victim arable land that would belong permanently to her mataqali. This is a major loss for the family that surrenders the land and benefit to the victim.

However, the nature of village life has changed dramatically during 150 years of contact with Europeans and colonialism and, since 1970, independence. The population is now largely literate and increasingly urban. About half the resi- dents of Fiji are people of Indian ancestry brought to work the sugarfields by the British colonial government and Australian sugar plantations. By 2000 about 40 percent of the ethnic Fijian population lived in urban or periurban settings (Lal 2002: 155). As village life has changed, so has the practice of bu- lubulu and the social pressure the village can exert on its members. My inter- views with judges, lawyers, and religious and political leaders in Fiji in 2003 in- dicated that bulubulu is increasingly rare even in villages. I talked to a variety of people in the urban areas who generally reported that ceremonies were not taken seriously and offenders were barely reprimanded. Some said that if a girl is raped in town, even by a boy from the same village, it is not seen as a problem by the village, only by the immediate family.

Bulubulu is being used in new contexts reshaped by urbanism and Christianity. A leading Methodist minister told me that bulubulu is a way of saying sorry to a victim or the victim's family, and is therefore similar to Christian forgiveness. The gifts bridge the gap severed by wrongdoing while recognizing our sinful nature and the possibility of repentance. Sometimes churches take a role in the process. One woman who had been battered twice by her partner refused to forgive the perpetrator but after he went to his church to apologize, the church leader approached her with the ritual drink, yaqona, and again asked her to take him back. She refused and sent him to jail for a month. But when she returned to his village, the villagers shamed her for putting him in jail. It is obviously much harder to resist accepting the ceremonial gift if a person lives in the offender's village. In urban areas, relatives are often distant and thus have less influence.

The Methodist minister I interviewed said that the church's position now is that the victim has to be asked if she accepts the apology. She said that victims need counseling and support, which was not provided in the traditional practice. She described a domestic violence case she herself handled through bulubulu, in which she revised the process to give the victim a greater voice. The victim was a relative who had been beaten by her husband for a long time. This woman took refuge in the minister's house in town. As an educated, financially independent urban woman, the minister was a powerful person and able to protect her. When the husband arrived with tabua, yagona, and the chief of his mataqali to offer bulubulu, she and her son told him his behavior was intolerable and that he had to talk to his wife before she would accept the bulubulu. The wife refused to accept. The man made several further attempts to persuade his wife to return, and after a year, she agreed to return to him.

In this case, a woman orchestrated the bulubulu rather than a man, but her son was present and spoke for her. She did not accept the apology on behalf of the victim but required the offender to speak with the victim directly and allowed the victim to live with her until she was ready to accept the offering and return to her husband. In village practice, the girl was not asked her opinion about accepting the apology and the apology was delivered to the kin group, not to the victim. If she refused, she was pressured to go along. Thus, as Fijian society changes, the custom has changed from a practice that focuses on preventing vengeance between clans to one that supports a victim and holds the offender accountable. Both a leader of the antirape movement and a Fiji magistrate told me that bulubulu can be good or bad depending on the gender sensitivity of the process and who is doing it.

There are also variations in the way the offender is treated after a bulubulu. In the past, he received a stern lecture from senior males and could be beaten by a stingray skin, which leaves permanent marks. In more recent times, severe sanctions from the offender's kin may still occur, but particularly in urban areas or where kin are dispersed, it is likely that nothing is said to him except "next time, do not get caught." Several people told me that if a bulubulu is preformed today, there is little effort to punish the offender afterwards. The process is often done in a pro forma way without any apology or repentance. Even the gifts can be minimal. Offenders who have been pardoned are likely to offend again. While village elders may be severe to young kinsmen who offend, when young people move to the city, elders often remain in remote villages. Thus, in recent times, the victim has greater voice but the offender feels less pressure. Indeed, the process is intended to "forget" (bury) the offense, and some claim it does just that for the offender.

Thus, the same practice — ritual presentation of tabua and speaking the words of apology — differs significantly depending on the social status of the parties, their interpretation of it, and the engagement of a wider community. The custom, which was powerful as a mode of making peace in a small remote village where senior males exerted considerable power over young people, takes on a very different meaning in urban settlements in which young people earn their own living and no longer depend on senior males for land, fishing rights, and social power. Despite these enormous changes, it is, confusingly, called by the same name.

BULUBULU AND THE LAW

There are fundamental differences between the logic of bulubulu and the law. The law punishes the offender to deter future offenses. Bulubulu makes peace to avert vengeance. In the absence of reconciliation, the family of the victim is entitled to attack, beat up, or possibly kill the offender. The goal of the process is forgetting the offense between the families and restoring community peace. The apology is offered to the senior males of the family, not to the victim. It is not directed toward providing support to the victim or punishment to the offender, since these responsibilities rest on individual kin groups.

Injuries are conceived and remedies imagined quite differently. The law holds the offender accountable and views the raped person herself as the victim. It punishes the offender but fails to compensate the victim for her injuries. Bulubulu envisions the injury as an offense to the husband's or father's kin group. The elders apologize for what their son has done, and those receiving the apology feel that the injury has been done to their whole mataqali. Each kin group is responsible for controlling the behavior of its members and is shamed by the offenses of close kinsmen (Arno 1993: 98). Elders of a kin group may intervene to criticize, lecture, and scold an offender and may themselves initiate a soro. If the conflict is between younger men of different mataqali, the elders of both may intervene directly and conduct a soro, taking the matter out of the individuals' hands and expressing "the accepted idea that a person's actions are attributable to his group, and that therefore there are no strictly interpersonal conflicts" (Arno 1993: 98). Following this logic, rape is an offense against the victim's husband or family rather than the woman herself. Indeed, in one rape case Arno describes from the early 1970s, the husband of the victim lodged a complaint with the police (1980). Restoring good relations between groups will not necessarily diminish the suffering of individual victims. Ratuva notes that shifting the responsibility from the offender to the kin group can undermine the individual rights of the victim for personal redress or compensation (2002).

Court and bulubulu are not alternative processes; they are interconnected and have been so for at least three decades. In the 1950s violence or the threat of violence was used to pressure defendants to apologize in cases of rape and domestic violence (Arno 1976: 62–63). With the advent of the threat of criminal prosecution, the police were used to force the offender to apologize. Filing a complaint with the police might encourage an apology. At the same time, ritual apology was used to avoid court penalties. If the offender can press the victim's husband into accepting his apology, he escapes the criminal penalties. Arno describes two cases from the 1970s where the victim filed a charge with the police, inducing the perpetrator to soro. One involved a rape (1980), the other a public attack on a senior man (1976: 59). If the offender apologized, the courts were willing to drop the cases. Accounts from the 1970s describe the courts dropping charges if a man has dealt with his offense through bulubulu. Magistrates sometimes sent cases back to the village to settle (Arno 1976). Hickson says that in 8 of 34 (24%) criminal cases involving Fijians heard in one magistrate's court between 1967 and 1971, charges were dropped after soro (1975: 228, n. 28). Indeed, the law stipulated that they were to seek amicable settlements (Wynn Furth, cited in Arno 1976: 52).

Arno gives a detailed account of a rape case from 1971–72 in which the aggrieved husband filed a charge with the police because the offender failed to apologize. A police officer came to the island and told the husband that the charge was very serious and that the offender faced prison. While admitting that he had done it, the offender said it was "only a game." Seven months later, a police official told the offender that he faced a prison sentence because the charge against him was very serious, but if the husband would accept a whale's tooth and send a telegram to the police headquarters saying that the matter had been settled by traditional means, the case would be dropped (Arno 1980: 348–54). The offender raced home to perform the soro as soon as possible. The husband of the victim forgave him and wired the police to drop the charge. Thus, there is a long history of using bulubulu to avoid court penalties. However, in the context of village life, bulubulu may have been more effective for the victim than was the court.

Since 1987, when some ethnic Fijian leaders engineered a coup to remove elected Indo-Fijians from power, there has been a resurgence of interest in Fijian custom along with Fijian cultural nationalism. A strong political and cultural movement celebrates Fijian custom and village life, including the use of bulubulu. One high-ranking Fijian chief condemned its use for rape, but for many, the new emphasis on Fijian culture makes it more difficult to criticize its use as an alternative to courts. After 1987, the government declared it legal to use bulubulu for rape cases. In 1988, a group of feminist activists met with the chief justice of Fiji to voice concerns about the spate of rapes and the lenient sentencing of rapists. In response, he issued new, more severe, sentencing guidelines for rapists (Fiji Women's Rights Movement 2000: 13).[11] The chief justice's circular memorandum no. 1 of 1988 recommended an immediate custodial sentence for rape (Beattie 1994: 74–75). This inspired an increasing use of bulubulu to escape custodial sentences. Eighteen months later the judge backed away from the more severe penalties.

Sparked by this retreat from more stringent penalties and the increasing use of bulubulu to get off, feminist organizations in Fiji, including the Fiji Women's Rights Movement, the Fiji Women's Crisis Centre, and the YWCA joined together in an antirape campaign (Bromby 1991: 19). From 1988 until 1994, the Fiji Women's Rights Movement lead the campaign, which included a critique of the court's use of traditional reconciliation practices for rapists. When I interviewed Peni Moore, the coordinator of the campaign, she said one impetus for the campaign was the 1990 decision by the chief justice to overturn the more stringent sentencing guidelines for rape. These guidelines had produced custodial sentences for rape of up to five years, but custodial sentences were no longer being given. Moreover, Moore was concerned about judges' acceptance of "traditional reconciliation," or bulubulu, as mitigation for rape cases. The anti-rape campaign focused on getting the judge to change his guidelines.[12] In

2003 Moore said that the objection was not to using bulubulu in a parallel track to the courts but using the process to undermine legal punishment.

In an early 1990s Radio Australia broadcast, Moore said that using bulubulu to settle rape offenses is a new practice, not an old one.[13]

> In fact, a very alarming new development is coming about because of a ceremonial practice called a bulubulu and this is when they present a tabua and all should be forgiven, and it is called a traditional reconciliation. In fact, from research we know that the bulubulu has never been used for situations of rape. Traditionally it was used when woman and man eloped. The man would go back to the woman's family and present the tabua as a bulubulu, or if two men fought and they wanted to reconcile, the bulubulu would be done. But a new development has come about where a bulubulu ceremony is performed and the rapist will come to the family and present it to the father. The girl isn't even discussed in this. If the family accepts the bulubulu, the girl must accept that. And then they try to get it out of court. If it has already been reported, then they go to court. The courts have started to recognize this. We've protested against this, and they are now accepting that it isn't correct and it shouldn't be accepted in court because rape isn't reconcilable. The problem is that because of this whole push about tradition, it's very easy to say, it's traditional and therefore you must do it. And what we're trying to say is, it's not traditional. It's a new invention, and in fact the women that we speak with, the Fijian women, say they believe it is the police who encouraged this in order to drop cases so they don't need to go through to court.

Thus, the antirape movement sought to return to an earlier, more stringent legal policy. It opposed bulubulu for rape because it was being used increasingly to provide offenders an escape from the new, harsher punishments such as jail time. There are accounts of forms of village and intervillage ritual apology and forgiveness dating back at least until the middle of the nineteenth century, but the use of this approach for rape seems to be relatively new. One Fijian commentator notes that bulubulu was never used in precolonial times to deal with the crime of rape, which was punished by death. But by the early 1990s, its use was on the rise in the courts and with the police (Emberson-Bain 1994: 32). The increasing popularity of bulubulu for rape reflected the mobilization of an old practice to deflect the new, more severe, court sentences for rape. Bulubulu offered rapists a new way to persuade police to drop charges and magistrates to reduce sentences. Thus, the antirape campaign was not against using an old tradition but against the new use of an old practice to escape the new, sterner penalties for rape.

One of the questions raised about the use of bulubulu in courts is whether courts should consider the nature of the gifts and their severity. One of the most ardent defenders of Fijian custom argued that the gifts for serious offenses could be quite significant, such as a piece of land that devolves permanently to the kin group of the victim. In order for courts to judge the significance of a bulubulu, she argued, they have to ask what the gifts were. However, courts apparently do not ask, although one magistrate I spoke to said that she did. Others apparently only note that the bulubulu took place, perhaps in an affidavit provided by the defendant. It is primarily "Suva lawyers," those in the capital city, who try energetically to use bulubulu as a strategy to get their clients out of court. Some are civil lawyers rather than criminal ones. The girl is pressured to accept bulubulu to protect her family's name and to avoid public attention.

Bulubulu enters the legal deliberations at two distinct points. The first is at the point of arresting and charging. Fiji has a system of police prosecutors for much of its criminal work, so that the police face the decision of whether or not to press charges. In the past, bulubulu was often raised as a reason to drop charges. In recent years, the police have enacted a no-drop policy for rape and domestic violence as a way of preventing this problem. Although prosecutors told me that they never drop these cases now, I have not carried out the empirical research to determine if this is in fact the case. One prominent lawyer told me that cases of rape and domestic violence are still being dropped because of reconciliation processes, and a prosecutor said that, despite their efforts, girls are sometimes forced to accept bulubulu and drop the charges. The second way bulubulu enters the legal process is at the point of sentencing. Some argue that the completion of bulubulu should mitigate the sentence of a rapist, particularly the custodial sentence. Rape is currently handled in magistrate's courts, but some advocate shifting it to the high courts, which might be more resistant to this argument.

BULUBULU AND CULTURAL NATIONALISM

Even as there is pressure to eliminate consideration of bulubulu in courts, there is an ongoing project to reestablish Fijian courts to enforce Fijian customary law. The debate about using bulubulu for rape takes place within a larger context of the struggle between the ethnic Fijian and the Indo-Fijian communities. These two groups were treated very differently by the British colonial authority. After Britain took Fiji in 1874, sugar planters imported large numbers of people from India to work as laborers in the fields. The populations reached parity in the middle of the twentieth century. Yet the British viewed the Indians as workers and the Fijians as villagers who needed to be protected and safeguarded in an unchanging way of life (see N. Thomas 1994). While the Indians, denied ownership of land, pursued education and business as the road to survival, Fijians remained in rural village enclaves, protected and isolated. By independence, some Indo-Fijians had joined the professional and business classes although most still lived as poor tenant farmers working land leased from Fijian clans on a limited-time contract. The British also established a system of communal voting in which each ethnic group voted for candidates of its own identity and seats in the legislature were allocated by group. Thus, British colonial policies created a situation of communal division and conflict (see Kelly 1991, 1997; Lal 1992, 2002; Kaplan 2004; Merry and Brenneis 2004).

In contemporary Fiji, bulubulu, like other village practices, is taking on new meaning within the politics of indigeneity. In the years following independence, Indo-Fijians have twice acquired power through electoral politics only to be displaced by an ethnic Fijian coup, once in 1987, when there were two coups close together, and once in 2000. The new Fijian nationalism excludes Indo-Fijians from political power. The doctrine of a paramountcy of Fijian interests, developed originally by Sir Arthur Gordon at the time of British annexation in 1874 and expanded in the early twentieth century, promises special privileges and preferential treatment for Fijians because of their indigenous status and primordial claims to land (Ratuva 2002). The concept of traditional Fijian culture and the values of the Fijian village are being mobilized to justify the continuing Fijian control of politics and more than 80 percent of the land. There is a need to justify land ownership in terms of the sacred link between the village and the land (Brison 2001; Kaplan 2004). The harmonious, sharing life of the village is contrasted with Indo-Fijian settlements that are portrayed as more individualistic and preoccupied with individual gain. Moreover, tourism has increased attention to this vision of the Fijian village, thus reinforcing the need to maintain the myth. As the Fiji Women's Rights Movement points out, practices that are described as traditional have now acquired new weight as essential to national identity. This contemporary political development makes it much harder to challenge the way custom is being used in Fijian communities.[14]

There is now a substantial out-migration of professional and educated Indo-Fijians, although poorer and less educated ones remain locked in rural poverty. Many Indo-Fijians have turned to a rights framework. On the other hand, Fijians are increasingly seen as bearers of the national culture. This pattern is reinforced by tourism, one of the major economic engines of the country, which features Fijian village life, arts and crafts, and traditions, such as fire-walking, but makes no mention of Indian cultural practices or festivals. Thus, Fijians defend their political control in terms of Fijian culture, epitomized in village life, while Indo-Fijians make claims to human rights. The opposition between culture and rights is being mapped onto ethnic differences. In this increasingly oppositional context, those who assert the importance of human rights do not think culture should trump rights, while those who defend culture see human rights, and particularly women's rights, as threats to culture. The juxtaposition of bulubulu and the law for rape cases replays this opposition. In this debate, culture is defined as national essence, even if it is shared by only half of the population.

BULUBULU AT THE UN

None of these issues came up at the CEDAW discussion. The CEDAW Committee adopted a straightforward view of bulubulu that did not include these complex considerations of urban-rural context and ethnic politics. There was no discussion of the fact that bulubulu could be helpful to a victim under certain circumstances nor that it is changing. Obviously, committee members did not have time to read the ethnographic literature, interview feminist, judiciary, and legal leaders in Fiji or develop a nuanced analysis of the practice. Bulubulu was only a small part of the issues in Fiji that the committee considered. The NGO shadow report did not discuss it nor did the NGO representatives raise it in their report to the committee. In the absence of detailed knowledge, the experts relied on the well-established category of harmful traditional practices and the assumption that village customs hinder women's equality. The idea of culture as tradition framed these customs as remnants of the past that must be changed to accommodate modernity, exemplified by human rights and gender equality, rather than as old customs newly deployed in urban contexts. From the vantage point of transnational modernity, such customs are part of traditional culture.

Why did the experts see bulubulu this way? And what does this tell us about the tensions between global law and local situations? The UN discussion did not deal with the complexity of the custom but focused on preventing its use for rape or eliminating it altogether. Neither the report, the NGO representatives, nor the government representative made clear how fundamental and widespread the practice was, or that it was used for many other offenses besides rape. They did not examine the practice of bulubulu in context or the ways it is

[handwritten margin note: lack of communication - misinterpre- "te bulubulu"]

changing. Their lack of detailed, specific knowledge is an inevitable feature of such transnational forums. Yet, there are at least two other contributing factors. The first is an interpretive one, the second a more structural one linked to the nature of law itself.

First, I think the committee moved quickly from condemning the use of the custom for rape to a condemnation of the custom altogether because many of the CEDAW Committee members assumed that the problem they confronted was one of a custom embedded in traditional culture. They were inclined to condemn the entire practice, not just the way it extracted rape cases from court in urban areas. They talked about bulubulu as a reprehensible custom for handling rape and as a harmful traditional practice that needs to be changed to improve the status of women. The custom was defined as a violation in and of itself rather than something used to derail legal penalties. It was presumed to be unchanging rather than adapting to a more gender equal, urban society.

In CEDAW hearings, as in other segments of the international human rights field, culture is used to describe the way of life of "others," usually the rural and urban poor. Culture is not found in the UN or among transnational elites, but only among those still living in what is often referred to as traditional society. This particular usage of the term assumes that people with culture live in circumscribed and unchanging ways governed by strict traditions and share the same set of values and practices. Such a perspective on culture is reinforced by human rights documents about women that repeatedly insist that no cultural, religious, or traditional practice should undermine women's rights. As experts listen to one country report after another, they often hear about customs that violate the terms of the convention and undermine women's rights. They share the widespread opinion that customs are a remnant of the past that must be changed to accommodate modernity and gender equality. Thus, they are predisposed to see customs such as bulubulu as problems.

Second, the experts are applying the law. They are acting as a legal body to enforce compliance with the terms of a treaty ratified by the country. The human rights system is a legal system committed to the universal application of a code of conduct to myriad particular situations. Its documents spell out this shared code, one legitimated by the process of consensual document production and ratification. The legal rationality at the heart of the process does not accept the existence of alternative normative codes as a reason to withdraw its scrutiny. Within the logic of legal rationality, there is no space to adjust the law to particular situations and contexts or to withhold its attention in favor of an alternative vision of justice. Of course, this universalizing approach is structured by the convention itself and the committee's mandate to apply it to all countries equally. Countries that ratify it assume the burden of conforming to its requirements, regardless of their specific cultural attributes.

The CEDAW Committee is not deliberately promoting a universalistic transnational modernity but is part of a process in which the convention itself is the moving force. Indeed, the whole human rights process is based on the assumption that local features of culture, history, and context should not override universal principles. Human rights documents create a universal vision of a just society in which cultural difference is respected but only within limits: it does not justify assaults on the bodily integrity of vulnerable populations. Local features of culture and history should not override universal principles concerning how societies should be organized and individuals protected. Nor does this system provide space to recognize other, non-rights-based understandings of social justice.

Furthermore, since governments often raise culture as an excuse for their failure to promote gender equality and the values of autonomy and choice that are at the heart of the human rights system, women's human rights activists see claims to respect the particularities of local cultures, traditions, or religious practices as resistance to women's equality. These claims challenge the universality of women's human rights. Consequently, transnational human rights activists have little sympathy for societies that allow separate personal laws for different religious communities or that practice customs that appear to violate the rights of women.

Conclusions

The contradiction between the desire to maintain cultural diversity and the effort to promote equality and rights universally is a fundamental tension within human rights practice. These two sets of goals are in conflict: applying a universalistic framework obscures local particularities, but yielding to local situations impedes applying universal categories. Rather than understanding how the practice of bulubulu meshes with a complex set of kinship interventions, police and court actions, and urbanization, the human rights actors criticized the practice itself. Ironically, this feeds into a resistant ethnic nationalism that attributes its problems to human rights. By misinterpreting the practice as the problem, the CEDAW Committee evoked a nationalist and resistant response even from feminists opposed to leniency for rapists. It fed into an ethnic nationalism that blames contemporary social problems on the expansion of human rights and celebrates a reified culture as national essence.

In both of these cases, human rights approaches have the potential to improve the position of women and to serve as a resource for marginalized ethnic groups. Under different political conditions, women's groups in India advocated a uniform civil code. Muslim and Hindu feminists recognize the need for reform of their personal law. Many Indo-Fijians see human rights as an important protection against ethnic Fijian claims to paramountcy. Ethnic Fijians are themselves claiming indigenous rights and developing affirmative action plans. Feminists of both ethnic groups in Fiji agree that in certain situations bulubulu allows rapists to escape punishment. Human rights are clearly an open resource, a source of political power available for mobilization by various groups in many different ways, but how they work depends on the context.

The tensions between the general and the particular arise frequently as the Committee deals with countries for which it inevitably lacks deep and detailed historical and particular knowledge. Government representatives, such as those from Fiji and Trinidad and Tobago, complained to me about the relatively limited amount of information the CEDAW Committee has about the particular history and situation of their countries. Despite the effort to solicit input from NGOs and the sketchy introduction each country provides in its report, it is impossible for experts to gain detailed knowledge of the social conditions of each country. In the absence of this information, the committee treats all countries more or less the same, as the convention requires. It does not judge local practices in context but applies the law as uniformly as possible. This means insisting on a uniform personal law in India despite the political uses of this demand by Hindu nationalists and seeking to eliminate bulubulu although even the Fiji feminists sought only to prevent using it as an excuse to get rape cases out of court. The committee has watched how claims to culture justify women's oppression and is deeply suspicious of cultural claims, even when they seem deeply rooted historically. Separate personal laws in India appear to be cultural traditions oppressive to women as does bulubulu. In both cases, the committee focused narrowly on gender subordination rather than viewing the intersections of gender with ethnic, religious, and class exclusions.

A more anthropological view of culture could highlight changes in the sociocultural life of village communities or urban neighborhoods. The cash economy, state bureaucracy, media, and warfare, for example, have penetrated deep into the most rural and remote places. Interventions that promote social equality for women now may be different from those of twenty years ago. Focusing on culture only as a barrier both ignores the extent to which change is taking place and deemphasizes the importance of economic and political factors in furthering those changes. It is part of "culturalizing" the social life of peoples remote from the urban middle and upper classes: seeing their behavior only in terms of culture rather than in terms of economics, politics, and social class. It subtracts the economic and political effects of globalization such as the spread of capitalism and the shrinkage of state services in favor of a focus on beliefs and values. It ignores the possibility that there are embedded in local communities alternative visions of social justice that are not founded on conceptions of rights but on ideas such as sharing, reconciliation, or mutual responsibility. Finally, it engenders national identity claims reminiscent of German romantic defenses of Kultur. A more elaborated theory of culture would underscore the ways local cultural practices and beliefs interact with global legal principles and the importance of seeing these in context.

Legal Transplants and Cultural Translation: Making Human Rights in the Vernacular

How do transnational human rights ideas become part of local social movements and local legal consciousness? Throughout the Asia-Pacific region, transnational activists, national elites, and middle-tier educated NGO leaders are energetically appropriating global human rights frameworks and translating them to fit into particular situations. This often means *transplanting institutions and programs* such as gender training programs, domestic violence laws, counseling centers for battered women, or human rights commissions. This is at heart a process of translation across boundaries of class, ethnicity, mobility, and education. Intermediaries who translate global ideas into local situations and retranslate local ideas into global frameworks play a critical role in the process. They foster the gradual emergence of a local rights consciousness among grassroots people and greater awareness of national and local issues among global activists. These actors include national political elites, human rights lawyers, feminist activists and movement leaders, social workers and other social service providers, and academics. Although grassroots groups are the ultimate target of these efforts, they are not typically the translators.

Movement activists, NGO leaders, and government officials create programs and institutions that are a blend of transnational, national, and local elements as they negotiate the spaces between transnational ideas and local concerns. These institutions incorporate indigenous social institutions such as kinship systems, transnational models such as shelters, and human rights ideas such as the right to safety from violence. The result is a bricolage of elements in constantly shifting relation to one another made up of elements that do not necessarily fit together smoothly.

This chapter examines the way programs and strategies are transplanted from one social context to another. Rather than providing a comprehensive view of national strategies for dealing with gender violence, it focuses on the transplanting process in five countries. Intriguingly, activists in each country are committed to developing models suited to their distinctive history and social conditions, yet the strategies they have adopted are all fairly similar. Although there is some reframing of reforms to fit local conditions, the array of programs and institutions being adopted in India, China, Fiji, Hong Kong, and the United States are roughly the same. Global processes, such as the worldwide feminist and human rights movements, account for the similarities.

Deterritorialized ethnography reveals these connections since it focuses on flows of information, funds, and personnel rather than the comparison of sites as discrete entities. Global and local are slippery terms in this process. Transplants are programs or models adapted from one local context to another, but the process of transplanting is a global one. For example, when shelters or hotlines are transplanted from one social and cultural context to another, the leaders are often feminist activists whose networks of knowledge are forged in international meetings such as global UN conferences or training programs. The programs are tailored to local contexts but arrive through paths of global circulation. Each was initially developed in some local place but is now being swept to a different local place on the currents of globalization. Transplantation is both global and local at the same time.

Transplanting institutions and programs involves appropriation and translation. Appropriation means taking the programs, interventions, and ideas developed by activists in one setting and replicating them in another setting. Appropriation is often transnational, as ideas and programs are discovered elsewhere and imported to a new set of circumstances at home. Appropriation requires knowledge of approaches in other countries and, in many cases, the ability to attract funding and political support. Successful innovations in one place feed back into global circuits and inspire other copies, arrayed in a different dress for the new location. Appropriation often depends on the availability of donors and the capacity of a program to deliver measurable change in a relatively short time period. Translation is the process of adjusting the rhetoric and structure of these programs or interventions to local circumstances. Appropriated programs are not necessarily translated, but they are more likely to be popular if they are. On the other hand, if they are translated so fully that they blend into existing power relationships completely, they lose their potential for social change.

Translation has three dimensions. First, the images, symbols, and stories through which the program is presented draw on specific local cultural narratives and conceptions. For example, domestic violence advocates in India tell stories about powerful Hindu deities to promote self-assertiveness among Hindu women while in China, feminists label abusive behavior as "feudal." Sociologists studying social movements describe this process as "framing" (Snow et al. 1986; Tarrow 1998). Frames are not themselves ideas but ways of packaging and presenting ideas that generate shared beliefs, motivate collective action, and define appropriate strategies of action. Frames can have powerful effects on the way situations are understood and on the tactics their supporters deploy (Khagram, Riker, and Sikkink 2002: 12–13). The frame is an interpretive package surrounding a core idea (Ferree 2003: 308).

Social movement theorists point out that the frame needs to be culturally resonant for the ideas to be adopted. However, Ferree argues that resonant discourses are less radical than nonresonant ones and that some movement leaders may choose the nonresonant approach in order to induce greater social change in the long run (2003: 305). Indeed, resonance is a costly choice since it may limit the possibility of long-term change. Choosing resonance requires sacrificing ideals, limiting demands on authorities, and possibly excluding significant groups and their demands from the movement (Ferree 2003: 340). This is precisely the problem human rights activists confront: If they frame human rights to be compatible with existing ways of thinking, they will not induce change. It is only their capacity to challenge existing power relations that offers radical possibilities.

The second dimension of translation is adapting the appropriated program to the structural conditions in which it operates. For example, in Hong Kong, shelters focus on getting social welfare department officials to move battered women higher up on the public housing priority list. In India, which lacks significant public housing, activists focus on giving battered women the right to remain in the matrimonial home through legal reform. In urban China, there are very few shelters since most housing is assigned on the basis of one's job, and it is the man who gets the housing. The woman who leaves her batterer for a shelter has few other housing options and must sooner or later go back to him. In China, activists rely on local leaders of the quasi-governmental mass organization for women, the All-China Women's Federation (ACWF), to deal with gender violence. In India, domestic violence is often handled by special dowry-focused police stations. Each location has a distinctive set of government and private services, laws, court and police systems, and political institutions that affect how the prototype is translated.

Third, as programs are translated, the target population is also redefined. For example, in China domestic violence occurs among many family members, not just within romantic relationships between men and women. Violence is common between adults and their co-resident elderly parents and between parents and children. The definition of the problem in China has been expanded to reflect these patterns. In the United States, domestic violence is more common in intimate, romantic relationships whether or not the couple is married than in larger family networks. Laws have gradually shifted from protecting women in marriage to women in households. There is a growing recognition that violence is also common in same-sex intimate relationships and that some programs need to be tailored to these populations (Ristock 2002).

However, even though programs are translated into new contexts and framed in culturally specific ways, they are never fully indigenized. They retain their underlying emphasis on individual rights to protection of the body along with autonomy, choice, and equality, ideas embedded in the legal codes of the human rights system. Inside the culturally resonant packaging is a core that radically challenges patriarchy. Despite arguments that human rights must be translated into local webs of meaning based on religion, ethnicity, or place in order for them to appear both legitimate and appealing, such transformations take place only at a relatively superficial level (see An-Na'im 1992a, b; Coomaraswamy 1994). When the aboriginal center in Australia developed its brochure for domestic violence services using Aboriginal art images, for example, it translated the program into local artistic forms, but it still produced a brochure. Moreover, this brochure listed the same kinds of services found in other women's centers around the world. In another example, the social worker running a treatment program in Hong Kong for men who batter sought to frame his curriculum in terms of Chinese ideas of masculinity and family headship, but he nevertheless ran a therapeutic discussion group for men whose domestic violence had been defined as a social problem. The focus on Chinese masculinity represents an adaptation to the Hong Kong context but not a complete transformation of ideas, an indigenization (Chan 2000b).

As the examples of appropriation and translation in this chapter indicate, human rights retain their fundamental meanings even as they become resources in local struggles. They grow out of a modernist understanding of the self and its capacity to act autonomously as well as an emphasis on equality and the security of the body. The power of human rights to change the way people think and act is their capacity to change existing cultural practices such as the husband's authority to discipline his wife through beating. It is not their ability to blend into preexisting cultural systems. Adopting human rights locally does not build on a preexisting similarity of cultural beliefs any more than introducing bureaucracy or traffic lights does. But proponents do dress them in familiar costumes.

Two different approaches to translating human rights concerning violence against women emerged in my research. The first was a social service approach inspired by feminists and social workers, largely middle-tier professionals and academics. Social workers and feminist activists transplanted from other countries social service programs that offered support services to victims and re-training for offenders. The second was a human rights advocacy approach led by lawyers and political elites. These groups worked to change national laws and institutions and transplanted institutions such as human rights commissions. Both social service provision and human rights advocacy are local appropriations of global ideas. The first transplants programs such as shelters, counseling, support groups, and legal aid through a transnational community of feminist social organizations. It uses sociological modes of analysis and grows out of an activist feminist community as well as NGO social service providers. It works with individual clients. The second develops mechanisms for defining human rights and responding to violations at the national level. This includes efforts to incorporate international standards into domestic law, to create human rights commissions and women's commissions, and to promote international human rights education programs. Governmental policymakers, legislators, and judges are key actors. They use legal modes of analysis and try to develop human rights complaint-handling mechanisms and enact legal reform through the legislative or judicial process.

Despite the disparate origins and fundamental differences between the two movements, there is a growing convergence between them. National interest in participating in the human rights system creates spaces for rights-based social service programs at the grassroots. As local social service programs encourage clients to frame their grievances in terms of human rights, they develop a rights-conscious local constituency that pushes governments to abide by the standards of the international system. Thus, human rights institutions benefit from the rights consciousness promoted by local social service programs and local social service programs benefit from adopting a nationally and internationally recognized rights framework. UN meetings and conferences punctuate this relationship by creating opportunities for consultation between the two tiers at international conferences, commission meetings, and during the writing of country reports for treaty bodies such as CEDAW. This chapter compares and systematizes a vast array of initiatives, using the five-country comparison to unearth common strategies and their global origins. This approach lacks the deep, contextualized form of analysis that anthropologists generally provide for a single site but shows gender violence reform efforts as part of global flows of knowledge and action.[1] It focuses largely on the capital cities of these countries, except for the United States.

Feminist Social Services

CRIMINAL LAW AND THE CRIMINAL JUSTICE SYSTEM

Four basic initiatives against domestic violence have been transplanted globally in these five countries: criminalization, provision of social services, public education, and survey research. Criminalization is usually the first step. Activists develop and pass laws against gender violence, train police to arrest offenders, encourage no-drop (i.e., mandated) prosecution, and train judges to treat wife battering and sexual assault seriously. Because the implementation of laws lags well behind the passage of these laws, activists devote considerable energy to implementation strategies. The justice system is often very lenient. When a man is arrested for battering in Fiji, for example, he receives a suspended sentence and if he offends again, he receives another suspended sentence. In the United States, the battered-women's movement, confronting a failure to enforce laws by police, prosecutors, and judges, has invested heavily in training programs. Deploying the police against batterers poses problems for some communities, however. Many groups experience the criminal justice system as hostile and racist. Groups such as Australian Aboriginal people, Native Hawaiians, Native Americans, and African Americans are already disproportionately incarcerated. In India, there is concern that the police are inefficient and corrupt.

INDIA

India's penal code covers domestic violence, defined as cruelty by a husband or relatives to his wife, in Section 498A of the Indian Penal Code. A legal aid handbook dates the law to 1983 and says it is the "first time the crime of violence specifically against a woman by her husband was recognized in law" (Lawyers' Collective 1992: 36). The term "domestic violence" was unknown until recently, according to an attorney at the Lawyers' Collective, and the term "cruelty" was used instead. It is now becoming far more widespread and the number of complaints is increasing dramatically. According to a police officer I interviewed in Delhi in 2001 who handles domestic violence cases, the sentence is a fine plus prison up to three years, and some men do actually go to jail. An activist working at Jagori, a feminist documentation and resource center in Delhi, said that the police complain that women often drop criminal charges under 498A.

So-called dowry deaths or dowry murders are a particular form of violence against women in India produced by the practice of providing substantial gifts from the bride's family to the groom's family at marriage. Quarrels over dowry gifts often last years into the marriage and contribute to abuse of the woman and possibly murder if her family fails to provide the promised dowry. This problem, along with rape of women in police custody, galvanized the women's movement in the 1970s. The Dowry Prohibition Act of 1961 made asking for dowry illegal, while amendments in 1984 and 1986 provided stringent punishments for giving and taking dowry (Poonacha and Pandey 1999: 179). Nevertheless, the practice continues. According to an amendment to the Indian Evidence Act, if a woman commits suicide within seven years of the date of her marriage and her husband or husband's relatives have subjected her to cruelty, the court may presume that the suicide is abetted by the husband or his family, and if a woman dies within seven years of marriage and she has experienced cruelty, her husband and relatives are assumed guilty unless it is proven otherwise (Lawyers' Collective 1992: 41; Jethmalani 2001: 60–61). The police officer I interviewed said that even a little harassment is enough for a criminal conviction. One consequence of the focus on dowry murders is that there is a tendency to see all incidents of domestic violence as economic struggles over dowry.

Special police stations focused on dowry conflicts were established starting in 1983 in Delhi (interview, Special Cell, 2001) and in 1989 in Bangalore as a branch of the detective units (Poonacha and Pandey 1999: 76–77). Each of the nine police districts of Delhi has such a cell. In 2001 I visited a dowry police station, called a Special Cell for Crimes against Women and Children. This station handles about 7500 cases a year and has 18 police inspectors working there. It also runs a police helpline that is available around the clock. Walking past a crowd of women and children as well as a few men waiting in the small anteroom, I was ushered into the office of the commissioner of police. This is not a police station, he told me, but a place that deals with domestic violence and dowry. After telling me that they generally reconcile couples and negotiate the terms of a settlement, he invited me to observe several cases he handled along with the social workers at the station. In 2000, 23 percent of cases were reconciled through counseling, including those resolved with the assistance of professional counselors from the Central Social Welfare Board. All the cases I observed in a two-day period were settled, often with the help of social workers, despite indications of significant violence in the relationship in several cases.

For example, in one case I heard in 2001, a young woman married for six months came to court because she was afraid of her husband's father. Her husband beat her as well. She came from a wealthier family than her husband. He offered to rent a room for her, but she did not want to live alone. She said that she could accuse him of harassment and beating, but then the marriage would fall apart. She wanted him to sign a paper so that he has something over his head if he does not treat her better. She does not really want a divorce. His parents, who attended the hearing as well, posted a notice in the newspaper saying that they have disowned him so that, if she accuses him of a dowry offense, they are not responsible. The police inspector worked out a compromise along these lines, and she stayed with her husband.

A second case involved both property and violence. A young couple, married seven years with one child, was supported by the husband who sells vegetables. He left her one month ago and his mother has taken all her jewelry. She says he beats her, but she will come back if he treats her better. The parents counter that this is a love marriage and since the couple eloped, it is not a real marriage. She insists that it is. She fled to her mother's house and he went to get her, but her brothers attacked him with a knife. He then filed a criminal complaint against her brothers. She wants to live with him but he beats her and she says she is black and blue. She would like some promise that he will not beat her and she wants her jewelry back. She cannot remain with her own parents. He insists that he never beats her, except "just to make her understand." He saw a woman of bad character going to visit her, so he beat her, he said. They left the hearing arguing with each other. It appears that the woman has little choice but to stay with him, but desperately wants him to be less violent. The hearing officer told me that his major goal in these cases is conciliation.

A third case followed a similar pattern. A woman came alone to tell her story and showed a list of goods owed to her, but the husband failed to show up. He drinks a lot and beats her. She works in a pen factory and gives all her earnings to her in-laws, but they still beat and harass her. She has left and the husband wants her to come back, but she is not persuaded. She has a list of the dowry articles she wants back, including gold chains, rings, clothes, blankets, ornaments, color TV, and washing machines. She wants to keep their child because the husband is an alcoholic. She was pregnant but lost another child because he kicked her in the stomach. The police commissioner pays little attention to the allegations of violence and works on negotiating a reconciliation.

These cases are quite similar to those handled by the *nari adalats,* or women's courts, discussed below (see Krishnamurthy 2002). Women typically seek return of their marriage goods and some reduction in violence yet need to stay with their husbands in order to have a respectable place to live. In general, it appeared that the police sought a compromise involving the exchange of money and the woman's return to her marital home. Money, rather than violence, was the focus of concern. These women seemed quite assertive, although they were not often supported by the police commissioner. I found the lack of attention to the violence quite striking. Cases were interpreted in terms of dowry and debt despite horrific stories. Reconciliation focused on the exchange of goods. The women clearly had no good alternative to returning to their violent husbands.

All-women police stations were formed in 1995 in twelve states and territories to deal with crimes against women, thus having a slightly different mandate than the dowry cells. The number has increased somewhat since then (Task Force on Women 2000: 28). They tend to be understaffed and unpopular among women police officers since they lack advancement possibilities (Poonacha and Pandey 1999: 76–77). They also tend to see violence in the home narrowly as a product of dowry claims (Sitaraman 2002). Legal aid and counseling are available at women's centers, but activists in Delhi pointed out that there are very few centers and that those that exist are only a band aid over a widespread problem. Family Courts were established about 1998, primarily in urban areas, and did not seem to have a substantial impact (UNIFEM interview 2000).

Indian law has some provisions for civil remedies such as the right to live in the matrimonial home and protective orders to restrain a spouse from further abuse of the woman and her children available in family court or civil court, but women's rights groups are working to expand these remedies (Lawyer's Collective 1992: 13). Several NGOs in India, led by the Women's Rights Initiative of the Lawyer's Collective with funding provided by the Ford Foundation, worked from 1999 to 2001 to develop new civil domestic violence legislation. After extensive consultations with women's groups, a draft was completed in 2001. When I visited the collective in October 2001, an attorney leading the project said they had been through 150 drafts of this legislation and had consulted extensively with NGOs all over the country and translated the text into many Indian languages. Although much of the text of the bill was borrowed from other countries — primarily South Africa but also Canada, Australia, Sri Lanka, Philippines, and some states in the United States — it has been adapted to the Indian context by taking a primarily civil law approach and by focusing on a woman's safety and her right to stay in the matrimonial home. The law is framed in rights language and emphasizes providing protection rather than punishing offenders. Section 5 of the 2001 draft contains provisions for protection orders prohibiting domestic violence as well as entering the home or workplace of the person aggrieved or making any attempt to contact that person or alienating any assets held by both parties, including a woman's *stridhan* (property a woman brings to the marriage). In a society in which divorce is extremely rare and virtually all women are married, it is not safe or desirable for a woman to live alone, so the bill protects a woman's right to reside in her home of marriage. The bill includes provisions for monetary relief for expenses and losses of the aggrieved person and any children as well as a residence order which prevents the respondent from dispossessing the aggrieved person from a shared household or for securing alternative accommodation if the shared accommodation is dangerous, in the view of the court (Ch. III, Secs. 6 and 7). Protection orders are accompanied by suspended arrest warrants to be executed if the order is breached (Jethmalani 2001: 73). The bill also specifies the creation of protection officers to assist the court in carrying out these provisions (Ch. IV). This officer is to investigate complaints of domestic violence, inform aggrieved persons of their rights to orders, and ensure that monetary relief is made available (Ch. IV, Sec. 20). Despite considerable debate about counseling for men, the Lawyer's Collective decided that a judge could require it, but it was not mandatory (interview Oct. 2001).

In December 2001, the government introduced its own bill on domestic violence, including provisions for protection officers and protection orders. Leading women's groups objected that the government law did not incorporate international human rights standards set by CEDAW into its definition of domestic violence and rejected this law (Emails on February 27, 2002 and September 30, 2002 to the end-violence and CEDAW listserves). Indira Jaising of the Lawyer's Collective argued in February 2002 that the government bill defined domestic violence in terms of conduct that makes the aggrieved person's life miserable rather than in terms of rights, failed to specify forms of violence, and did not include the broad range of abuses identified in the UN Declaration and the Platform for Action. Most important, it did not specify that the woman has a right to remain in the shared household. Although it provides for the creation of protection officers, it includes no funding proposal to make this possible. Jaising contrasts this absence with the US Violence against Women Act of 1994, which committed substantial funds to preventing violence against women. An email posting from the Lawyer's Collective in December 2004 indicated that the law had still not been enacted (esaconf.un.org).

144

In Fiji, activists have been working since the mid 1980s to develop and implement laws to criminalize domestic violence. Historically the police and courts have been reluctant to prosecute violence against women and impose penalties. A 1988 study of the Suva area found that police reconcile 64 percent of reported cases of domestic violence, generally by persuading wives to drop the charges (Jalal 1988: 35–36). At the time, the police were reluctant to prosecute husbands. Between 1993 and 1997, police still reported reconciling 38 percent of cases (Fiji Women's Crisis Centre c. 2000: 45). Both police and courts find these cases embarrassing and often do not support women who complain. In the 1990s, the government, police force, judiciary, and military were overwhelmingly male.

Fiji's active women's movement has focused on rape and domestic violence. The Fiji Women's Crisis Centre (FWCC), a feminist battered-women's center, was founded in 1984 with considerable initial input from overseas feminists (anon. 1999). Its energetic leader, Shamima Ali, makes public statements critical of the police and the government. She started to work in the anti-rape movement in England during a stay of three and a half years, then volunteered at FWCC in 1985 and became its coordinator in 1986. She participated in the Center for Women's Global Leadership in Rutgers University, New Jersey. The FWCC now operates four centers providing counseling and legal advice for battered women. I visited the main office and one of the branch offices, where counselors were busy talking to women who had come for help with their violent home situations. In 1986, the Fiji Women's Rights Movement (FWRM) developed as a sister organization to work on policy issues of women's rights, human rights education and public awareness of gender discrimination. By the 1990s these groups had separated into two quite distinct but still complementary organizations, one focusing on battered women's service and advocacy and the other on women's human rights.

Fiji now has a no-drop policy in the prosecutor's office, although some prosecutors still prefer to reconcile cases. FWCC trained police and military officers, but does not maintain batterer education programs. It initiated a Pacific network of organizations working on domestic violence, supported by the Australian government's aid program. Another feminist NGO in Fiji, the Regional Rights Resource Team (RRRT), worked for eight years to develop a new family law bill, finally passed in 2003. The Family Law Act is based on principles from the Convention on the Rights of the Child and CEDAW. It created the Family Court with mediation, a fairer distribution of matrimonial property, and greater priority for the interests of children in custody situations. The enforcement of maintenance payments is increased. NGOs are still working on a domestic violence bill.

The Fiji feminist movement was a collaborative effort among leaders from Fiji, Australia, and Canada. A workshop in 1991, early in the movement, brought together 25 activists, community leaders, and housewives with sponsorship by the Canada Fund and content developed by an Australian. At the time, the FWCC was being supported by the Australian Freedom from Hunger Campaign. The organizer of the workshop, Shamima Ali, stressed counseling as a major part of the center's function (Singh-Wendt 1991: 11). The workshop discussed the meaning of feminism, oppression, sexism, classism, and racism as different forms of oppression. Peni Moore, then head of FWRM, spoke on the antirape movement and discussed efforts to change the laws on rape (Singh-Wendt 1991: 16). Participants came from both Fijian and Indo-Fijian backgrounds and talked about the role of women in overcoming the deep ethnic divisions in the country (see Prasad 1989). Both FWCC and FWRM emphasize working across this ethnic divide.

Fiji focused on criminal justice reforms in its 1998 Women's Plan of Action 1999–2008 (Vol. II, by the Ministry for Women and Culture [Suva, Fiji], at www.unescap.org/pop/database/law_fiji/fiji_017.htm, February 2, 2001). In the section Violence against Women and Children, this plan recommends law reform, supportive services, and the training of care providers and law enforcement agencies to deal with "ingrained bias against women and the stigma attached to victims of sexual violence." The plan argues that it is important to promulgate specific laws to deal with violence against women and to improve the law and practice for child abuse. It is also important to provide victims of violence with a safe haven in urban and rural areas and to improve data collection and analytical services to assist in designing strategies beyond the legal system. Violence against women is defined as "the most pervasive violation of human rights and for women it is considered as a major impediment to their participation in development." The report focuses on the role culture plays in perpetuating this violence: "Some forms of violence against women, particularly those that occur within the family, are entrenched and not recognized by society and our institutions as they are explained as 'family discipline' and therefore ignored, condoned, or tolerated. These social attitudes perpetuate violence and it requires more than punishment of the perpetrators to change these attitudes and behaviours" (p. 8).

This report advocates law reform and criminal justice education, safety systems, attitude change education, and research as basic strategies for violence against women, the same basic package of reforms that is found around the world. This report attributes the origins of this movement to Europe and North America two decades earlier and in other parts of the world in conjunction with development issues. It stresses the contribution of the UN in its decade for women (1975–85), women and development efforts, the 1995 World Summit for Social Development at Copenhagen, and the 1995 Beijing Conference (p. 9). It makes clear that Fiji's attention to this issue was inspired by international movements and the expansion of women's human rights. In this report the government presents itself as deeply concerned with violence against women, influenced by international conferences and feminist movements, and working to ameliorate the problem using the standard set of approaches.

CHINA

In China, domestic violence has appeared quite recently as a public issue and to a large extent in response to international interest and pressure. Until the mid 1990s, government and public awareness of the problem was very limited (Human Rights in China 1995: 25). As late as 1990, the government was able to deny that there was a problem in China (see Liu and Chan 1999, 2000). The world conference on women in Beijing in 1995 galvanized public concern about violence against women and spawned the development of hotlines, legal services clinics, and counseling centers in urban areas. The impact was far less in the rural areas. In most areas, a woman's only recourse in a battering situation is her family or the ACWF.

The ACWF is a mass governmental organization representing women's interests, although it presents itself as an NGO at international meetings. It is the main organization protecting women's rights and providing legal aid. The policy of gender equality was fundamental to the New China established by the Chinese Communist Party (Hecht 1998: 72). In 1983, rights departments were established within every Women's Federation Branch down to the county level (Hecht 1998: 79). A report by four women's NGOs to the 2000 Beijing Plus Five Conference states that 85–90 percent of all counties have set up legal counseling centers to protect women and provide legal counseling and assistance and notes that several provinces have passed legislation against domestic violence (China Working Group against Domestic Violence 2000a: 11). A survey of women's status in China in 2001 by the ACWF reported 1759 counseling centers for legal aid in the country established by the ACWF (*Women's Daily News,* November 5, 2001, trans. by Wei-ying Lin). However, the ACWF's mandate is to implement government policies, so that it cannot represent women's interests when they conflict with those of the ruling party (Human Rights in China 1998: 8).

With a turn toward greater reliance on law to implement policy in China along with concerns about the social disruptions of the economic liberalization process since the 1980s, the government asked the ACWF along with other organizations to draft legislation on women's rights. The result, the Law of the People's Republic of China on the Protection of Women's Rights and Interests, was passed in 1992 after three years of investigation and refinement (Hecht 1998: 72–74). It was intended to bring CEDAW principles into Chinese law. Although it clearly articulates a policy of gender equality, it specifies that men and women should be treated equally, not that their conditions of life or social status should be equal. The law protects women's bodily integrity and contains considerable protective legislation for the workplace, which emphasizes women's biological differences and the need to protect maternity (Hecht 1998: 76–77). However, it does not define discrimination nor provide an enforcement mechanism (Human Rights in China 1998: 13). It prohibits violence and abuse against women but does not specifically mention violence in the family, nor are remedies provided. Instead, the language is abstract and general. A report at a domestic violence conference in Beijing in 2002 on police effectiveness said that the police are often reluctant to intervene, and neither the police nor the public is aware of the problem. Even many women police officers think the antidomestic-violence movement is too "feminist."[2]

China's 2001 Marriage Law prohibits domestic violence but does not define it nor specify any mechanisms for preventing or punishing it. However, activists recognize that it is very important that this law names domestic violence as a problem rather than as a necessary form of discipline. Some worry that the law does not expand the concept beyond hitting to threats and mental and sexual abuse (Wang Xingjuan in *China Women's News,* November 16, 2000, trans. by Wei-Ying Lin). Since it is civil law, it does not delineate punishments but offers the victim mediation and the opportunity to press criminal liability claims (Article 43, trans. by Wei-ying Lin). The victim has the right to bring a lawsuit to the people's court. The public security division will carry out the investigation and the people's court will bring the lawsuit (Article 45). Despite the efforts of activists, the law does not include a provision for a protection order and it requires the victim to take the initiative in going to the law. A 2000 survey of 10 provinces and cities by the ACWF reported that 96 percent of respondents thought this revised Marriage Law should include regulations on domestic violence (*China Women's News,* August 3, 2000, Wei-Ying Lin, trans.).

Between 2000 and 2002, a Domestic Violence Research and Intervention

Project (DVRIP) engaged in major research and intervention initiatives concerning violence against women. Funded by the Ford Foundation, NOVIB of Holland, SIDA of Sweden, and the Human Rights Center of Oslo University in Norway (Domestic Violence in China: Research, Intervention and Prevention *Newsletter* 2 [October 2001], typescript), it culminated in the first international conference on violence against women held in Beijing in 2002, which I attended. In 2001 I interviewed many of its leading researchers and the director. At the final session of the 2002 conference, the chair presented a draft bill on domestic violence prepared by the research team after two years of intensive effort and consultation of domestic violence laws collected from forty countries. The presentation of the law was the culmination of the conference. Many of the conference participants expressed the need for a strong and effective domestic violence law in China.

In addition to legal aid services provided by the ACFW, there is a prominent legal aid clinic in Beijing established in 1995 that offers legal assistance to women who are victims of violence or rape and pursues high visibility policy-making cases. I visited the center in Beijing in 2001 and 2005. It is a small two-room office, festooned with banners given by grateful beneficiaries, but hardly capable of providing services to much of populous Beijing. It does not have the resources to handle a large volume of cases. Its clients range from highly educated people to low-status women such as migrant workers, housekeepers, and peasants (Guo 2000: 3). Between 1995 and 2000, the center provided consultations to 7000 clients through its hotline, interviews, letters, and email. These cases cover domestic violence, sexual crimes, employment discrimination, distribution of joint property after divorce, and child custody. The center has strong international connections and tries to use CEDAW in its legal work. Some of its funding comes from the Ford Foundation, and a 2001 research report on women's rights and the implementation of CEDAW was supported by the British government (Centre for Women's Law Studies and Legal Services of Peking University 2001).

Although cases of domestic violence are handled in court, they pose difficult dilemmas for victims. The DVRIP reported some of its research findings on the legal situation of domestic violence victims in its newsletter. Wang Kairong observed a case in the appeal court in Tianjin in 2000. The court of first instance had already decided in favor of the appellee, a 26-year-old housewife married to a young peasant living in Tianjin City for almost two years. She was said to be battered by her husband because she had been slow in caring for her ill mother-in-law. She filed a criminal suit and a civil claim against her husband in the Jing County People's Court with a private prosecutor. Forensic evidence confirmed that she had a fractured rib, and the court sentenced the husband to 10 months' imprisonment with one year's probation and a fine of 2000 yuan for medical expenses, damage compensation to the plaintiff, and a lawsuit fee. The husband appealed the judgment. He claimed he did not beat his wife's chest and cause the fracture. The case was the first one heard in the Domestic Violence Criminal Collegiate Tribunal since its establishment within the intermediate court. A legal aid agency lawyer was appointed for the appellant and the Tianjin Women's Federation recommended two lawyers from its affiliated law firms for the appellee.

The appeal was witnessed by over one hundred visitors including family members, women's federation leaders, judicial administrative officials, and law school students and was broadcast live by Tianjin television. The court upheld the earlier judgment. The woman was successful because her husband confessed that he did beat his wife and the village clinic doctor and other villagers testified to the violence. Finding witnesses willing to testify would have been far more difficult in a city. The audience had some sympathy for the man, however. An older woman said, "I found the woman too aggressive and deserved beating. The husband looks really pitiable!" Even though the woman won the appeal, the fine will probably be paid out of family resources, which are jointly owned by husband and wife, so that he will use part of his wife's property to pay for the damage he has inflicted on her. Wang, the author of the newsletter article, concludes that there are still problems in the legal resolution of domestic violence cases (Wang c. 2001: 4–6).

In the same newsletter, a lawyer who handles domestic violence cases in court notes the many difficulties battered women face in court: a lack of concern by law enforcement officers in comparison to other criminal cases, a lack of effort by police and court to gather evidence, and an unwillingness of other family members, neighbors, friends, coworkers, and relatives to serve as witnesses. They may be afraid of the perpetrator or reluctant to interfere in other families' business. Even brothers and sisters of the abused woman may feel intervention is inappropriate (Liu Donghua c. 2001: 6–7).

Even as China eagerly examines programs for dealing with domestic violence in other countries and relies on the social science literature produced in North America for its theoretical framework, national leaders insist that their approaches have Chinese characteristics. The leaders of DVRIP as well as other domestic violence activists want to develop a Chinese model of preventing violence against women, more kin-based and less focused on spouses and romantic/sexual relationships than are Western models (see Li Hongxian 2000: 75). Because Chinese families are typically three-generational, violence is not restricted to husband-wife battering but occurs among a variety of relatives and often against elderly parents or children. In rural areas, the husband's family is very important, and if a woman sues her husband, the whole family will hate her. She has often lost ties with her natal family and has no place to go if she leaves her husband's family.

These family conditions affect patterns of violence and forms of intervention. They make recourse to shelters or the use of restraining orders very difficult. Instead, the domestic violence intervention program focuses on raising awareness among the police so that they see domestic violence as their responsibility and on working with local hospitals and women's federation workers. A Chinese NGO, the Maple Women's Psychological Counseling Center, recommended strengthening the Peoples' Mediating Committees to prevent and halt domestic violence since they are a mass organization with a long history spread all over China (China Working Group against Domestic Violence 2000b: 9). There are also neighborhood committees made up of retired people and chosen by the party who sometimes get involved. But, even though there are many local organizations such as work units, they rarely view domestic violence as a problem they must handle.

At the 2002 conference, there was little talk of "Chinese characteristics" for domestic violence reforms, however, nor of clans, lineages or even neighborhood groups as sources of support. Instead, the focus was on the institutions of the state: the police, the courts, and hospitals. Many participants spoke of the need to "catch up" and of being "behind" the United States, Canada, the Nordic countries, and Japan. Despite the desire to tailor the understanding of the problem and its solution to Chinese kinship characteristics, the focus was on state intervention and the goal was creating a more modern society. The DVRIP director pointed to the need to change traditions, such as eliminating the common Confucian proverb that a man needs to beat a woman every three days or she will climb up on the roof and destroy the house (Liu and Chan 2000: 74). The activists in this project were highly educated urban elites with significant international travel and knowledge of international human rights.

HONG KONG

Hong Kong has a specific piece of legislation for domestic violence, the Domestic Violence Ordinance. This law, passed in 1986, provides for temporary restraining orders and the possibility of arrest (Yeung 1991: 35; Man 2001: 4–5). However, by 2002 there was some concern among activists, including the executive director of the first shelter, that the law was too narrowly defined and overly restrictive since it only covered marital relationships (*South China Morning Post,* March 14, 2002, p. 15). Women's groups have trained police officers in handling domestic violence cases and prepared guidelines. In 2000, a Domestic Violence Policy Unit was established in the police department (Man 2001: 22). Nevertheless, researchers commonly observe that the police are still reluctant to intervene and consider battering simply a domestic disturbance (Yeung 1991: 35).

USA

In the United States, although the battered-women's and antirape movements of the early 1970s emphasized criminalization, by the mid 1980s there was growing interest in civil protective orders as well (Schechter 1982; Ptacek 1999; Schneider 2000). A centerpiece of the US effort has always been increasing the severity of criminal penalties, improving policing to make arrests more frequent, and developing more certain prosecution through no-drop mandates. These efforts have improved the likelihood of arrest and prosecution, but penalties are still relatively light. Significant police training has improved intervention, yet many still fail to take this offense seriously. Those who violate restraining orders are subject to criminal penalties, at least in theory. In my research in a small town in Hawai'i, I found that a woman getting a restraining order can still have contact with her violent partner, but he will probably be required to attend a psycho-educational violence control program (1995a, 1995b). If he fails to attend or violates the order, he will usually be sent back to the program. Many battered women I talked to in Hawai'i did not want criminal penalties for their partners but preferred to get a protective order and send them to a program that tries to train them not to be violent.

Thus, there are substantial similarities in the criminal justice and legal interventions being developed for men who batter in all five countries and roughly contemporaneous program and legal innovations. This is clearly a transnational social reform movement.

SOCIAL SERVICES AND VIOLENCE CONTROL TRAINING

Some social service initiatives seek to improve the woman's safety rather than to punish the offender. The most important of these initiatives are shelters or refuges for women fleeing from their batterers, an idea that emerged in both the UK and the United States about 1974. Although shelters have now spread through the urban areas of many countries, they are far from universal.

Women's violence advocates in Beijing told me that there were very few shelters in China, with one existing for a time in Wuhan and one being developed in Tianjin (see Wang 1999a, b). The director of a counseling center in Beijing told me she was under pressure from foreign donors to set up a shelter and asked my advice about how to do it. According to some of the people I interviewed, shelters are difficult because China lacks a civil society with NGOs who might be able to develop and run one. It is currently difficult to establish an NGO under Chinese regulations. Shelters are also expensive.

Activists in Delhi told me that there were virtually no shelters in India either. There were two shelters for the whole of Delhi in 2001. Some women's activists said shelters do not mesh well with a kinship system in which a woman must either live with her husband's family or her natal family. Accounts of incidents of domestic violence indicate that women generally flee to their natal families when violence becomes severe (Poonacha and Pandey 1999; Krishnamurthy 2002; ICRW 2002: 26). Some said it was not safe for poor women to live outside a family setting. A study of West Bengal argued that shelter homes set up by the state are not a good idea because they isolate women from their communities rather than encouraging the community to respond to such problems (ICRW 2002: 30). Some activists I talked to in India thought there was a desperate need for shelters but that there were no resources to set them up.

Fiji has only one small private shelter for its population of about 800,000, but its dynamic and high-profile women's center offers counseling and legal aid for battered women as well as considerable community education and political advocacy. This women's center attempted to set up a shelter in the early 1990s but found it too expensive and security too difficult (Fiji Women's Crisis Centre Report 1996: 19).

Shelters require substantial investment by governments or donors. Their absence reflects resource deficits more than kinship structures. For example, Hong Kong has four shelters, one of which was started in 1985 by an NGO, one in 1986 by the government, one by a Christian church that has since become secular, and one sponsored by the government but run by Caritas, which opened in 2002 in response to concerns about rapid increases in rates of domestic violence and demands for shelter services (*South China Morning Post,* Feb. 16, 2002, p. 4, Ella Lee). These shelters typically offer hotlines, counseling, legal, financial, and housing assistance, and support groups plus tutorial groups for children (Yeung 1991: 35; Tang, Lee, and Cheung 1999: 50–51). The pioneer shelter, Harmony House, was started in 1985 by Americans and Britons using models from the United States and the UK. Its current executive director spent ten years in Canada working on family violence. In its early years, Harmony House was described as offering treatment and shelter for abused women rather than promoting women's human rights in order to diminish opposition, according to a social worker who worked at Harmony House at the time (interview March 2002). Human rights sounded more Western. Only when they began to develop publicity pamphlets did they talk about family violence.

Activists in Hong Kong told me that their dilemma was that the city was now too affluent to interest international donors and they had to fund the shelters and domestic violence programs with government money. The government offers substantial subventions to many NGOs, thus guaranteeing their survival for service delivery but inhibiting innovation and advocacy. Although the directors of these programs typically emphasize their efforts to "indigenize" the program, they also rely on concepts of gender equality, understanding feelings, and the icon of a power/control wheel developed in the United States. "Chinese traditional culture" is cited as a factor contributing to the occurrence of gender violence rather than a mode of combating it (Yeung 1991: 34).

Shelters are widespread in the United States, but they too face challenges in receiving sufficient government funding. The first shelter in Hilo, Hawai'i, set up in 1978, was a rambling old house with little staff or support run by formerly battered women (Merry 2001a). Like shelters elsewhere in the country, it has gradually become more established and professional, but shelters continue to run on limited government funding. Around the country, they face cutbacks when local governments run short of funds. Discussions with activists in each of these countries suggest that shelters are only feasible in urban areas where women can live outside a kin group. If a woman's only housing option is within a family, moving to a formal state institution is not a viable solution. Moreover, shelters are expensive, and even in relatively affluent nations there are constant concerns about the expense of providing a secure space and offering the broad set of services necessary to allow a woman to find housing and employment away from her violent partner.

Other widespread innovations are hotlines to receive emergency calls, counseling for women seeking to escape battering situations, legal aid if they decide to go to court or pursue a divorce, and supportive discussion groups to help women talk about their problems. There is an NGO counseling center and hotline in Beijing, but it handles relatively few cases and a wide variety of family problems, including a significant minority who are men having difficulties with the sexual aspects of their marriages. The *China Women's News,* an ACWF-affiliated newspaper, ran a hotline for a year, called Household National Defense, until the lawyer who answered calls left (interview 2001). The first specifically anti-domestic-violence hotline was established in Shaanxi Province in 2001 by the Shaanxi Women's Federation (*People's Daily* May 15, 2001). The main organization for most women is the local office of the ACWF, the place they typically turn for help. As one activist told me, the ACWF is the only institution that cares about domestic violence; police, judges, and lawyers do not seem concerned. In rural areas, however, the ACWF is primarily responsible for enforcing the one-child population policy so that it may not be trusted by women for other types of problems, according to a China human rights organization based in the United States (Human Rights in China 1998: 70).

Most of the innovative programs that address women's rights are located in cities. For example, the Maple Women's Psychological Counseling Center in Beijing, established in 1992, offers counseling and a hotline. The center's hotline has increasingly focused on issues of gender violence (interview with director, 2001). About 70 percent of the phone calls about domestic violence involve husbands beating wives, while 30 percent concern children beating parents. The first in the country, it is now joined by five others in other provinces. This organization has significant transnational linkages: it is supported by the Ford Foundation (which is now pushing them to set up a shelter) and a German foundation. A few years ago, this group received training in how to handle domestic violence calls from a hotline in Korea. It was also aided by Harmony House in Hong Kong. Its director attended the Beijing Plus Five Conference and was involved in the DVRIP program.

Women's support groups, while common in the United States, are not so widespread globally. The Fiji Women's Crisis Centre offers counseling to individual women who are battered, but not in groups. While the core of the Fiji intervention is counseling, it is more concerned with jobs and legal aid than with psychological adjustments. I visited a branch center in 2003 and talked with the counselors who described talking to women who dropped in for advice or support on a regular basis. China has recently developed women's support groups that meet once a week for six weeks under the supervision of a social worker. This initiative came from the ShangXi Province Women, Marriage, and Family Counseling Center.[3] However, this process can only help a small fraction of the people in the country and there are very few social workers available to do it.

In India, some NGOs in Delhi such as Sakshi and Jagori offer counseling, but support groups are rare. Women typically turn to their families for help. However, a report on organizations that provided services to women, including domestic violence, in the Indian states of Karnataka and Gujarat found a large number of organizations, at least some of which offered shelter homes.

The study identified 480 organizations working in these two states and studied 20 of these that dealt with domestic violence (Poonacha and Pandey 1999: 2). These ranged from all-women's police stations to counseling cells associated with the police or private organizations and shelter homes. Many offered legal aid as well as counseling. Most of these programs focused on helping women in general rather than just victims of domestic violence. The report found that counseling in the centers, as well as in the police stations, generally sought reconciliation between husband and wife. They found that women typically want reconciliation unless their children are being harmed. Only then, as a last resort, do they seek divorce (1999: 30, 58). Many programs also offer job training and education for women. In 1990 the Central Social Welfare Board in New Delhi began a countrywide initiative to set up Family Counseling Centers to counter family breakdown and the violence it caused, growing out of a 1980s efforts to provide "preventive, referral, and rehabilitative services to victims of domestic violence and counseling in cases of 'marital maladjustment'" (UAB Annual Report, Karnataka, 1995–96, quoted in Poonacha and Pandey 1999: 132–33).

Violence control programs for batterers were developed in the United States in the early 1980s but have not spread globally to the same extent as these other initiatives. They are fairly common in the United States, and there were several in Hawai'i. Hong Kong has had therapeutic groups for male batterers since 1995, and they are currently being run on a voluntary basis by several of the shelters. I spoke to the leader of one group in 2002. He commented that the intervention was valuable for the men but that they participated on a voluntary basis rather than under court mandate and it was very difficult to persuade men to participate at all (see Chan Ko Ling 2001). Their experimental treatment programs relied on anger control techniques and on changing abusers' belief systems using a US approach similar to the Duluth model, the Domestic Abuse Intervention Project (Pence and Paymar 1993; Chan Ko Ling 2001: 49). However, court-mandated counseling for batterers also reflects Confucian values of harmonic interpersonal relationships and reeducation (Man 2001: 14–18).

In many ways, the provision of services in Hong Kong was more similar to that in the United States than either India or China. It seems likely that the relative affluence of the government and the influence of the British expatriate community both played critical roles in generating this level of services. It is noteworthy that these differences developed despite the similarity in the culture between China and Hong Kong. Economic and political resources are as important as kinship systems and religious beliefs in explaining the differences.

Fiji also had relatively more services, again inspired and funded by Australian and British expatriates and governments.

156

Although many of these programs copy transnational prototypes, some build on local feminist activism and forms of village political organization to a far greater extent than others. For example, in India, nari adalats, or women's courts, emerged in the mid 1990s from a government-initiated program to develop women's collectives in the villages and a long tradition of women's movement activism addressing violence against women. The parent program, called Mahila Samakhya, is a village-level women's empowerment program (ICRW 2002). Started by the Department of Education in 1989 with funding from the Dutch government, Mahila Samakhya (MS) endeavored to promote development by collectivizing and empowering poor women through knowledge and the confidence to make changes (Poonacha and Pandey 1999: 161; ICRW 2002: 32–65; Sharma, forthcoming). Promoting women's equality was an important part of this effort, along with health, literacy and nonformal education, savings, political involvement, and community development initiatives. During the first four years of the MS program, the training in Uttar Pradesh was carried out by Jagori, a feminist resource and training center I visited in Delhi in 2001, which adopted a radical feminist approach (see Krishnamurthy 2002: 42). The philosophy of the MS program is that decision making should rest with local collectives. The program depends on a cadre of women activists, *sahyoginis,* who develop and encourage *sanghas,* or women's collectives, in each village. Each sahyogini works with a cluster of ten villages.[4]

Since violence in the home was a major concern to many of the women, the women's collectives focused on this problem. A system of nari adalats emerged from the women's cooperatives in Gujarat in 1995 and in Uttar Pradesh in 1998 (ICRW 2002: 34). These were informal courts intended to handle women's legal problems. A 2001 study reported that since they were initiated in 1995, the four adalats in the Vadodara district handled about 1200 cases of marital violence, harassment, divorce, maintenance, property, and child custody and successfully resolved a majority of these. The clients were mostly low-caste and tribal women (Krishnamurthy 2002: 3, based on MS Annual Reports).

The nari adalat consists of a core team of selected sangha women and sahyoginis, most of whom have poor literacy skills and many of whom are *dalits,* people of low-caste status (ICRW 2002: 36).[5] The members of the nari adalat tour the district, meeting at regular days and times in public places near government offices to dispense legal advice and settle marital disputes (Poonacha and Pandey 1999: 161–78). They are not paid nor is their transportation covered. They have no legal authority but rely on pressure and shaming. Like the parent MS program, they straddle the government-NGO divide, claiming either identity as it seems helpful (Sharma, forthcoming). Krishnamurthy's ethnography describes how nari adalats move creatively between community and state to gain recognition in the villages and access to formal institutions (2002: 12, 51). The women meet in government compounds close to police and local government offices, assert their status as part of the official MS program, use state symbols such as files, stamp paper, and seals, call on the police for protection, and cite formal laws to support their decisions as they were trained to do by urban activists. At the same time, they reflect the communities they come from. They use humor and shaming to pressure litigants, adjust their meeting times to the rhythms of village life, and use their knowledge of local practices, customs, and social networks to gather evidence and negotiate agreements. They do not try to end marriages but emphasize the rights of the woman within marriage (ICRW 2002: 51). Their authority is limited, and they seem to be most successful in helping women arrange divorces and escape violent marriages, particularly among poor families. They are less successful with wealthy families and with cases of rape and molestation, which require greater evidentiary effort (2002: 99).

Nevertheless, an International Center for Research on Women (ICRW) study in 1999–2000 indicated that the operation of these courts and the closely related *mahila panch* (Women's Councils) made violence in the home a more open and public offense. ICRW evaluations of these programs indicate that sangha and sahyogini women and those who experienced the nari adalats were more aware of their rights and better able to speak up (ICRW 2002: 40–41, 54). This initiative claims to introduce human rights concepts to poor, illiterate women, many of whom are tribals or dalits. The goal of the MS program itself is to deal with domestic violence and to raise consciousness about women's rights (ICRW 2002: 70). A counterculture based on resisting violence in terms of the intrinsic rights of women is developing slowly, largely in local terms: "Research documented the innovative ways in which activists use their local knowledge to reshape and reinterpret community idioms, phrases and beliefs to create and persuade the community to adopt new perspectives" (ICRW 2002: 72). At the same time, they push the ideology of human rights.

In sum, this overview reveals many similarities in the repertoire of social services in these five countries although the more costly initiatives, such as shelters, are found only in richer countries. As in Hawai'i, the informal social network is the first place women turn for help and often the most important one. Women's centers of various kinds are common, some patterned after US or UK models such as those in Fiji and Hong Kong, but others more locally shaped, such as the nari adalats. These program transplants are a bricolage of local and international elements. Unlike the United States, these centers focus less on psychological support than on housing and legal problems. Gender violence was more often seen as a structural problem related to poverty, alcoholism, or patriarchy and less as a psychological issue of childhood trauma or learned behavior.

COMMUNITY EDUCATION AND PUBLIC AWARENESS

The third initiative against domestic violence is community education. This includes public awareness campaigns in the media, curricular development in schools, gender training, and public events such as marches and demonstrations. Local adaptation is important since messages must be presented in ways that are understood, in mediums that are heard, and in places where people will notice. This may mean TV or radio spots, tee shirts or coasters, brochures with local designs, or community meetings. The medium and the message are tailored to the particular community. However, the fundamental message, that women have the right not to be beaten under any circumstances, comes from the transnational feminist movement and is grounded in rights concepts and ideas of gender equality. Moreover, the idea of doing community education is itself a transnational concept.

There are many similarities in approaches used for community education. One NGO I visited in Fiji was training Fijians to conduct street theater about domestic violence. The DVRIP program in Beijing developed street theater, a billboard campaign using media personalities, and a TV soap opera on domestic violence. Celebrities were termed "image ambassadors." Starting in 2001, a group in the rural area of Yangqing County distributed more than 45,000 publicity flyers, information sheets, and posters, while women formed a local group to perform stories on stage based on their experiences (2002 DVRIP conference). The group says that this effort reduced the frequency of domestic violence in the county. Public education and awareness campaigns have been actively pursued in Hong Kong since the war-on-rape campaign of 1977 (Tang, Lee, and Cheung 1999: 49). Community education is an important dimension of the work of the first shelter, Harmony House. Among the numerous forms of community education in India, the *Mahila Suraxa Samiti* focuses on preventive measures to curb crimes against women. It intervenes in some cases of violence that are brought to it, as well as collaborating with NGOs in performing street plays, cultural programs, workshops and classes for housewives on sex education, marriage, and family life (Poonacha and Pandey

1999: 157–58). The US battered-women's movement has worked for many years to develop music, film, and media messages about the problem.

SURVEY RESEARCH

A fourth category of intervention is survey research. Survey data on the frequency of battering and rape along with statistics from the police and courts are used to document the extent and causes of the problem. Surveys documenting the extent of the problem in Fiji, India, China, Hong Kong, and Hawai'i as well as elsewhere in the United States helped to build political support for the movement. For example, in India, the National Family Health Survey, which is a major study done of 90,000 households, asked questions about domestic violence for the first time in the 1998/99 survey. It reported that 56 percent of ever-married women thought it was legitimate for their husbands to beat them for infractions (NFHS-2, 2000: 73). The same study reported that 21 percent of women have been beaten or mistreated since they were 15 and 19 percent of women by their husbands, although it is likely that this figure is underreported because of shame and fear (NFHS-2, 2000: 74–75). The ICRW conducted a large empirical study in India to map out the extent of domestic violence, which researchers told me in 2001 was the first effort to create a large empirical database on domestic violence in India. It began in 1995 and was at least partially funded by USAID and included a household survey on domestic violence in seven locations involving almost 10,000 people (letter from ICRW, Jan. 19, 2000).

The Fiji Women's Crisis Centre (FWCC) carried out a major survey on the frequency of domestic violence through 1575 survey questionnaires, qualitative research, and an examination of police statistics and FWCC data from 1993 to 1997. The research was supported by the UNIFEM Trust Fund, the Asia Foundation, and the Fiji government (Fiji Women's Crisis Centre 2000). This survey found that 65.8 percent of women with partners (1500 people) have been hit by their partners, while 47 percent of all married male respondents said they hit their wives (2000: 16–17). Of those women who reported being hit, 30 percent said they were beaten repeatedly (2000: 24). The report found that domestic abuse is widely tolerated and is increasing in frequency and that women most commonly think they are hit for disobedience, laziness, or adultery, while men most commonly say they hit their wives because of disobedience (2000: 32).

A survey of research on domestic violence in Hong Kong notes that there was virtually no data prior to 1980, but in the early 1980s some research began to document the scope of the problem (Yeung 1991: 32–33). As early as 1984, police in Hong Kong recorded "battered wife" as a separate category, facilitating research on the problem. Several studies examined frequencies of domestic violence and sexual harassment during the late 1980s and early 1990s (Tang, Lee, and Cheung 1999: 46–47). The social welfare department also began to collect statistics (Yeung 1991: 33). A 1996 survey of 1132 cohabiting women randomly sampled in Hong Kong revealed that two-thirds reported at least one incident of verbal abuse and a tenth one incident of physical abuse by their husbands in the past year (Tang 1999a: 180; see also Tang 1999b). More recent research has explored the impacts on children and children's perspectives (Chan Ko Ling 2000a, b; Yeung and Lok 2001).

The earliest studies on domestic violence in China were in the 1990s (Wang 1999b). A 1990 nationwide ACWF survey in China reported that about 29 percent of women said they are beaten at least occasionally (Human Rights in China 1995: 23). In 1994 the Beijing Women's Federation did a survey of surrounding counties and found domestic violence in 20 percent of families surveyed (Human Rights in China 1995: 23). The DVRIP program in Beijing included in its many research projects a survey of the frequency of domestic violence. They collected 3780 questionnaires in wealthy, middle, and poor provinces and did 30 in-depth interviews and monitored hotline calls. The survey showed that 24 percent of women reported fighting at least once a year and 38 percent of those with fighting said that there was some violence in the marriage. A survey of 2351 households in urban and rural Shanghai by the Shanghai Women's Federation in 2002 reported 93.5 percent of urban women and 94.5 percent of rural women said they had never experienced family violence (Xinhua News Agency 2002.6.14). On the other hand, another news report said that the ACWF survey found that domestic violence occurs in 30 percent of all Chinese families (Impress Service, 2000). A 2000 survey of 2500 men and women reported that 33.9 percent of families face domestic violence, probably an underreported statistic because of the "traditional" idea of Chinese people of keeping family problems within the family (*China Women's News* March 25, 2000, Wei-Ying Lin, trans.). A 1999–2000 national survey of 3323 men and women between 20 and 64 reported that 34 percent of women experienced violence by their male partners and 18 percent of men were hit by their female partners, most of the latter in the course of mutual fighting. Male on female hitting was more common in rural areas than urban (21% vs. 14%; Parish et al. 2004: 177). Statistics from ACWF showed that domestic violence increased in the late 1990s as a result of women's increasing economic dependence on men and the increase in extramarital affairs (*China Women's News*, August 3, 2000, Wei-Ying Lin, trans.).[6]

Disparities in survey data come from many sources, but one is the term used. There is no term for "domestic violence" in Chinese. One word, *bao-li,* refers to brute force, while another, *nue-dai,* refers to cruel treatment or abuse, and a third, *qin-fan,* refers to violation. A focus group in Hong Kong found that the latter terms provided a broader definition of abuse (Tang et al. 2000). The term used will clearly affect reported frequencies. A 2002 survey of 3692 rural and urban men and women in China using the term bao-li found 2.7 percent reported violence by their spouses, 1.3 percent of men and 3.9 percent of women. However, when couples are asked if they quarrel, of the 80 percent who say they do, 35 percent said they used violence in the quarrel and 29 percent of women said that their husband verbally insults or abuses them, suggesting different patterns depending on the term used (Liu and Zhang 2002, trans. by Wei-Ying Lin).

Most people think males cause the violence with the wife being the victim, and a quarter think that the children are also victims (*China Women's News,* March 25, 2000, Wei-Ying Lin, trans.). Over a third (38%) thought respecting and taking care of each family member were the best ways to deal with domestic violence, but 17 percent thought each family should take care of its family problems itself, 27 percent advocated resort to law, and 14 percent to other organizations such as the local women's federation.

To a significant extent, shared academic work and conferences spread ideas about domestic violence globally. There are several global Internet listserves on violence against women, sponsored by INSTRAW, UNIFEM, International Women's Rights Action Watch of Asia Pacific, the Rutgers Center for Global Leadership, Amnesty International, the CEDAW Committee, and a women's rights organization in Nigeria. UNIFEM sponsored an end-violence listserve that included perhaps 2500 people in 130 countries and ran, more or less continuously, for about two years in 2001–2002. A six-month seminar sponsored by the UN training agency INSTRAW focused on men's violence. Cedaw4change is an online discussion forum with 683 members.

Major conferences play similar roles. The Ford Foundation facilitated the development of a Chinese program on violence against women by hosting a conference for Indian and Chinese activists in Jaipur, India, in 1998. Chinese activists said this meeting was the impetus for their domestic violence intervention project and that they learned a lot about developments in the United States and Britain. There was also an important training program in India on judicial attitudes toward violence in India that helped to galvanize women's rights activists in Fiji. In the early 1990s, the NGO Sakshi studied judicial attitudes toward women and violence against women by interviewing 109 judges in a project supported by the Canadian International Development Agency, finding widespread gender bias (Sakshi 1996). In 1997, Sakshi held a training session in gender equality for the judiciary with the support of the chief justice of India (Sakshi 1997). This program was attended by judiciary leaders from Bangladesh, India, Nepal, Sri Lanka, Pakistan, Fiji, Canada, Australia, and Kiribati. Judges from Canada and Australia discussed the problems of gender bias and judicial discretion in their countries. Both of the representatives from Fiji who attended this workshop have continued to work for human rights and women's rights subsequently and one of them is still very central to the movement. This is only a small fraction of the international meetings and conferences regularly attended by the leaders of the NGOs dedicated to stopping violence against women in these countries.

COMPARISONS

Thus, a basic set of social service strategies circulates globally. These strategies are appropriated and translated into local social and cultural conditions. Despite claims to national distinctiveness, approaches to gender violence in all of these countries take place within a shared discourse of feminism and social work. The activists who develop these strategies are part of a transnational feminist movement whose members routinely meet and exchange ideas at transnational conferences and through publications and the Internet. Transnationally educated national elites and expatriates play critical roles in the transfer of service intervention models. Expatriate communities contributed to the relatively early and extensive adoption of services in Fiji and Hong Kong. Many of the leaders of gender violence interventions in these countries traveled widely for their academic education and now journey to conferences around the world.

Despite talk about the need to indigenize these approaches, they are the same feminist ideas and techniques rephrased in local cultural terms. In Hong Kong, for example, the power and control wheel is translated into Cantonese. Examples of independent women are drawn from Chinese history and Confucianism in a process one scholar described as "Chinese packaging." Men's groups in Hong Kong emphasize Western ideas of gender equality rather than Chinese concepts of lineage solidarity or Confucian family harmony. Similarly, advocates in India draw on images from Hindu mythology of strong, independent women, but they still see gender inequality as the basic problem and understand battering as the product of social and economic conditions. While family and economic systems shape the opportunities for exit and the costs of leaving, the basic approach to controlling male violence is surprisingly similar across these broad economic, political, and social differences.

THE MEANINGS OF CULTURE

Insofar as culture is discussed in social service settings, the concept is more like contentious culture than tradition or national identity, ideas common in national and transnational human rights debates. The national and local level social service providers I talked to rarely blamed culture in any simple or essentialized way for the violence women encountered. Although activists thought that cultural beliefs supported domestic violence, they focused on state indifference, a lack of services, and a failure of laws and their implementation. The inability to find a satisfactory life outside marriage was often mentioned, not as a problem of culture but as a difficulty with housing, social stigma, and economic survival. They recognized variations by religion, region, urbanism, and social class in the extent to which women experienced violence and could leave their family situations but did not see women trapped by culture. Female feticide is recognized as a growing problem in India, for example, but it is attributed to patriarchal views found in only some regions in the north of the country.

Sometimes culture was described as contributing to violence for minorities or people in rural areas. National minority or immigrant characteristics were raised in discussions of the Muslim community in India and the mainlanders in Hong Kong. In China, activist leaders sometimes attributed the problem in rural areas to "feudal ideologies" because there "traditional feudal concepts and customs are stronger" (Wang 1999a: 1502). In Hong Kong, a disproportionate number of shelter residents are women from mainland China, and their greater vulnerability to violence is understood as a product of their more traditional culture as well as their isolation from networks of family support. Chan Ko Ling, on the basis of his study of male batterers in Hong Kong, argues that it is not traditional culture that is at fault but rigid gender-role expectations in the face of rapid economic and social changes and a changing status for women (2000). He advocates a Chinese approach that emphasizes face and the man's responsibility for the family as well as gender equality.

Allowing local community control over programs is one way to help them adapt to local cultural and social conditions. For example, Merilyn Tahi has been running the Vanuatu Women's Centre for many years and, with funding from the Australian aid agency AusAID through the Fiji Women's Crisis Centre (FWCC) has set up about eighteen local committees in different parts of the country. These committees are working to develop violence intervention programs in their communities. In my interview with her and in her lectures, she stressed the importance of bringing the local chiefs or church pastors into the process, inviting them to meetings, including them in discussions with her when she comes from the capital, and getting them involved in opposing domestic violence. Several grass-roots activists have developed strategies for involving local male and female leaders. These are examples of efforts to tailor programs to local cultural conditions in a way that recognizes and works through the power relationships of the local community.

Thus, local activists doing service delivery tend to see culture not as a reified entity but as a set of resources. If donors do not allow grassroots control of programs, they may import notions of "culture" from the transnational domain rather than allowing local groups to define for themselves what culture means at that particular moment and place. There is an important difference between a top-down program seeking to be culturally sensitive in terms of an essentialized idea of culture and a locally controlled program that recognizes the complexity of local cultural ideas but allows local groups to tailor the program to the power dynamics and symbolic resources of the situation in which they work.

Human Rights Advocacy

Human rights advocates rely on the international legal system far more than local social service providers do. International treaties and principles can be incorporated into national legal systems either by legislation or by reference in judicial decisions. Human rights are also promoted by human rights commissions that handle individual complaints. It is primarily at the highest levels of government that international human rights instruments are important. National NGOs, national commissions for women, human rights commissions, and the upper layers of the judiciary are most likely to invoke international human rights treaties. These international standards may be used to interpret the meaning of gender equality for constitutional jurisprudence (Economic and Social Commission 1997: 14).

In contrast to the social service tier, human rights advocacy is primarily an activity of national and transnational elites. By and large, these ideas have little resonance at the grass roots. The major actors in human rights advocacy at the national level are typically educated, transnational elites who are part of the same transnational world as those who serve as experts and government representatives in UN meetings. Many are lawyers, academics, or NGO leaders. Political and economic elites in postcolonial societies often feel that they belong to the modern transnational world more than the local village one. Although many retain ties to their villages, some elites in Delhi, Beijing, and Hong Kong view the rural village as farther away than London, Paris, and New York.

In none of the countries I studied did activists think human rights were widely understood in poor communities. Even for countries with a British colonial legal legacy, human rights are far less salient than national rights at the grass roots. In India, for example, many people said that although rights language in general was widespread, knowledge of human rights and of specific documents such as CEDAW was limited to those working internationally. Delhi activists working on violence against women said that the national discourse of rights is far more important for promoting reforms in the area of gender violence than international human rights principles. According to a leader in the Joint Women's Program in Delhi, only women's groups are aware of CEDAW. CEDAW is good for lobbying at high levels with government officials such as those in the Department of Women and Child Development, but poor urban and rural people do not understand these ideas (interview, October 2001). For most people, the Indian Constitution is the basis for rights. A prominent feminist lawyer in Delhi, the director of the Women's Rights Initiative of the Lawyers' Collective, said that she uses local laws rather than international conventions in her cases, but international laws can be invoked in support of arguments as a form of setting standards, perhaps influencing judges who have open minds toward international treaties. A member of the Human Rights Commission in India told me that the Indian Constitution is so strong that most people draw their faith in rights from that document and pay little attention to the international standards (interview, October 2001).

A central feature of human rights advocacy is generating international pressure on one's own government. By appropriating human rights language, advocates gain access to international expertise, funding, and political pressure that may influence decisions at home. There are symbolic, economic, and institutional pressures on states to conform to the norms of the international community. International pressure is important for countries concerned about international opinion and economically dependent on international trade, aid, and investment. Large and economically powerful countries, such as China with its vast markets, can more easily resist this pressure (see Foot 2000). As CEDAW experts point out, the impact of their concluding comments depends on the pressure that national NGOs can mobilize. Some NGOs, such as Sakshi, in India use international law itself as a resource.[7]

International donors are as important for human rights advocates as they are for social service providers. Advocacy organizations, human rights education programs, and conferences where governmental and NGO leaders learn the treaty-monitoring process, all require donors, as does NGO attendance at UN meetings. UN agencies such as UNIFEM and UNICEF usually have national or regional offices that develop programs and promote transnational policies and sometimes fund NGO participation in UN events. On the basis of my discussions with Ford Foundation representatives in India and other donors at UN meetings, observations of international funding procedures, and participation on the board of a regional NGO, it appears that international donors allow some flexibility in specific projects but set the general agenda. A funder may wish to support human rights education, for example, but allow local groups to determine how to carry this out. This means that the broad agendas for intervention are defined internationally although the scope of work is defined locally.

The rest of this chapter discusses four specific ways that international human rights law shapes policy toward violence against women. First, human rights ideas may be incorporated into domestic law through legislation or judicial decision-making. Second, human rights commissions and women's commissions encourage citizens to complain about their problems in human rights terms. Third, international workshops and training programs educate the judiciary about the treaty process, human rights standards, and treaties such as CEDAW. International and national donors also sponsor programs to provide human rights education and advocacy at the grass roots. And fourth, the frequent demands for country reports, NGO shadow reports, and attendance at UN meetings and conferences encourages stocktaking by governments and fosters communication between government and civil society.

INCORPORATION OF CEDAW THROUGH
LEGISLATION AND JUDICIAL DECISIONS

In most countries, particularly those that follow the UK model, ratified treaties do not automatically become state law but must be incorporated through legislation and administrative regulation or indirectly through judicial interpretations of court cases (Economic and Social Commission 1997: 12). In India, for example, ratified treaties do not have the force of law without an additional act of Parliament (interview October 2001). A former Supreme Court justice of India, now on the Human Rights Commission, said when I interviewed her that the Indian Constitution is actually better than the international instruments since it can be enforced. But the international documents can be used to interpret the laws. A 1997 Supreme Court judgment on sexual harassment in the workplace, which this judge wrote (Vishaka v. State of Rajasthan, AIR 1997 SC 3011), provided guidelines proscribing sexual harassment in the workplace. The opinion used CEDAW in support of its decision (National Commission for Women 2001: 6–7). A UN study found that the Indian superior courts have used constitutional interpretation creatively to develop a human rights jurisprudence, providing an example for other countries in the region (Economic and Social Commission 1997: 29). New legislation can draw on international treaties. The Indian 2001 draft domestic violence law mentions CEDAW and the UN Declaration on the Elimination of All Forms of Violence against Women, while a UN document advocating a uniform civil code for personal laws in South Asia notes that international principles can serve as the standard for these new laws (Economic and Social Commission 1997: 24). Both the Family Law Act in Fiji and the Law of the People's Republic of China on the Protection of Women's Rights and Interests are based on CEDAW.

Attorneys may also refer to international law in their briefs. A former chief justice of the Indian Supreme Court, interviewed in October 2001, said that it is common for briefs to the Supreme Court to refer to international human rights treaties. For example, a case filed in the Supreme Court in 1994 by Women's Action Research and Legal Action for Women (Writ Petition [Civil] No. 684 of 1994) used CEDAW (Jethmalani 1995: 106–7). The petition asked the court to order the government to show what steps were being taken to end discrimination in the personal laws consistent with the principles of CEDAW and relied on the preliminary report of Radhika Coomaraswamy and the 1994 Protection of Human Rights Act of India. The petition suggests that initial efforts should be directed toward the personal laws of Hindus until other groups are ready to change their personal laws. It focuses on gender inequalities in Hindu laws of inheritance, adoption, and guardianship (Jethmalani 1995: 113, 114–16). When I interviewed the head of Women's Action Research in 2001, the Supreme Court had not yet acted on this petition.

In Fiji, a High Court judge said in a 2003 interview that Section 43:2 of the Fiji Constitution makes provision for applying international law in cases of human rights violations. She looks at court of appeal decisions from the Canadian, Namibian, South African (post-apartheid), and New Zealand supreme courts to see how other countries have applied these international laws. Fiji ratified CEDAW in 1995, but the judge uses conventions that Fiji has not ratified as well for issues such as that on the treatment of offenders. The Fiji Human Rights Commission also relies on international law. When the Fiji government presented its first report to CEDAW in 2002, it said it was reviewing legislation in the light of Convention on the Rights of the Child and CEDAW. A women's rights activist in Fiji said that CEDAW is helpful in rape and family law cases and has been used domestically on several occasions. Judicial decisions in Fiji sometimes rely on CEDAW, such as State v. Filipe Bechu (1999), heard in the magistrate's court.

In the run up to Hong Kong's incorporation into China in 1997, Hong Kong leaders turned enthusiastically to international human rights treaties. The 1991 Basic Law incorporated much of the International Covenant on Civil and Political Rights (ICCPR). CEDAW was ratified in 1996 and was mentioned in debates over social welfare. Hong Kong presented its first report to CEDAW in 1999 with considerable participation by women's NGOs (Erickson and Byrnes 1999: 359–61). In March 1999, the Home Affairs Panel of the Legislative Council held hearings to consider the concluding comments and the government's response to them. Although it did not accept the major recommendations of the committee, especially the creation of national machinery for women's issues, Erickson and Byrnes argue that the reporting exercise still forced government officials to engage in analysis and justification of their policies in light of the convention's requirements in front of the Legislative Council and the international community (1999: 363–64).

Although China ratified CEDAW in 1980, the government has only recently made efforts to educate the people about it. There are ongoing debates about whether or not CEDAW can be considered law (interview May 2001). A feminist journalist in Beijing said that she finds the UN's documents and mechanisms useful for her activism and another journalist said that the national-level support for interventions in violence against women is far less than the international support (interviews 2001). CEDAW is sometimes used by feminist lawyers in their arguments. For example, a lawyer I interviewed at the Centre for Women's Law Studies and Legal Services of Peking University in Beijing, one of the most influential centers on women's rights in China, said that the center sometimes referred to CEDAW in their complaints (interview May 2001). In one case, CEDAW was not mentioned in the final judgment but reference to it in the briefs probably helped the center prevail.

HUMAN RIGHTS COMMISSIONS AND WOMEN'S COMMISSIONS

National and state commissions are important institutional mechanisms for implementing international treaties. These are typically government-funded but semiautonomous institutions that advise on policy and receive and manage complaints. India and Fiji have human rights commissions and Hong Kong has an Equal Opportunity Commission. Both India and Hong Kong have National Women's Commissions. These commissions are, of course, transnational transplants. The Human Rights Commission in India was established in 1993 by the Human Rights Protection Act. It provides a forum for the investigation of human rights violations including those against women (see generally Mohapatra 2001). About 70,000 people file complaints every year at India's Human Rights Commission, mostly about police behavior. In the area of women's rights, complaints are about dowry deaths, reproductive rights, rape, and female feticide. The commission will investigate the complaint and make recommendations to the government. The number of complaints has increased dramatically from 400 in the first year to about 70,000 in the late 1990s, according to the annual reports of the commission. In 2001 I interviewed one of the five members of the commission who is a former chief justice of the Supreme Court. She said that many people from the villages complain and that this avenue of complaining is spreading. They get faxes from the villages, as well as postcards, telegrams, and letters. She thought that world conferences, such as the 1993 Vienna Conference on Human Rights, helped to generate an increasing interest in human rights. Interest in human rights seems to be spreading into the countryside. The commission makes policy proposals to Parliament and has recently pushed hard for reform of Hindu personal laws to eliminate ceilings on maintenance for women after divorce (interview 2001). The NGO developing a new domestic violence law consulted the commission on several occasions. In 2001 the Human Rights Commission defined female feticide as a human rights violation after an investigation into the sharp disparity in numbers between boys and girls aged 0–6 in certain provinces revealed in a recent census.

Fiji established its Human Rights Commission in 1999 as an autonomous body supported by the government (interview with director, February 2002). Although its primary focus is labor relations, it also supports women's rights. It works on the prevention of sexual harassment in the workplace and does considerable education and outreach promoting human rights. Decisions of the commission frequently refer to UN treaties. The director is from Fiji, but spent 14 years in New Zealand and has both a Ph.D. and a law degree. She is a member of a prominent family in Fiji. She travels widely internationally and knows judicial and legal leaders around the world. The commission played an important role in facilitating international scrutiny of Fiji's racial policies, cooperating with the committee monitoring the Convention on the Elimination of Racial Discrimination (CERD) in 2002. During the CERD hearings in 2003, the government published a long statement in the national paper defending it-self against its international critics (*Fiji Times,* March 5, 2003: 15; see also Ecu-menical Centre for Research, Education and Advocacy 2002).

Hong Kong formed the Equal Opportunity Commission instead of a Hu-man Rights Commission. The EOC was developed in 1996 to implement the 1995 Sex Discrimination Ordinance, a law enacted in part to permit the ex-tension of CEDAW to Hong Kong (Byrnes 1999: 13). The Equal Opportunity Commission has broad jurisdiction to review laws, policies, and practices re-lated to gender-based violence and other forms of gender discrimination by the ordinance (Byrnes 1999: 13; Tang, Lee, and Cheung 1999: 51). In a flagship case, the EOC demonstrated that school admissions procedures discriminated against girls and, through litigation, succeeded in changing the policy.

Hong Kong and India have national women's commissions, while the ACWF serves as the political spokesman for women's issues in China. The Na-tional Commission for Women (NCW) in India was set up in 1990 to safeguard women's interests by reviewing legislation, intervening in individual com-plaints, and undertaking remedial actions. It has examined laws, made recom-mendations, and participated in the planning process for women's socioeco-nomic development. It has some autonomy from the government because of its legislative basis. For the NCW, international law is very important. It uses ratified treaties to pressure the government. I interviewed a former member of the commission in 2000 and its member secretary in 2001. According to the member secretary, the commission receives about 5000 complaints a year and either calls the accused into the office and tries to sort out the problem or re-fers the case to state governments and state women's commissions. In 1993–94 the NCW drafted a bill on domestic violence and sent it on to the gov-ernment. The NCW also established *Pariwar Mahila Lok Adalat* (Women's Family Courts) to provide speedy justice to women (NCW Annual Report 1996–97: 7, quoted in Poonacha and Pandey 1999: 179–80). A UNIFEM rep-resentative said only a few had been established by 2000, primarily in urban areas. These courts are for family disputes and use social workers instead of lawyers. They deal largely with divorce, maintenance, marriage, adoption, and dowry (NCW interview January 2000). However, many NGOs complain that the NCW lacks power. For example, a member of the Women's Rights Initia-tive of the Lawyer's Collective complained on an electronic listserve that al-though the NCW did a report on the communal violence in Gujarat in 2002 and referred to CEDAW and other international conventions, the report was weak and did not pinpoint the police's role in this violence (May 20, 2002 post-ing, end-violence listserve).

The Women's Commission in Hong Kong was established by the Hong Kong Special Administrative Region in 2001 after a long period of pressure by Hong Kong women's NGOs and strong support from the CEDAW Committee. Its mandate is to advise the government on strategies for the advancement of women, review service delivery measures, initiate research, and encourage education on women's issues (Leung 2002: 2). At a major conference sponsored by the Women's Commission in 2002, CEDAW was raised as a resource for the women's movement. Yet, the Women's Commission in Hong Kong has also been criticized for its weakness. These transnational institutions operate in relatively similar ways and are clearly part of a single global network of institutions.

INTERNATIONAL HUMAN RIGHTS TRAINING

An important way that human rights ideas and activists circulate globally is through training programs. I encountered several forms of internationally supported human rights training. The UN runs training programs on treaty ratification and report writing that bring together government and NGO representatives as well as international experts such as CEDAW members. A series of workshops in both South Asia and the Pacific organized by UNIFEM and the Division for the Advancement of Women to teach about CEDAW ratification and report writing took place during the 1990s and early 2000s. In the Pacific, there was a subregional meeting on Pacific women in 1980 (Rasmussen 1980), a training program for Pacific nations on the process of ratifying CEDAW in 1991 run by the Division for the Advancement of Women (1991), and a workshop on CEDAW in 1992 (Singh 1992). In 1998, the Secretariat of the Pacific Community held a regional consultative meeting on the implementation of CEDAW (Secretariat of the Pacific Community 1998). In 2001, another workshop on CEDAW took place in Auckland, New Zealand. In 1998–99, FWRM served as the secretariat for CEDAW in Fiji and organized national workshops, local legal literacy training, and media campaigns to increase awareness of its benefits for women (ESCAP 2000: 13–19). This project culminated in a subregional meeting on CEDAW in the Pacific region in 1999 (ESCAP 2000: 63). UNIFEM and several South Pacific regional organizations sponsored a workshop for NGOs and government representatives on report writing in 2003.

A similar series of meetings took place in South Asia. In November 1999 and December 2001, UNIFEM held workshops on CEDAW report writing that brought together government representatives from India, Nepal, Sri Lanka, and the CEDAW Committee, UNIFEM also held pre- and post reporting meetings for Nepal, India, the Maldives, and Sri Lanka.

Some UN workshops focus directly on violence against women. In 2003, the UNIFEM regional office in Fiji held a workshop inspired by a similar one for the Asian region in 2002. Some women from the Pacific attended the earlier workshop and thought that it was needed in the Pacific region. This workshop was part of a UNIFEM global scan to assess the status of violence against women world wide, a project discussed at the 2003 CSW meetings in New York.

Training is also done by national NGOs with international funding. For example, Jagori, one of the oldest women's organizations in India, provides gender training for development projects, including the MS program that produced the nari adalats. In 2001, I visited Jagori's office and resource center in Delhi, a set of small rooms packed floor to ceiling with books and resource materials, desks, and computers and a small staff of energetic young women. The director, Kalpana Vishwanathan, told me that they talk about rights and CEDAW in workshops they run. Although they have not used CEDAW extensively, they refer to the convention to indicate global support for women's rights. Jagori chose to accept donor funds to run its programs, although it recognized that this compromised its autonomy. Its busy office differed from that of other NGOs who refused external funding and achieved greater independence but were not able to maintain an office, staff, and services.

In 1997, some women activists in China approached the ACWF and offered to do training in gender awareness. They used a UNDP training manual, *Gender and Development* that I had also seen in India to provide participatory gender-training seminars for judges, court personnel, members of the ACWF, hospital staff, police, and subdistrict leaders (interview May 2001). Many of the participants resisted at first because they were used to a far more authoritarian style of teaching instead of sitting in a circle and talking. Over time, many came to like it. In my interview with the feminist journalist who ran these programs, she spoke Chinese to an interpreter but used the words for "facilitators" and "trainees" in English, suggesting that this training approach was originally in English. There are very few NGOs in China and those that exist are largely dependent on foreign funding.

In Fiji, the FWRM has worked since 1993 on legal literacy campaigns, focusing on CEDAW and women's rights (FWRM 2000: 2–3). It seeks to improve the socioeconomic and political status of women through legislative and attitudinal change (FWRM 2000: 8). It handles complaints, provides paralegal services, and serves as an advocacy and lobbying group for women's human rights in a wide range of areas. Some of the FWRM leaders attended the Global Leadership Institute for Women's Organizations at the Center for Women's Global Leadership at Rutgers University in 1997 (FWRM 2000: 25). The Regional Rights Resource Team (RRRT) grew out of FWRM. Since 1995 it has provided grassroots human rights education focused on women's rights and CEDAW. In 2003 RRRT was working in Vanuatu, Kiribati, and Fiji with funding from the British government. In 1999, the crisis center, FWCC, received A$2.2 million for five years from AusAID, the Australian government's aid agency, to provide counseling and community education and to develop a Pacific network of programs addressing violence against women (Fiji Women's Crisis Centre, *Pacific Women against Violence* 5 [4]: 3). Funding for Pacific human rights programs comes largely from wealthy Pacific donor countries such as Australia, New Zealand, and Japan as well as Britain and Canada.

International foundation or government funding is essential to these programs. Many of the programs I visited in Delhi, Beijing, and Fiji had international donor funding, as did the major research study on domestic violence in Beijing. I talked to Macarthur and Ford program officers in Delhi who said both foundations are interested in funding human rights and women's rights projects. Ford has a budget of about $25 million in India and has had a program there for fifty years; in China the Ford program is a little over ten years old (interview with Ford official Oct. 2001). In India, 50 percent of the human rights work is on women's rights, both in funds and in proportion of grantees. The human rights program officer in Delhi said that most of these projects work on violence against women, sexual harassment, domestic violence or women's property and inheritance. Ford also supported groups going to Beijing and Beijing Plus Five. A sociology professor I interviewed in Delhi in 2001 said that since the late 1990s, human rights have become increasingly important as the basis for funding. She both welcomed the ideas and worried that NGOs often operate outside the state with little accountability.

In China, the Ford Foundation now funds community legal services and university-based programs such as legal education. My trip to China in May 2001 was funded by a grant from Ford to develop university training in the sociology of law. It provided me the opportunity to interview many activists and academics working to reduce violence against women, including those in the DVRIP research project on domestic violence. Because I heard about the DVRIP project in 2001, I was invited to attend the final conference in November 2002 as one of nine international participants. The Ford program in China defines its work as falling in the area of rule of law, governance, and judicial administration. Hong Kong, in contrast, no longer receives international funding because of its affluence. Human rights advocacy and social services are now supported by the government or by local funders, such as the Jockey Club.

According to officials at Ford, their general practice is to decide on a focus and consider proposals or look for groups that do work in this area. They may encourage groups to take up such issues. Once a project is started, they try not to direct it, although there are differences in the personalities of program officers. Program officers recognize the power imbalance between them and the recipients and that any comments they make may be taken as authoritative. In Delhi, both the Ford Foundation program officer and one of its recipients, the Lawyer's Collective, said that although the funder sets the general agenda, the recipient has considerable flexibility in how the work is carried out. Close scrutiny is reserved mostly for questions of finances and accountability. Another feminist Indian NGO said that the funders set the issues and the organization has to respond. For example, they now do a lot of gender training because all the funders insist on including gender training in their programs. Ford recipients in China said that they discussed the project with them at some length but had a free hand to work it out as they wanted. Thus, the extensive training and educational programs funded by foreign governments and foundations on behalf of human rights draw people together transnationally, promote global ideas, and reflect agendas that circulate globally.

UN EVENTS AND NGO-GOVERNMENT COLLABORATION

UN events punctuate the exchange of information among NGOs and governments. They are fundamental to transnational consensus building, program transplants, and the localization of transnational knowledge. UN conferences and commission meetings provide NGOs opportunities to work together at the national and international level and to work with their governments in what is often a more accessible environment. When government representatives and NGOs prepare country reports and make presentations about the conditions in their countries in international forums, they are often forced to talk to each other. Writing reports together fosters interchange, even when governments and NGOs do not agree. UN training for convention ratification and report writing typically includes both NGO and government representatives.

Large meetings such as the 1995 Fourth World Conference on Women in Beijing spread human rights ideas to those who participate and beyond. These world conferences pull together large numbers of NGO representatives — about 30,000 in Beijing — plus government delegations that include both

NGOs and government representatives. A large proportion of the activists and academics I interviewed had attended the Beijing meeting and many said they found it transformative. Even a woman from the tiny Pacific nation of Kiribati whom I met at the Fiji Women's Crisis Centre said she went to Beijing and was very impressed by the excitement of the event, all the marching, carrying of placards, and assertion of opinions. In India, I met a 60-year-old woman activist living in a remote rural village who described her first plane ride and her trip to Beijing with great excitement. Feminists I interviewed in Beijing all agreed that the conference had galvanized work on domestic violence and made clear the links with women's health and the enjoyment of human rights. Many of the reforms I heard about in Beijing in 2001 and 2002 dated from the 1995 conference. People I talked to throughout the Asia-Pacific region referred to the Beijing Platform for Action. In Fiji, the Platform for Action served as the basis for the government's Women's Plan of Action drawn up in 1998.

Since the late 1990s, both UNIFEM and UNICEF have incorporated more of a rights perspective in their work. UNICEF organized two conferences on violence against women and girls in South Asia in 1997 and 1999, for example (UNICEF 1999). While UNICEF supports the Convention on the Rights of the Child, UNIFEM has been increasingly active in supporting the CEDAW process. After 1998, UNIFEM put more emphasis on sending NGO representatives to CEDAW meetings, often through the International Women's Rights Action Watch of Asia Pacific, based in Malaysia. In an interview in India in 2001, a UNIFEM staff member told me that UNIFEM supported NGO participation in the CEDAW process by training governments and NGOs in report preparation and by sending NGO representatives to CEDAW hearings. When India reported to CEDAW in 2000, UNIFEM encouraged NGOs to prepare a shadow report and sent nine NGO representatives from India. One of those who authored the report said that the experts at CEDAW used the shadow report to ask the government many pointed questions. Under the pressure, inspiration, challenge, and financial support of UNIFEM, NGOs in India brought out a shadow report for Beijing Plus Five called Task Force on Women 2000, according to one of the activists who organized the project. This 80-page report assessed the progress of the government on each of the 12 points of the Platform for Action. The task force had 25 members, but according to one of its leaders, it took considerable networking among the NGOs to get them together and, after completing its task, the task force disbanded (interview 2001).

CEDAW reports also generate consultation between NGOs and governments. In Fiji, several women's NGOs worked with the government on the

CEDAW report and also produced an independent shadow report. Three NGO representatives attended the 2002 CEDAW meetings in New York representing FWRM and RRRT. China also sent a delegation to Beijing Plus Five and organized informational meetings when the delegates returned from the conference. Two factions from Hong Kong went to Beijing Plus Five, divided between a more establishment and a more feminist group. Two working groups from China went to Beijing Plus Five, one on media and one on violence against women (interview 2001). The working group against domestic violence, made up of four China NGOs (the Women's Legal Research and Service Center, the Female Counseling and Developing Center of the Social Work Department of the Chinese Women's College, the Maple Women's Center, and the ShanXi Women's Legal Research and Service Center) prepared two reports for Beijing Plus Five. The reports discussed government and NGO actions against domestic violence and were funded by Hong Kong Oxfam (China Working Group 2000a and 2000b). Two NGO observers watched China make its report to CEDAW in 1999 and an expert from China sits on the CEDAW Committee. However, the shadow report by Human Rights in China, a New York-based NGO, and three other NGOs outside China complained that the government's 1999 CEDAW report failed to incorporate the substantial research and publication within China on women's status. It failed to circulate the report or to allow these groups to participate in its preparation even though the report was produced by the ACWF (Human Rights in China 1998: 5, 12–13, 27).

Thus, UN events and conferences provide rich opportunities for collaboration and conversation among NGOs and governments domestically and internationally. The British Commonwealth sponsors other international collaborations such as a conference sponsored by the Commonwealth Secretariat in the mid-1990s in Hong Kong for Commonwealth countries on using CEDAW in domestic courts (Byrnes, Conners, and Bik 1996) and regular meetings among Commonwealth countries and their judiciaries.

Conclusions

Social service programs and human rights advocacy are complementary. Although human rights workers are usually transnational NGO and government elites while social service providers are more often middle-class professionals, the two initiatives support each other. The successful delivery of services, such as shelters and support groups, may create a greater rights consciousness among service recipients. Programs encourage clients to define themselves as rights-bearing individuals. Rights-conscious clients are more willing to support other human rights projects. Moreover, leaders of social service NGOs themselves become important promoters of transnational human rights. They often attend international meetings, write shadow reports, and pressure their governments with UN documents and concluding comments. Some push governments to write more thoughtful reports to international treaty bodies. Many find that their governments are more responsive and more vulnerable to shaming at international meetings. At home, NGO leaders and their rights-conscious clientele promote human rights institutions that respond to rights claims. Thus, the provision of services framed in rights terms fosters the development of rights consciousness by middle-level social service providers and grassroots service recipients and generates pressure on governments to expand their human rights systems.

On the other side, human rights advocacy at the national level creates political space for local social service delivery focused on women's rights. Those eager to expand services for women find that nationally ratified international documents help to mobilize national support. Human rights commissions and women's commissions generate political support for rights initiatives. In countries with few social service resources, the provision of services is shaped less by domestic political agendas and more by international definitions of problems and solutions since these are the principal funders.

This chapter has described how transnational feminist approaches to violence against women have been appropriated by country-based activists and tailored to specific contexts. The most striking finding is the extent to which, despite significant variation in cultural background, political power, and history of each country, the palette of reforms is similar. Domestic violence laws are developed through prototypes in other countries; shelters and other services are built on Euro-American models; community education campaigns and brochures conform to modern communication techniques; and surveys rely on shared social science methodologies. Countries develop similar commissions to support women's human rights. These are not parallel inventions but the product of transnational flows of knowledge, actors, programs, and funds. Mechanisms such as UN conferences foster circulation and exchange, drawing people from different countries together to learn about activities in other countries. The circulation is never free, however, but always channeled by global inequalities in wealth and power.

Transnational programs and ideas are translated into local cultural terms, but this occurs at a relatively superficial level, as a kind of window dressing. The laws and programs acquire local symbolic elaboration, but retain their fundamental grounding in transnational human rights concepts of autonomy, individualism, and equality The programs are appropriated and translated but not fully indigenized. To blend completely with the surrounding social world is to lose the radical possibilities of human rights. It is the unfamiliarity of these ideas that makes them effective in breaking old modes of thought, for example, denaturalizing male privilege to use violence against women as a form of discipline. On the other hand, it is only when they take a familiar form that they are readily adopted. Like the tee shirt developed by the Aboriginal teenagers, human rights are appropriated when they draw on transnational ideas but present them in familiar cultural terms. These appropriations promote global cultural homogeneity, but the impact is greater on transnational elites and middle-level NGO activists than on people at the grass roots.

Localizing Human Rights and Rights Consciousness

How do people come to see their problems as human rights violations? How are human rights incorporated into local cultural systems? In this chapter I examine the process of *localizing transnational knowledge* of rights. In the preceding chapters I showed that despite the divide between transnational activists and national and local leaders, human rights concepts and approaches are being energetically appropriated and adapted to local contexts. But do poor urban and rural women think about their problems in human rights terms? Has this movement changed rights consciousness at the grass roots? Have those most vulnerable and in need of rights protection recognized their entitlements and asserted their rights? Human rights must become part of local legal consciousness in order to fulfill their emancipatory potential, yet activists in several countries told me that the knowledge of human rights within village communities was quite limited. Moreover, even in the United States, reputed to be a highly rights-conscious place, research indicates considerable reluctance to assert rights even among disabled people who have a clear legal basis for these rights (Engel and Munger 2003). In this chapter I use two case studies to explore when and how powerless people take on a rights framework for understanding their problems.

Many have argued that in order for human rights to be culturally legitimate, they must fit into existing normative structures and ways of thinking (An-Naʿim 1992b; Ignatieff 2001). An-Naʿim, for example, argues that human rights in Islamic countries are most effective when they use Islamic models and approaches (1992b, 2002). Presenting human rights ideas through culturally familiar images and sources of authority, such as the Qu'ran in Islamic societies, facilitates their adoption. However, it is the challenge that human rights conceptions offer to traditional ways of understanding relationships that gives them their power to change local legal consciousness. An-Na'im recognizes this dilemma in his proposal for a crosscultural dialogue on human rights. He envisions a conversation over incompatible values that respects cultural difference and at the same time asserts the importance of universal standards (1992b; 2002). His solution is a pragmatic one, focused on developing dialogues within and among countries. The activists described in the last chapter and this one often use such pragmatic, dialogic approaches to localizing human rights ideas.

Yet, in the area of violence against women, human rights ideas are powerful precisely because they offer a radical break from the view that violence is natural and inevitable in intimate relations between men and women. Defined as a human rights violation, gender violence becomes a crime against the state that the state must punish. In the United States, redefining battering as a crime rather than a life-style choice encouraged women to resist the violence and persuaded the criminal justice system to take the offense more seriously. The power of human rights, like the power of criminalization in domestic law, is its capacity to challenge existing social relationships and power structures. Indeed, human rights ideas are appealing because they provide a radically different frame for thinking about the relations of power and inequality in society. In the French Revolution, asserting rights was a way to demand radical social change (Chanock 2002). Human rights today are legitimated by their origins in transnational consensus-building processes and packaged by translators into local cultural terms.

In examining how grassroots individuals take on human rights ideas, I argue that the rights framework does not displace other frameworks but adds a new dimension to the way individuals think about problems. In both case studies women who are angry about the way their relatives have treated them turn to rights, but rights are only one way of thinking about their injuries and about justice. Many women in these two places attributed their injuries to their relatives' failure to abide by the norms of kinship and care. Local activists and reformers encouraged them to see their injuries as violations of their rights that the state is obligated to protect. In adopting this framework, victims do not abandon their earlier perspectives but layer the rights framework over that of kinship obligations. These grassroots individuals take on human rights discourse through a double subjectivity as rights-bearers and as injured kinsmen and survivors. There is not a merging and blending, but two somewhat distinct sets of ideas and meanings that coexist. It is possible that over time, and with shifting circumstances, one of these identities will become stronger at the expense of the other.

Yet, adopting a human rights subjectivity does not happen quickly or easily. It is a slow process. It means adopting a new sense of self that incorporates rights and testing it experimentally to see if it makes a difference. Only if there is institutional support for this perspective will this new subjectivity be sustained. A feedback model that emphasizes responses to rights claims provides the best explanation for how people take on rights consciousness. In the previous chapter I examined how human rights ideas were transplanted through rights-based social services and human rights activities. In this chapter I look at the impact of these reforms on their targets: the people who experience injuries in their daily lives that have been defined as human rights violations.

Battered Women in Hawai'i

The battered-women's movement in the United States has long encouraged abused women to see their violation as a crime and to turn to the legal system for help (Schechter 1982: 157–83; Schneider 2000: 44–49). Yet, my research in Hawai'i during the 1990s showed that despite considerable emphasis on rights by shelter staff and court advocates, battered women are often slow to take on rights. Even after calling the police for help and filing for temporary restraining orders, battered women are likely to drop the restraining order or refuse to testify. They clearly fear retaliation by the batterer, but they also resist the shift in subjectivity required by the law. This is often a sense of self deeply at odds with others rooted in family, religion, and community. Taking on a rights-defined self in relation to a partner requires a substantial identity change both for the woman and for the man she is accusing. Instead of seeing herself defined by family, kin, and work relationships, she is invited to take on a more autonomous self protected by the state. At the same time, her actions allow the law to define her husband/partner as a criminal under the surveillance and control of the state. A battered woman may be pressured by kin to feel she is a bad wife, while her partner may claim she is taking away his masculinity. The only way she can rescue him from this loss is to deflect the very legal sanctions she has called down upon him. It is hardly surprising that abused women will ask for help from the law, back away, and then ask again. Such women appear to be difficult or "bad" victims since they typically file charges, then try to drop them, or fail to appear for restraining order hearings. Yet, these women are tacking back and forth across a significant line of identity transformation.

The adoption of a rights-defined identity under identity-shifting circumstances such as battering depends on the individual's experience with the law. One of the powerful consequences of bringing gender violence cases to the attention of the legal system is the victim's and perpetrator's encounters with the new subjectivity defined within the discourses and practices of the law. Interactions with police officers, prosecutors, probation officers, judges, shelter workers, feminist advocates and even bailiffs affect the extent to which an individual victim is willing to take on this new identity. Do the police make an arrest or tell him to take a walk? Does the prosecutor press charges or nolle pros (i.e., fail to prosecute) the case? Does the judge impose prison time or dismiss the case? Does she offer a stern lecture or mumble the charge and penalty? These are all indications of how seriously the legal system takes her rights. If the police are friendly to the man and fail to arrest him, if the judge suggests that battering is not a serious offense, and if the court imposes no prison sentence, this experience undermines the woman's rights subjectivity. If police act as if women do not have the right to complain about the violence of their husbands, battered women are discouraged from seeing themselves that way. If their partners, relatives, friends, and neighbors tell battered women that a "good wife" does not take her husband to court and that he was violent because she provoked him, she may also be deterred. Thus, an individual's willingness to take on rights depends on her experience in trying to assert them. The more state institutions reflect back serious attention to her as a person with rights not to be battered, the more willing she will be to take on this identity. On the other hand, if these rights are treated as insignificant, she may give up and no longer think about her grievances in terms of rights.

My ten years of research on battered women in Hawai'i showed that women gradually took on a sense of themselves as people whose rights had been violated with continued experience with the law (Merry 2003). They initially imagined themselves as wives or girlfriends injured by those who loved them, seeing their grievances in terms of specific wrongs committed by particular people who violated codes of marriage and intimacy. As in many other parts of the United States, such injuries were often experienced as painful and debilitating, but not as violations of the woman's rights. Instead, the injuries formed a part of gendered relationships. A woman reported, for example, that when she complained to her mother about violence from her husband her mother said that she had made her bed and now she had to sleep in it. Until the battered-women's movement of the 1970s and 1980s, violence in gendered relationships was seen as a natural, albeit regrettable, fact of life.

However, as they turned to women's centers for help, battered women heard that violence was a violation of their rights. As a result of extensive pressure, laws were passed naming domestic violence as a criminal offense and police were encouraged to arrest, prosecutors to press charges, and courts to sentence convicted batterers to prison and/or to batterer education programs. Women began to think of themselves as having rights and of "standing up for themselves," but they also continued to see themselves as wives, girlfriends, and daughters who had been hurt by those they loved now or at least had loved in the past. When asked during support group meetings how they thought of themselves, these women were more likely to say they were survivors than that they had rights. Thus, the women developed a double consciousness of injury, both as people whose relatives failed to treat them properly and as people whose rights had been violated.

To explore subjectivities produced by the encounter with the legal system, my research assistants and I interviewed 30 women and 21 men about their experiences with the legal system, and their reactions to the experience. We did this research in the small town of Hilo, Hawai'i, a place typical of rural agricultural regions of the United States but different in its colonial and plantation past and contemporary ethnic diversity (see Merry 2000). All of those interviewed had experiences with the family court and/or the district court as well as participating in a court-mandated batterer intervention program or women's support group. The interviews were supplemented by observing many hours of discussion within women's support groups and men's batterers groups.[1] These interviews were part of a larger project that involved observations of criminal and family court hearings, men's violence-control training programs, women's support groups, and discussions with judges, prosecutors, probation officers, feminist activists, and members of the community (see Merry 1995a, 1995b, 2001a).

The town of Hilo is a small port city of about 45,000 that serves a sprawling agricultural region and provides a hub for governmental, educational, medical, and retail services as well as some tourism. Local feminists started a shelter in Hilo in 1978 (Rodriguez 1988) and in 1986, working with an active and committed local judiciary developed a violence-control program that offered training for batterers and a women's support group. The dominant ethnic groups in the town are Japanese-Americans, whites, Native Hawaiians, Filipino-Americans, Portuguese, along with people with ancestries from Korea, China, Puerto Rico, South Pacific islands, and Mexico (see Merry 2001a).

In this town, the number of cases in court of violence against women expanded dramatically over the last twenty-five years, particularly during the period of the early 1990s. While the population of the county surrounding this town has doubled over the last 25 years, the number of calls to the police for help has grown eight times, the number of requests for protective orders has jumped from one or two a year to 710 in 1998, and the number of arrests for abuse of a family or household member from none to over 1200 reports to the police and 855 cases in the courts in 1998. This dramatic increase in the number of court cases of wife beating may reflect an increase in battering, but it also shows a major increase in seeking help from the law. In most cases, the victim has taken the initiative to call the police for help or to ask the family court for a restraining order. Those who call on the legal system for help have taken a step toward seeing themselves as defined by the promises and protections of rights even in the domain of the family. At the same time, there have been substantial changes in law, the police, and especially the courts that have encouraged women to use the law. And, most important, a strong battered-women's movement in Hilo has developed a shelter, a women's support group, and a batterer's intervention program in the town and has done substantial community education.

SHIFTING SUBJECTIVITIES

The poststructuralist concept of the self as the location of multiple and potentially contradictory subjectivities, each established within discourses and discursive practices, provides a helpful way to conceptualize the complex positioning of women who turn to the law in crises of violence. In Henrietta Moore's description of the poststructuralist gendered subject, each individual takes up multiple subject positions within a range of discourses and social practices, so that a single subject is not the same as a single individual (1994: 141). What holds these multiple subjectivities together are the experience of identity, the physical grounding of the subject in a body, and the historical continuity of the subject. "If subjectivity is seen as singular, fixed, and coherent, it becomes very difficult to explain how it is that individuals constitute their sense of self—their self-representations as subjects—through several, often mutually contradictory subject positions, rather than through one singular subject position" (Moore 1994: 141). Instead of seeing a single gender system, anthropology has moved toward understanding gender by examining how "individuals come to take up gendered subject positions through engagement with multiple discourses on gender" (1994: 142). Although this framework appears to emphasize choice, Moore stresses that there are dominant and subdominant discourses that are both reproduced and in some ways resisted. This model opens up the possibility of multiple femininities and masculinities within the same context, onto which gender differences are again inscribed, so that some masculinities appear more feminine and others more masculine, with the hierarchical relationship between the genders reinscribed on these variations within a gender in a particular social context (1994: 146–47). Moore notes that this theory of gender as consisting of multiple, possibly contradictory competing discourses enables the question, how do people take up a position in one discourse rather than another? (1994: 149).

This framework provides a way of thinking about battered women's experience with the law. In going to the law, a woman takes on a new subject position, defined in the discourses and social practices of the law. She tries it on, not abandoning her other subject positions as partner/wife, member of a kinship network that usually includes her partner's family as well as her own, along with other subject positions such as "local," Christian, and poor. She is, in a sense, seeing how it goes. The experimental subject position includes assertiveness, claims to autonomy, and mobilization of the power of the law. The encounter with the courts is an exploration of the dimensions of this position, the experience of taking it on, of seeing how it conforms with or contradicts other subject positions she occupies. There are risks: going to court typically precipitates an angry and hostile response from the partner. Indeed, her assumption of this new legally constituted subject position may be interpreted as a direct challenge to his masculinity. Insofar as women are required to confirm a man's masculinity by their adoption of a feminine subject position, "The inability to maintain the fantasy of power triggers a crisis in the fantasy of identity, and violence is a means of resolving this crisis because it acts to reconfirm the nature of a masculinity otherwise denied" (1994: 154). Violence is then a sign of the struggle for the maintenance of certain fantasies of identity and power. Violence emerges, in this analysis, as deeply gendered and sexualized and as a consequence of her turning to the law for help.

The woman calling the police and pressing charges is thwarting the fantasy of power and identity of masculinity in dominant discourses. As her partner struggles to reassert his masculinity through reestablishing his control over her, she may find her new subject position within the law an alienating and empty one. It may disrupt her relations with her kin and her partner as she is pressured to leave him and turn to a new source of support in social services and legal officials. This is a subject position shaped by the discourses of autonomy, choice, and reasonable behavior, not by love, anger, hurt, and ambivalence. The move into this subject position initiates a period of tension, a continual questioning whether it is worth it. Those who press on are people for whom this new position has something to offer. Or perhaps they have less to lose by antagonizing those who support their partner.

Although there has clearly been a substantial increase in the number of women willing to turn to the courts, many try this position on and discard it, returning to a subjectivity less challenging to their partners and perhaps to their kin. Such discarding can be temporary or permanent; individuals frequently proceed through a long sequence of putting on and taking off this subject position, perhaps holding it a little longer each time, depending on what the discursively constituted position of battered woman has to offer and the extent of contradiction with other subject positions. Indeed, women are choosing between two incompatible subject positions, one the rights-bearing subject, the other the good wife. Each represents a vision of the self that produces self-esteem, but the battered woman cannot simultaneously enact both. Choosing either one represents a failure of the other. The practices of the legal system are thus of critical significance to the woman's decision as she ambivalently moves in and out of this subjectivity. Fragmentary evidence around the country of an explosion of cases in the late 1980s followed by a leveling off in the mid 1990s suggests some deep and enduring ambivalence about the legally defined subject position for situations of battering.[2]

Judith Butler's performative conception of gender provides one way of thinking about the contribution of law. There is no "natural" or presocial sex: it is the doing of gender that creates it. Gender is an identity that is "performatively constituted by the very 'expressions' that are said to be its results" (1990: 25). Among the regulatory practices that generate the identities of gender is law. Following Foucault, Butler argues that juridical power produces what it claims only to represent. "In effect, the law produces and then conceals the notion of a 'subject before the law' in order to invoke that discursive formation as a naturalized foundational premise that subsequently legitimates that law's own regulatory hegemony" (1990: 2). Thus, gender is continually transformed through its performance in legally regulated contexts. It is constituted and reconstituted through regulatory practices such as the law that shift the conditions for performing gender. Thus, a change in legal practices for handling violence in intimate gendered relationships has produced a new doing of gender within a changing system of regulatory constraints.

Gendered subjectivity is redefined by doing legal activities: through acting as a legally entitled subject in the context of these injuries. As women victimized by violence call the police, walk into courtrooms, fill out forms requesting restraining orders, tell their stories of violence and victimization in forms and in response to official queries, they enact a different self. Such performances reshape the way these women think about themselves and the relationship between their intimate social worlds and the law. This means disembedding the individual from the structure of kin, neighbors, friends, and churches in favor of a new relationship to the state. The state's obligation to protect a wife from her husband's violence has until recently not been a recognized aspect of selves even in the legally constituted American society. The idea of the private domain of the family, insulated from state supervision by the patriarchal authority of the husband (although constituted by the state in its capacity to marry and divorce) exists at the level of the taken-for-granted world. The penetration of rights into this patriarchal sphere represents a radical break. The rapid movement of gender violence cases into the courts in the United States reveals a diffusion of a new definition of the self as protected by law from violence even within this sphere. It is not that the right to protection from assault has changed, but that the meaning of the sphere of the family as a private domain secluded from legal scrutiny has changed to one more porous.

It is not surprising, given the significance of this cultural change for concepts of privacy and the family, that there are significant class differences in how much women participate in opening the family to legal surveillance. Wealthy and middle-class women are far less likely to appear in court than poor ones (see Merry 1995a). One of the consequences of opening the family to legal surveillance is a loss of control. The law takes over the case and imposes penalties on the perpetrator, whether or not the victim wishes it. There may also be a public announcement of the problem, at least in court if not in the local newspaper. In Hilo, the town paper prominently publishes the names of all men arrested for abuse of a family and household member or for violation of a protective order, listing them by name, age, and place of residence. As the law has constituted women as legal subjects no longer mediated by their embeddedness in family relationships but standing alone in relation to the state, it has reduced the patriarchal privileges of males within the domain of the family. For poor families, such an opening of the family was already well established by the regulations of welfare and charity in earlier periods as well as ongoing legal control over drinking, child abuse, welfare, and vagrancy.

As women approach the legal system, they encounter widespread lenience concerning these cases. When police fail to arrest, prosecutors to push a case forward, or probation officers to compel an offender to attend the battering program, the rights-endowed self is compromised. As women confront the demand to testify against an offender in open court, unsure of the penalty that will follow but certain of the anger he feels as a result of her testimony, the new subjectivity offered to her by the law appears uncertain and risky. When women find that their batterers are not punished, they see that there are limitations to their rights.

Moreover, the law puts conditions on its help. The new self, now no longer enclosed in the private sphere of the family but constituted by the law, is wrapped in expectations of a continued commitment to prosecution and severing the relationship with the violent man. The good victim in the law is not a woman who fights back, drinks, or takes drugs along with the man, or abuses her children. When women act in violent and provocative ways or refuse to press charges or testify, legal officials are often frustrated. Women who do not fit the image of the good victim become redefined as troublesome and difficult and are likely to receive less assistance. Good victims are also those who follow through with their cases. To begin a legal case, then to drop it, then to go back for another civil protective order (called a temporary restraining order) or to call the police again but not testify in court, earns a woman the label of difficult and "bad" victim. Thus, women's very hesitancy and ambivalence about making this identity change as well as their desire to defend themselves against violent men conspire to define them as "bad" victims and therefore less deserving of legal help.

Thus, turning to the legal system for help is a difficult decision, in which the practices of the legal system itself are critically important. Even when a new law specifically criminalizing gender violence was passed in 1973 in Hawai'i, very few women filed cases. It was only after substantial changes in police practice, the elimination of the requirement to use an attorney to get a temporary restraining order, and greater attention to these cases by prosecutors and judges, that women began to turn to the law in larger numbers. The impact of an active feminist movement in the town as well as greater media attention increased women's willingness to complain. But the new terrain is ambiguous, offering a new legal self protected from violence by men but providing in practice a protection never fully guaranteed or experienced. Even as the law restricts men from using violence to control their partners, it does so in a contingent and variable fashion, incorporating the possibility of unmaking as well as making this change. There is a tension between the construction of new discourses of rights and the practices through which these promises are disclosed which mediates the reconstitution of both male and female subjectivity.

EXPERIENCES OF TURNING TO LAW

The interviews indicate that the encounter with the law affects the way these people think about themselves in fundamental ways, but that there are enormous differences in the impact on men and women. While women respond by trying on and sometimes discarding what they usually see as a more powerful self whose adoption is scary, men resist and reject a diminished self which is not heard, is sometimes humiliated and ignored, and is subject to penalties both restrictive and expensive. The women talk about gaining courage and appreciating the help of the law while the men talk about shock, anger, surprise, and a sense of betrayal by the women who have accused them. In an excruciating turn, the women typically feel some concern and even love for the men they have helped to humiliate while the men find solace in moments when the women drop charges or switch from a no-contact to a contact temporary restraining order. A woman's willingness to join with her partner in opposing or subverting the law recuperates some of his damaged masculine identity and allows him to confront the legal system not as a diminished man whose wife no longer submits but as a strong man who still controls his wife and can count on her support. Thus, the woman assaults his masculinity by turning to the law, adopting its definition of her autonomous personhood and protection from violence, while gaining for herself greater control over his violence and domination in her relationship with him.

Insofar as gender hierarchies are mapped onto these new subjectivities, the woman could be said to become masculinized and the man feminized in this encounter. Concepts of masculinity and femininity are, of course, cultural products, derived from particular histories and highly variable, but within a single social space there is some level of shared understanding. I am referring to these concepts as they are located within the dominant American framework of masculinity and femininity, recognizing that there are regional, ethnic, class, and other variations within this general pattern. In the shape that gender takes within the Hilo community, the woman who gives in and withdraws from the legal process returns to a more feminized self and allows her male partner to recuperate his masculinity. Since gender is produced by such performances, the way that women and men chart courses through the tensions of violence and its legal regulation shapes their gendered selves. As they do law, they also do gender.

It is not surprising that women would adopt a tentative stance toward this transformation — trying it on, dropping it, trying it again — given the significance of the change and the mutually constitutive nature of gender. In a het-erosexual relationship, the way she plays gender affects the way the man with whom she is in relationship can play gender. The move back to the more famil-iar femininity in which the man can oppositionally be a man is undeniably se-ductive, while the stance of refusing femininity opens her to his sense of be-trayal, to the extent to which he is diminished both by the performances of the court and by her very rejection of feminine submissiveness. It is hardly surpris-ing that this position seems scary to women and that they enter and leave it many times before finally seizing it more or less permanently as a new identity. Those women who have fully taken on this subject position no longer express a sense of fear and anxiety about court hearings, instead eagerly pursuing their assailants in court. Such women are not necessarily those most seriously vic-timized, leading some critics to argue that trivial incidents are coming under the scrutiny of the court. They are, however, the women who have moved through a series of experiments and reinforcements from others into a new subjectivity within the law. This probably accounts for what Judith Wittner finds is the court's central problem and most baffling contradiction: "women with the genuine and serious complaints of the type the court was designed to help frequently drop out, while women with the most minor and trivial com-plaints were often those who were most energetic about prosecuting, eager to see the perpetrator punished, and willing to return to court many times" (1998: 88–89). As Ferraro and Pope observe, at the point of arrest there is a dramatic and irreconcilable clash between the culture of power embodied in the law and the relational culture within which battered women live (Ferraro and Pope 1993).

Women's ability and willingness to move into this subjectivity depends, of course, on how the law treats them. As the interviews indicate, the police play a critical role in either taking them seriously or telling them their bruises are in-significant or the assault minor. Women notice if the police chat and joke with the batterer. Both men and women attend closely to the demeanor of the judge, the things she says, and the extent to which penalties are actually imposed. As they move into this subjectivity, the support or opposition of kin and friends, including the man's kin, friends, and other women in the support group, are ex-tremely important. One woman said that when she consulted with her friends, for example, she discovered that they were all in the same boat with her and that they all had battering relationships. They talked about their problems but did not urge her to leave the man. Many of the women I interviewed said that their mothers played a critical role in supporting their rejection of the violence.

The staff of the feminist advocacy program in Hilo, Alternatives to Violence

(ATV), and its shelter also play critical roles in fostering this transformation of self. One woman, for example, said that the support of the ATV advocates in court was very helpful. "They really changed my life around." With the support of other women in the ATV women's support group, this woman said she was able to "tell off" her batterer, letting him know that he was "playing with her mind" and that she wanted him to leave her alone. She said in an interview that in the group she learned that despite her boyfriend's constant insults, she had nothing to feel ashamed of. She was proud of the certificate she received from attending the support group and noted that she and others had framed it and hung it on the wall. Taking on this new identity requires a social shift of some magnitude. For many abused women, their most important relationship is with their partner. Taking on this subjectivity excludes him from her life unless he is willing to adopt the new identity the law offers him. Her ability to make this change depends on the social support she receives from others.

Difficult as the change is for women, the transformation for men into a new subjectivity as batterers is far more challenging. For men, the law offers a new identity as a batterer, with a loss of class status and self-respect along with humiliating appearances before the police, the judge, and the ATV program, settings in which a man is either refused the opportunity to speak or not heard if he does. His wife or partner is ultimately the source of this humiliation; it is she who holds the key to supporting and even constructing his masculinity. If she tries to undermine the process, drop the charges, change the temporary restraining order from a no-contact to a contact order, or even sneak visits with him despite the legal prohibition of a restraining order, this mitigates the pain of a damaged masculinity.

New images of egalitarian gender relations based on negotiation and responsibility for naming and knowing feelings are taught to men in a violence control program mandated by the court. Batterers meet in quasi-therapeutic settings in which they are encouraged to share their experiences and their feelings and learn to name and understand those feelings. Men resist the new masculinities constructed in the law by joking and sexual innuendo in the violence control program, by failing to appear for court and ATV meetings, by denying the construction of their violence as inappropriate battering, and by pressuring their partners to withdraw charges. The joking, back talk to the facilitators, and talk about sex in the group meetings asserts a masculinity of sexual potency and interpersonal power that defies the model of collaborative masculinity promoted within the law and the feminist program. It challenges the elite, white identity of the program that appears feminized to many of these working-class men (Merry 1995b; Connell 1995).

There is an important class dimension to men's encounters with the law as well. The intervention of the law into the inner workings of the family — the police at the door, the judge reading the description of the blows — is generally experienced as humiliating by men as well as women. This opening of the family seems both a sign of a subordinate social status and, in many ways, an effect of that status. A lack of resources renders families open to a variety of legal interventions from welfare supervision to child protective investigations. The inability of many of these men, who are typically poor and unemployed, to perform the breadwinner task impinges on their own sense of masculinity and their ability to assert control over their wives. It also diminishes their ability to live a more middle-class life outside the scrutiny of the law. Women seeking help are also subjected to the kinds of intrusions characteristic of lower-class lives. One woman said, for example, that she hoped one day for a two-car garage and not to have to call the police about violence in the home. It is not surprising that women's entrance into this subject position is ambivalent, hesitant, and intermittent.

This analysis suggests that the adoption of rights consciousness requires a shift in subjectivity, one that depends on wider cultural understandings and individual experiences. It is in particular interactions and encounters that this subjectivity shift takes place. That the adoption of rights depends on individual experiences in the social world has significance for a range of rights-based social movements from pay equity and mental health rights to human rights. Such adoptions depend not only on educating people about the availability of rights but also putting into place practices within legal systems that will reinforce the experience of these rights. This reinforcement depends on social encounters in which those endeavoring to exercise rights and thus redefine their previous relationships find positive reinforcement for this change. Human rights are difficult for individuals to adopt as a self-definition in the absence of institutions that take these rights seriously. Implementation is fundamental to establishing human rights consciousness.

The Female Inheritance Movement in Hong Kong
Coauthored with Rachel Stern

A case study of a successful human rights movement supporting women's inheritance rights in the rural areas of Hong Kong provides another perspective on when and how women at the grass roots adopt rights consciousness.[3] In the spring of 1994, a small group of poor and mostly illiterate women in Hong Kong challenged the Chinese customary law that forbade female inheritance of family land, a system that had long maintained the continuity of the patrilineage. Using the language of rights and gender equality, these women joined forces with a variety of Hong Kong women's groups and staged dramatic demonstrations and protests in the plaza in front of the Legislative Council building demanding a change in the law. The indigenous women lived in relatively rural areas and these demonstrations were the first time they had ever been to the central business district. In the midst of shining towers of office buildings, they dressed in the oversized hats of farm women and sang folk laments, replacing the old words with new lyrics about injustice and inequality. Demonstrators from women's groups attached paper chains to their necks, tearing them to symbolize liberation from Chinese customary law (Chan 1995: 4). Across the plaza, a conservative group representing rural elite interests, the Heung Yee Kuk, gathered in large numbers to protest any change in the law. Their songs and banners claimed that female inheritance would undermine tradition and destroy the lineage.

In the demonstrations, these poor, rural women claimed that their inability to inherit land was a violation of their rights to gender equality. In other words, they framed their grievances against the patrilineal system of inheritance as a violation of their human rights. They turned to the legislature and law to solve their problems. They became active in a public protest even though many of them needed directions even to find downtown. This is an example of human rights made vernacular as the centerpiece to a local protest. How did these rural village women come to interpret their grievances against kin as human rights violations?

A detailed look at this movement shows that their activism depended on a complex layering of distinct groups with quite divergent ideologies. Although the village women campaigned on behalf of their human rights to equal inheritance, their commitment to this vision was limited. It was transnational elites in Hong Kong who initially developed a human rights analysis of women's rights to inherit. Local women's groups translated the grievances into a rights language that the legislature and political leaders could hear. They taught rural women how to frame their inheritance problems in the language of rights and to talk to reporters this way. This example shows the importance of translators, people who navigate between more or less separate social worlds, helping each group to understand the perspectives of others. It also shows that it was not necessary for the rural women to have a deep commitment to human rights, since other parts of the movement translated global human rights approaches into the vernacular.

The female inheritance movement represented a coalition of groups with significant ideological differences that worked collaboratively to link local systems and global ones. It was made up of a series of separate social layers, roughly organized as local to global but also ranging from poor to rich, lower social class to elite, rooted to transnationally mobile, ethnic/racial minority to dominant group, and uneducated to educated. Each layer had a distinctive way of framing the problem and acting on it. Activists in one layer saw the problem as one of human rights and gender equality while another layer saw the problem as a product of patriarchy and feudal thinking. The indigenous women themselves, whose stories formed the narrative core of the movement, generally saw themselves as the victims of unfeeling and rapacious male relatives. These grassroots women came to think of themselves as having rights, but did not understand their problems in terms of human rights conventions. Nevertheless, they were able to create an effective working relationship with educated elites who did.

The translators were people who helped the members of one layer reframe their grievances in the language of others. They showed each layer how to understand the perspectives of adjacent layers, but they did not produce a homogeneous movement. The translators' ability to switch between different ways of framing the problem enabled collaboration even though people in various layers did not say the same thing or think about the issue in the same way. For example, a social worker in a women's group helped the indigenous women recast their stories as gender discrimination. These intermediaries played critically important roles in the movement. They provided a bridge between global human rights discourse and anger at selfish relatives who ignored kinship obligations. Human rights need not be adopted by participants at all levels of the movement and throughout society to be politically effective. But it is important to have translators who can redefine particular problems in terms that flow across national and class lines.

The historical origins of this issue lie in British colonialism. When Britain leased the New Territories from China in 1899, they promised to respect Chinese custom and Chinese customary law. The colonial administration fossilized this law, resisting change even as laws in Hong Kong were reformed. Part of the ossification of Chinese customary law was the retention of the principle of male-only inheritance, although such laws were reformed in China, Taiwan, and Singapore. Massive numbers of people moved from Hong Kong into towns in the New Territories in the postwar period, transforming much of the formerly rural district. By the early 1990s, Hong Kong was facing the handover to China in 1997 in the wake of the crackdown at Tiananmen Square in 1989. Hong Kong leaders and citizens were very concerned about protection for individual rights (Chan 1995: 27; Petersen 1996). This political situation gave added force to the arguments of a group of transnational elite academics, including British and American expatriates, that denying women the right to inherit property was a human rights violation.

THE MOVEMENT, 1993/1994

An indigenous woman, Lai-Sheung Cheng, who lived in the rural section of Hong Kong called the New Territories, played a significant role in mobilizing the village women denied inheritance rights. She made contact with other poor rural women facing difficulties as a consequence of the male-only inheritance laws and with Hong Kong women's groups. As the leader of the indigenous women, she was the subject of a great deal of media attention during the movement. Rachel located her and interviewed her in June 2003.[4] When Ms. Cheng's father died without a will, a common occurrence in the New Territories, her two brothers inherited her house.[5] In May 1991, Ms. Cheng's brothers decided to sell the family's two-story home in Yuen Long, a town in the New Territories, to a private developer. The only problem was that Ms. Cheng was still living on the second floor. Ms. Cheng refused to leave unless she was given a share of the proceeds from the sale, citing a Qing dynasty custom that allows unmarried women to reside indefinitely in the family's home after a father's death (*South China Morning Post,* August 23, 1993; also Cheng interview 2003). For the next two years, Ms. Cheng was harassed by the buyer of the house to force her to leave. The buyer routinely broke into the house, once smearing excrement and urine around the interior and, on another occasion, releasing mice (*The Sunday Telegraph,* October 24, 1993; Cheng interview 2003). The harassment was so intense that Ms. Cheng said she had to call the police nearly every night.

Fed up with the harassment, Ms. Cheng decided to make her story public. Her first step was to write a letter to Chris Patten, then governor of Hong Kong. In the letter, Ms. Cheng told Governor Patten that, in her words, "I was persecuted because of the law" (Cheng interview 2003).[6] Not content with alerting Governor Patten, Ms. Cheng wrote a letter to the Chinese newspaper *Oriental Daily* explaining her situation. *Oriental Daily* did not publish the letter, but someone at the paper put Ms. Cheng in touch with Linda Wong, a social worker at the Hong Kong Federation of Women's Centres.

Ms. Cheng told Linda Wong over the phone that she knew several other indigenous women in a similar situation, including Ying Tang, a patient at Ms. Cheng's Chinese medicine clinic. Ms. Cheng also said several women had contacted her after they saw her name and story in a Chinese newspaper, *Wah Kui Daily*. Ms. Wong asked Ms. Cheng to contact these women and bring them to a meeting. Several indigenous women met with Ms. Wong for the first time in 1992 (Wong, interview 2003). After this first meeting, the women began to publicize their stories. At some point, they met informally with various government officials, including Hong Kong Legislative Council members Anna Wu and Christine Loh, to figure out their legal options. The first formal step, they finally decided, was to file a complaint at the Complaints Division of the Office of Members of the Legislative Council (Wong, interview 2003).

Discrimination against New Territories women had been on the radar screen of women's groups for a long time. When the Association for the Advancement of Feminism (AAF) was founded in 1984, abolishing discriminatory laws in the New Territories was mentioned in its position paper (Tong 1999: 64). In addition, five women's groups asked the government to set up a working group to look into New Territories discrimination in July 1990 (Howarth et al. 1991: 17). However, the specific issue of female inheritance took on increased importance after a 1991 shadow report by the Hong Kong Council of Women which was prepared in conjunction with Hong Kong's report to the Human Rights Committee in Geneva concerning compliance with the International Covenant on Civil and Political Rights (ICCPR). Hong Kong's Bill of Rights had just been passed in July 1991 and civil liberties and discrimination were hot public issues (Petersen 1996; see also Petersen and Samuels 2002: 47–48).[7] Although the Heung Yee Kuk, a political organization representing rural villages, lobbied to exempt "traditional rights" of male villagers from the Bill of Rights, they failed to win an exemption (Petersen 1996: 353–55). As a result, the Hong Kong Council of Women's ICCPR report was able to claim that this was a form of gender discrimination that contravened the newly passed Bill of Rights (Howarth et al. 1991: 16).

Founded in 1926, the Heung Yee Kuk has acted as a leader in protecting the interests of indigenous villagers, particularly with reference to land. It is the highest tier of the representative organization of the villagers (Chan 2003: 67, 87). Kuk members consist of the chair and vice-chair of each rural committee. There are 27 rural committees in total and they are comprised of village representatives elected by the village (Asia Television News 2001). The Kuk consists of conservative clan leaders who opposed development in the past but since the late 1950s have stopped resisting development and sought to increase compensation for land from the government (Chan 2003: 71).

The ICCPR shadow report was important because it framed the female inheritance issue in legal human rights terms. The four authors, all Western women with strong academic backgrounds, argued that male-only inheritance violated both the Convention on the Elimination of Discrimination against Women and the ICCPR (Howarth et al. 1991: 12).[8] They further explained that Hong Kong's legislation governing succession — the Intestates' Estate Ordinance and the Probate and Administration Ordinance — did not apply to New Territories women (Howarth et al. 1991: 14). The report also includes a well-reasoned argument concerning why male-only inheritance is not protected by either the Joint Declaration or the Basic Law, the two documents outlining the terms of the handover (Howarth et al. 1991: 16–17). These legal arguments were critical to the female inheritance movement because they provided the intellectual framework for activists and legislators to push for equal inheritance. They also helped clear up confusion about the complicated dual legal system, which differed between the New Territories and Hong Kong. The government could no longer claim, as the Attorney General did in 1986, that they were "not aware of any provisions of [Hong Kong] law which discriminate against women" (quoted in Lui 1997: chaps. 3, 5).

While doing research for the section on New Territories women, one of the authors of the ICCPR shadow report discovered that the jurisdiction of the New Territories Ordinance was based on territory, not on indigenous identity. In other words, Chinese customary law applied to all residents of the New Territories, not just indigenous villagers. In 1994, 42 percent of the population of Hong Kong lived in the New Territories (Tong 1999: 53). Most of the people lived in public housing estates or private flats that had not received any special exemption from the New Territories Ordinance. As a result, women were ineligible to inherit property throughout most of the New Territories (Petersen 1996: 341; Jones interview 2003). Amazingly, practically no one had realized this.[9]

The news of this discovery broke in the Chinese newspaper *Ming Pao* on September 6, 1993 and immediately created a crisis for the government (Wong 2000: 299; see also Fischler 2000: 215).[10] The 340,000 owners of apartments and houses in urban parts of the New Territories suddenly discovered that Chinese customary law applied to them (Home Affairs Branch 1994). Clearly, the New Territories Ordinance would have to be amended to allow female urban residents to inherit property when the owner died intestate, following the laws in place in urban Hong Kong.

On November 19, 1993, the government introduced the New Territories Land (Exemption) Ordinance (NTL[E]O).[11] The bill exempted only urban land in the New Territories from the New Territories Ordinance, but discussion of the issue created a window of opportunity for indigenous women in the rural areas. A legislator, Christine Loh, proposed an amendment extending this bill to all women, rural as well as urban. This political opening led to the creation of the Anti-Discrimination Female Indigenous Residents Committee. In addition to indigenous women, the group also included Linda Wong, a social worker from the Hong Kong Federation of Women's Centres. Other participants were a representative from the AAF, a Radio Television Hong Kong reporter, an anthropology graduate student, and a labor organizer.[12] With the help of these outsiders, the indigenous women began to tell their stories to a wider audience. Most important, they learned to tell these stories in a way that was politically effective.

In the beginning, the women saw their situations as personal wrongs perpetrated by evil relatives. They first tried to persuade their relatives to act in more filial ways, then sought help for their individual situations from a legal aid office. According to Linda Wong, the women were not thinking about changing the law until the first demonstration outside the Legislative Council. Rather, they were hoping that Legislative Council members would address their individual cases (Wong, interview 2003).[13] Eliza Chan, the anthropologist who studied the movement (1995), argues that most of the women saw their claims in terms of kinship obligations, not equal rights. They justified their claims on the basis of affection for their fathers, not rights to equal inheritance. Most of the women did not criticize the lineage system itself but blamed particular relatives who reneged on their obligations to provide them financial and emotional support in lieu of their father's land. One woman interviewed by Chan was angry that her relatives had failed to keep in touch with her. They should not have forgotten that she is her father's "root and sprout" and "flesh and blood." If she had inherited, she said, she would have allowed her relatives to live in her father's house as long as they maintained close ties with her (Chan 1995: 88–89).

When the women did make inheritance claims, they justified inheritance rights on the basis of ties to their father. In telling their stories, several of the women emphasized the role they had played in their father's funerals to underscore their close ties to their fathers (Chan 1995: 82–85). Because they had been filial, affectionate daughters, they argued, they were entitled to inherit.[14] By using kinship ties to justify inheritance, the women in some sense reinforced the patrilineal system even as they asserted their rights (Chan 1995: 97). Tellingly, only one of the women in the Anti-Discrimination Female Indigenous Residents Committee had a brother. The rest of the women were all "last of line" daughters (*juefangnu*) and, as a result, their father's land was inherited by distant male relatives.[15] In Chan's interviews, most of the women said they would have been willing to give up their inheritance rights if they had had brothers (Chan 1995: 72).[16]

Yet, these women had exhausted the appeals they could make to their kins-men for better treatment. Political activism offered a more promising path. Through the Anti-Discrimination Female Indigenous Residents Committee, the indigenous women learned how to translate their kinship grievances into the language of rights and equality. This translation was critical because, in or-der to be politically persuasive, the women had to phrase their needs in a lan-guage acceptable to those hearing their claims (Chan 1995: 56). The Legislative Council and the media were not interested in family disputes over property, but they were interested in stories that spoke to wider themes of gender equality and human rights.[17] In order to talk about their stories from a rights perspec-tive, the women had to learn to generalize their grievances. Not uncaring rela-tives but gender discrimination and inequality were the root of the problem. Chan describes how the social workers helped the indigenous women put a broad concept like gender equality into the context of a woman's personal story, thus making the story more powerful and more convincing (1995: 119). The social workers "drilled" the women, urging them not to use slang and teaching them how to present themselves to the public (1995: 120). The solution they proposed was not mediation and a more equal division of property, but a broad-ranging change to an unfair law. As part of this process of generalization, the women needed to present a united front regardless of differences in age, eth-nicity, and education. They had to negotiate a common identity as indigenous women, an identity forged through a series of small decisions within the group. When the women rewrote a traditional song to include new lyrics about injus-tice, for example, they had to find a song that everyone knew. In the end, they chose a Hakka mountain song (*shan ge*) even though the majority of the indige-nous women were not Hakka (Cheng interview 2003).

Although the Hong Kong Federation of Women's Centres claimed that the "women took all the initiatives by themselves while the Centre just concen-trated on providing resources and support," the process was more complicated (Hong Kong Federation of Women's Centres 1994: 20; see also Lui 1997: 20). The outsiders on the Residents Committee played an important role in fram-ing the indigenous women's stories and, more generally, facilitating the transi-tion to a more generalized, rights-based perspective. On several occasions, the outsiders in the group groomed the women in dealing with the media, particu-larly teaching them how to respond to reporters. The emphasis was on keeping the women's stories short and quotable, as well as avoiding slang and speaking with sufficient detachment. The women practiced responding to tough questions like: "There are some women in the New Territories who said that they do not need the rights of inheritance. Why do you insist on it?" (Chan 1995: 117–19; see also Chan interview 2003 and Cheng interview 2003). In addition, the Residents Committee helped the women branch out into different modes of expression, creating dramas and songs to illustrate the injustice of male-only inheritance. A labor organizer, one of the outside voices in the group, became the "stage director" for the dramas. As one interviewee put it, "she put together elements to strike those cameras," like suggesting that the women dress in traditional clothes (Chan, interview 2003; see also Cheng, interview 2003).

In creating the dramas, the organizers were responding to the stereotypes they knew the media wanted to see. The media discussed female inheritance in terms of dichotomies. The Kuk were portrayed as traditional, rural, and male whereas the female inheritance coalition was urban, modern, and female (Chan 1995: 50). For the most part, the indigenous women were seen as victims of "tradition" and lineage hegemony (Chan 1995: 100). One TV series broadcast during the movement depicted the lineage system as a "living fossil" of Chinese tradition (Chan 1995: 107). In 1994, these dichotomies were deeply entrenched. The media had long seen the New Territories as a bastion of outdated tradition. In a 1986 documentary on New Territories life, the narrator closes by saying "traditional modes of thinking vastly out of step with the modern world are still deep rooted in the hearts of indigenous villagers in the New Territories" (Radio Television Hong Kong 1986).

Indigenous women who failed to reframe their particular grievances into general stories of rights violations were silenced. In the middle of one Legislative Council debate, for example, an indigenous woman, the oldest participant in the movement, suddenly interrupted the chairperson and started shouting in Hakka about how badly her relatives had treated her. The chairperson cut the woman off, saying "your story is not related to our discussion" (Chan 1995: 131–32). Portraying the women's stories as individual disputes without broader significance was also a way to discredit the indigenous women (Chan 1995: 5). During the debate over the passage of the NTL(E)O, one legislator dismissed the indigenous women by saying: "As regards the case of Ms. Cheng Lai-Sheung . . . her family members have already clarified publicly that it was only a matter of dispute on fighting for legacy [sic]" (Hong Kong Hansard 1994: 4553).

In contrast, the women's stories were very effective when filtered through the lens developed in the Anti-Discrimination Female Indigenous Residents Committee and presented as examples of gender inequality. Social movement scholars have noted the degree to which individual testimonials can help legitimate a cause and, by extension, rally support behind it (Keck and Sikkink 1998: 19–20). In the female inheritance movement, the women's stories played a critical role in giving a human face to the problem and in discrediting the Heung Yee Kuk's claim that they were the sole voice of indigenous villagers. During the October 1993 motion debate, several of the legislative councilors mentioned meeting the indigenous women and were personally moved by the women's stories. Referring to the women was also a way to refute Kuk claims that there were no complaints about male-only inheritance (Hong Kong Hansard 1993: 249, 253, 256).

It would be easy to believe that the indigenous women lost control of their stories and were exploited for political change, as has occurred elsewhere (Keck and Sikkink 1998: 20). The reality, however, is more nuanced. While the outsiders on the Residents Committee helped the women present themselves to the outside world, the women themselves played an active role in shaping the strategy. The idea of rewriting lyrics to indigenous songs, for example, came from the women (Chan 1995: 108; see also Cheng, interview 2003). The idea was a public relations coup: the image of indigenous women singing traditional songs became an icon of the movement. The women also had a voice in the wider women's movement through the chairperson of the Residents Committee, Ms. Cheng, who attended meetings of a coalition of women's groups. Perhaps most important, the women spoke for themselves. While the outside members of the Residents Committee coached the women, they also felt strongly that the women should have their own voice (Chan 1995: 117; see also Wong, interview 2003).

As the indigenous women learned to tell their stories differently, the ways they thought about those stories also began to shift. They were not initially critical of the patrilineal system, only of their relatives' failure to provide for them. They began to think of the family inheritance system as unfair to all women. Over time, the women decided that the inheritance law needed to change and came to see themselves as victims of gender discrimination. This shift in consciousness seems to have been an additive process. Although the women developed a new perception of the problem as gender discrimination, they retained their old sense of individual wrongs perpetrated by male relatives. Violations of duty by male relatives became violations of rights they held as women and, to a much lesser extent, rights they held as human beings.

Consciousness is a slippery, unquantifiable concept and it is difficult to know how many of the indigenous women fully incorporated the gender equality framework. It seems that their consciousness fell along a spectrum from those who adopted a largely kinship-based perception of the problem to those for whom the rights layer of thinking predominated. The women occupied shifting points along this spectrum. For example, over the course of the movement one woman learned to talk about her story using terms like "gender discrimination" and "injustice," vocabulary that she literally did not know before joining the Residents Committee (Chan 1995: 146). Another still told a story in the Legislative Council of abusive relatives, as I mentioned above. The Hakka mountain song covers both ends of this spectrum. The first two lines of the song say that the indigenous women are poorly treated in general: "Female indigenous women are the most unfortunate people / This world is unfair to them" (Chan 1995: 98). The second two lines locate the injustice in the legal system and ask the Legislative Council to change the law: "The Hong Kong society is unjust / I hope that the Legislative Councilors will uphold justice" (Chan 1995: 98).

But there is little evidence that the indigenous women developed a sustained critique of their problems based on human rights. Despite one woman's statement that "Now and after [the handover in] 1997, I will continue to bravely stand up and fight for the rights of indigenous women," the indigenous women entirely dropped out of the women's movement after the NTL(E)O was passed (Hong Kong Women Christian Council 1995: 126; also interviews). No doubt the women were tired of fighting, but this may also be a sign that they were not deeply committed to seeing female inheritance as part of a larger struggle for gender equality. It is more likely that they saw their problems primarily as violations by particular male relatives and to a lesser extent as the product of unfair Hong Kong laws. Another indication that the women never developed a sustained rights perspective was their frustration with demonstrations that did not focus exclusively on them. Chan reports that some of the women were upset when their stories were subsumed by the larger themes of gender equality or antidiscrimination against people with disabilities and other groups (Chan 1995: 146).

DEFENDING CULTURE

The major opponent of the indigenous women was the Heung Yee Kuk, a political organization of rural male leaders who positioned themselves as defenders of tradition and culture. Traditionally, women leave their home village and adopt their husband's lineage as their own. Allowing female inheritance, the Kuk argued, would lead to a disintegration of clan identity because land would eventually be owned by nonlineage members (Chan 1998: 45). One placard used during the demonstrations held the plaintive message (in English) "Why are you killing our culture?" (Chan 1995: 30). To buttress their claim, the Kuk appealed to the authority of the ancestors. Male-only inheritance is "in accordance with the wishes of [the] ancestors" and, as a result, "any outsider tampering with these customs shall not be tolerated" (Heung Yee Kuk Proclamation, quoted in Chan 1998: 45). In order for this claim to be seen as legitimate, the male-dominated Kuk also realized that they would need the support of indigenous women. They found women who believed that, in the words of Angela Li York-lan, women "do not think we are discriminated against. We love our traditions. We have the right not to accept any change" (*South China Morning Post,* April 4, 1994). In a canny public relations move, these women were often placed at the front of Kuk demonstrations (Wong, interview 2003). At one demonstration, Kuk Vice Chairman Daniel Lam said, "We have shown the community that villagers are able to demonstrate endurance, calm and reason in the fight against the destruction of our customs (*Hong Kong Standard,* December 4, 1994). After the legislature voted to approve the new bill, the Kuk chairman threatened to prosecute the government and challenge the legality of the bill, then left in his Silver Spur Rolls-Royce (*South China Morning Post,* June 23, 1994).

As defenders of tradition, the Kuk placed emphasis on being Chinese. One song often sung at demonstrations was "The Brave Chinese," renamed "The Brave New Territories People" (Chan 1998: 47). Being Chinese also meant renewed attention to the anticolonial strands of indigenous history. In April 1994, a thousand villagers gathered to commemorate an 1899 uprising against the British at Tai Po (Chan 1998: 45; see also *South China Morning Post,* April 18, 1994). Ironically, it was the first time the uprising was ever commemorated (Chan 1998: 46).

Kuk demonstrations lent themselves to dramatic media coverage. The inheritance issue stayed steadily in the public eye from October 1993 (the motion debate) through June 1994 (the passage of the bill) because Kuk members did things like beheading a doll representing Governor Patten (*South China Morning Post,* April 18, 1994). On another occasion, angry villagers threatened to rape Loh if she dared set foot in the New Territories (*South China Morning Post,* March 26, 1994). When it came to media attention, as Loh put it, "one couldn't have better opponents than the Heung Yee Kuk" (Loh, interview 2003).

Although there were times when the outcome of Loh's amendment was unclear, the issue was pretty much settled by May 1994. The Hong Kong public overwhelmingly supported female inheritance rights, by a margin of 77 percent in favor to 9 percent opposed (*South China Morning Post,* May 9, 1994). There was little sympathy for the Heung Yee Kuk both because the public generally believed in gender equality and because they were resentful of the special privileges long granted indigenous villagers. Recognizing the extent of public support, the government incorporated Loh's amendment into its own bill, along with suggestions from several other Legislative Councilors (Tsang and Wan 1994: 13). On May 24, 1994, the Bills Committee of the Legislative Council accepted the government's amended bill and voted down Heung Yee Kuk Chairman Wong-fat Lau's suggestion to hold a referendum in the New Territories to settle the issue (Tsang and Wan 1994: 12). By the time of the actual vote on June 22, the result was a foregone conclusion. The NTL(E)O passed easily, with 36 votes in favor, two against and three abstentions (Hong Kong Hansard 1994: 4656).

THE LAYERS AND THE TRANSLATORS

The female inheritance movement consisted of four relatively distinct groups or layers: expatriates, the Legislative Council, women's groups, and the indigenous women. Each layer differed in its level of education, extent of international travel, degree of international exposure and rights consciousness of its members. In interviews with movement participants, the extent of separation between these four layers was striking. Despite outward unity, the layers had relatively little contact with each other and saw the issues quite distinctly. The layers had quite different ideologies and even spoke different languages, including Hakka, Cantonese, and English.

EXPATRIATES

Expatriates were clearly oriented toward transnational human rights perspectives. They played a critical role in bringing the female inheritance issue to prominence and framing it in rights terms. When they found out about the land problem, they published news stories in both the Chinese and English press. One of the leaders of the Hong Kong Council of Women said that they approached a more grassroots women's group, the AAF, to see if a Chinese-speaking women's organization would be interested in pursuing the issue. In a meeting chaired by Christine Loh, the Hong Kong Council of Women also discussed female inheritance with the Legislative Council Subcommittee on Women's Affairs on October 1, 1993 (Samuels 1994: 1).

This layer was the main place where female inheritance was discussed in reference to international covenants. The 1991 Hong Kong Council of Women report clearly stated that male-only inheritance "should have been declared *unlawful* long ago, as [it is] contrary to Article 26 of the ICCPR" and is "in conflict with the principle of equality between sexes contained in the internationally accepted Declaration of Elimination of Discrimination against Women" (Howarth et al. 1991: 16, 12). This emphasis on international law stemmed from the background of the individuals involved. This group of expatriates was made up mostly of either academics or lawyers, several of whom dealt with international law professionally.[18] They were mostly from the United States, UK, or Australia and spoke English fluently, mostly as a first language. On a local-global continuum, they were undeniably global. As cosmopolitans, they saw denying women inheritance rights in international terms as a violation of women's human rights to protection from gender discrimination. Some of these women participated with the Women's Centre although most did not.

THE LEGISLATIVE COUNCIL

The Legislative Council, Hong Kong's national elite, saw female inheritance primarily as a choice between tradition and modernity. In the final debate over the NTL(E)O, supporters of the Heung Yee Kuk claimed that the bill would "attack the age-old fine tradition of the clan system" and "disturb the peace in the countryside" (Hong Kong Hansard 1994: 4579).[19] Others sympathetic to the Kuk complained about the pace of change.[20] In the words of one legislator: "This is an attempt to change the social customs of the indigenous population. Such thinking will gradually be overtaken by newer concepts. In view of this, should we take the hasty move of enforcing the changes through the legislative process?" (Hong Kong Hansard 1994: 4544). In a petition submitted to the Legislative Council in May 1994, the Kuk claimed that women's rights to inherit would disperse clan land, promote the collapse of the clan and undermine social stability (Wesley-Smith 1994: 8). Not even opponents of the bill, however, dared question the tenet of gender equality (Lee 2000: 248). Heung Yee Kuk Chairman Wong-fat Lau maintained that the indigenous women "are not actually treated unequally. In fact, they are equal in other respects. Many of them may even often bully their husbands" (Hong Kong Hansard 1994: 4559).

On the other side of the debate, supporters of the bill argued that Hong Kong could not be an international city as long as it had laws that discriminated against women. As one legislator put it, "Hong Kong is a prosperous and progressive metropolis. The fact that the indigenous women of the New Territories are still openly discriminated against is a disgrace for the people of Hong Kong" (Hong Kong Hansard 1994: 4565). Many felt that the Heung Yee Kuk's rowdy behavior and verbal abuse left them with no choice but to support the NTL(E)O. Legislator Anna Wu remembers it as a choice between the "law of the jungle" and "civilization" (Wu, interview 2003). Others made an explicit connection between the Kuk's behavior and support for the NTL(E)O: "When the 20th century is coming to a close, that someone should so shamelessly and overtly threaten to rape is indeed a shame on this modern international city of Hong Kong. Today members of this Council must use their vote to remove such a stigma on Hong Kong" (Hong Kong Hansard 1994: 4542).

Christine Loh, originally attracted to the issue because she saw it in rights terms, continued to talk about equality and human rights. What, Loh asked rhetorically during the motion debate, "would justify excluding the wives and daughters of indigenous villagers from the rights they are guaranteed under the Bill of Rights and under the ICCPR?" (Hong Kong Hansard 1993: 270). In Loh's words, "The idea of human rights is that we have to protect every individual's basic right. Not to mention that there are 200 indigenous women complaining, even if there were only two of them, we as legislators still have the responsibility of ensuring their equal right before the law" (quoted in Lee 2000: 250).

Some legislators also referred to international rights, echoing the rhetoric used by the expatriate layer. Legislator Anna Wu, herself a lawyer, was one of the first legislators to pick up the connection between female inheritance and international law. In a December 1993 letter to members of the Bills Committee, Wu wrote: "The 1976 extension of the ICCPR to Hong Kong and the 1991 enactment of the Bill of Rights Ordinance should have cast serious doubt on the continuing validity of the system established by the NTO (New Territories Ordinance)" (Wu 1994: 1).

For legislators, there were two appealing aspects of international law. First, international law could be used to shame the government into action. In question-and-answer sessions with government representatives, legislative council members occasionally inquired about international covenants as a way of holding the government responsible to the ideals expressed in UN documents (Hong Kong Hansard 1993: 156–57, 159–60). The other appealing aspect of international law was its perceived connection to modernity. In the debate over the passage of the NTL(E)O, Legislator Fung called it "both out of date and inappropriate to deprive women of their land rights," particularly because the Bill of Rights, the ICCPR, and CEDAW all state that all citizens should be equal before the law (Hong Kong Hansard 1994: 4547).

Women's groups used concepts of gender equality and a critique of patriarchy to frame the issue. In 1989, twenty women's groups formed a coalition to lobby for a women's commission and the extension of CEDAW to Hong Kong (Wong 2000: 60–61).[21] Until the Coalition for Equal Inheritance Rights was founded in March 1994, the women's groups shared information and coordinated action on female inheritance through regular meetings of this coalition. Unlike the Legislative Council or expatriates, the coalition functioned entirely in Cantonese. Like the wider women's movement, it consisted primarily of middle-class, educated women, including students and social workers (see Tong n.d.: 648). Although the Cantonese-speaking group welcomed coalitions with expatriates, they did not encourage them to participate. The women's groups mainly conceptualized the female inheritance issue in terms of gender equality. T-shirts and banners from the movement often carried the simple slogan "♂ = ♀." In keeping with this theme, one women's group issued a statement that: "Based on the principle of equality, land inheritance right is the right of every indigenous inhabitant. If women inhabitants are not entitled to it because of their gender, it is blatant discrimination, something we cannot accept" (quoted in Lee 2000: 250). The women's groups treated gender equality as a self-evident tenet and, for the most part, saw no need to justify it in terms of law. When they did talk about the law, women's groups borrowed their arguments and even their language from the Hong Kong Council of Women ICCPR report. One AAF publication directly quotes the Hong Kong Council of Women report, saying male-only inheritance rights "should have been declared *unlawful* long ago, as they are contrary to Article 26 of the ICCPR" (Association for the Advancement of Feminism 1993: 14). Like the Legislative Councilors, the women's groups were focused on changing the law, not on providing solutions for individual women.

However, there were some important differences between the perspectives of the women's groups and the Legislative Council debate. The women's groups saw male-only inheritance as a product of patriarchy, a strand of thought that never emerged in the Legislative Council.[22] One group accused the Heung Yee Kuk of "patriarchal hegemony" (Wong 2000: 192). Another group suggested that the majority of indigenous women were not aware of their oppression because of "patriarchal socialization. . . . A harmony that conceals injustice is not one to be applauded" (quoted in Lee 2000: 250–51).

This critique of patriarchy was closely mixed with antifeudalism, a term associated with postrevolutionary thought in China. The term feudalism functioned as a kind of shorthand to connote backward customs in need of change. During the rally outside the Legislative Council while the October motion was debated, demonstrators shouted "Down with feudal traditions!" (*Hong Kong Standard,* October 14, 1993). Antifeudalism was even the theme of the May 4, 1994, demonstration outside the Legislative Council in honor of China's May Fourth movement (Chueng 1994: 7).[23] By "feudal traditions," the women's groups generally meant gender inequality, usually stemming from patriarchy. Male-only succession "reinforces the feudalistic idea that women are inferior to men" (AAF 1993: 7). Another women's group wrote that "depending on fathers, husbands and children is exactly what the 'three subordinations' teaches in feudal society" and is in opposition "to the principle of independence for women" (quoted in Lee 2000: 250). Postrevolutionary China also has a long tradition of promoting gender equality.

Many of the other concepts used by the women's groups — nondiscrimination, human rights, and critique of patriarchy — were appropriated from Western thought. Although they were used in a Hong Kong context, their essential meanings were not transformed. The critique of patriarchy is a standard feminist message, as familiar to the US National Organization of Women as to Hong Kong's Association for the Advancement of Feminism. The women's groups' techniques of activism — demonstrations, t-shirts and banners — are also familiar from Western feminism, as is the ♂ = ♀ logo.

While the broader themes were appropriated from abroad, both from China and the West, the women's groups used local symbols to express these international ideas. Hakka songs, for example, were used to illustrate inequality and injustice. While singing the songs, the women wore traditional hats, colloquially known as "Hakka hats." Hakka women have a reputation as hard workers so the hats connoted both ruralness and hardiness. Even the slogans about feudalism were a way to put gender equality in a regional historical context.

The extensive appropriation of Western feminist concepts and activist techniques is somewhat ironic since many of Hong Kong's women's groups were founded specifically to indigenize Western feminism. AAF, for example, was founded "to bring together people who speak our language and share a similar background" and "work within our own culture" (AAF founder quoted in Choi 1995: 95).[24] Perhaps it was enough that the female inheritance movement was led by Hong Kong women and conducted primarily in Cantonese. In discussing the role of the Hong Kong Women Christian Council, one of the founding members emphasized the importance of local leadership: "[We are] a local Christian women's group, not the expatriates. If they join us, then they may play a supporter's role . . . but we have a local basis" (quoted in Choi 1995: 97).

During the movement, this concern with indigenization was manifested in attempts to bridge any divide between the women's groups and the indigenous women. "Urban and rural women share the same heart" was another slogan often seen on banners (Chan 1995: 5). This emphasis on urban-rural solidarity was meant both to solidify the coalition and to authenticate the claims about gender equality that the women's groups were offering on behalf of the indigenous women. In addition to being sincerely felt, slogans like "urban and rural women share the same heart" helped gloss over any tension between the indigenous women and their urban champions.

INDIGENOUS WOMEN

The indigenous women were the only lower-class voice in the female inheritance movement. The core members of the Residents Committee were relatively poor and the majority were illiterate. None of the women spoke fluent English and one woman spoke only Hakka (Chan 1995: 20). The women came from the lineage underclass, a group glossed over in egalitarian lineage ideology (Watson 1985: 54). Comparing the women to the Kuk elite, it is clear that there was a class-struggle dimension to the movement. One of the indigenous women remarked "Before, when all the villagers were poor, we helped each other out. Now we are enemies" (Chan 1995: 30–32).

However, the movement was nearly always discussed in terms of gender, not class. One of the few references to class came from Ms. Cheng. After the law was changed, Ms. Cheng said: "Before we had nothing while the male villagers had everything. There was a wide gap between rich and poor and women were inferior at that time" (Asia Television News 2001). In Ms. Cheng's view, women have an inferior status not just because they are women but also because they are poor.

Over the course of the movement, the indigenous women slowly shifted from seeing their stories as individual kinship violations to broader examples of discrimination, as discussed above. In public, the theme of rights and gender equality emerged in documents jointly written by all the members of the Residents Committee. In an article published in the Hong Kong Federation of Women's Centres Annual Report, the Residents Committee calls the denial of female inheritance "a century-long discriminatory barrier to the indigenous women's basic rights" (Hong Kong Federation of Women's Centres 1994: 88).

Another submission to the Legislative Council talks about the "inherent right" to succession and mentions "the protection to women that has been laid down in the United Nations Universal Declaration of Human Rights" (Anti-Discrimination Female Indigenous Residents Committee 1994). The majority of the indigenous women were illiterate, so such articles and statements must have been guided, if not written, by Linda Wong or the other outsiders on the Residents Committee.[25] It is impossible to reconstruct what happened, but it is unlikely that references to rights and international law were introduced by the indigenous women themselves.

On an individual level, Ms. Cheng was the person most comfortable talking about female inheritance in terms of discrimination, equality, and rights as well as the person most comfortable talking to the press. In one interview, she said clearly, "what I am fighting for is sexual equality" (*Sunday Telegraph,* October 24, 1993). At another point, she said that if the government refused to change the law, they "would be violating the Bill of Rights" (*Hong Kong Standard,* October 14, 1993). In contrast, another indigenous woman's critique of the New Territories Ordinance was limited to the fact that "the legislation does not take care of situations where families do not have any sons, which is my case" (*South China Morning Post,* February 25, 1993). Because she spoke rights language, Ms. Cheng could bring the women's concerns to a wider public. For other core members of the group, this frame was probably less familiar.

TRANSLATORS

In order to communicate, the different layers relied on a select few people we call translators. Translators are people who can easily move between layers because they conceptualize the issue in more than one way. It seems likely that they saw these issues in multiple ways from the start. As they move between layers, these intermediaries translate between one set of principles and terms and another. They played key roles in creating a movement where rights language and indigenous women's stories could come together to create political change. Through their mediation, human rights became relevant to a local social movement even though the oppressed group itself did not talk about human rights. Although the women acquired some consciousness of rights through participation in the Residents Committee, rights language was mainly promoted by others. Through the mediation of the translators, the indigenous women joined their stories to a larger movement concerned with human rights and discrimination.

At least three people acted as translators: Lai-Sheung Cheng, Linda Wong, and Anna Wu.[26] Ms. Cheng, in essence, created the Residents Committee by finding other women with similar stories who were ready to step forward. For many of the women, Ms. Cheng was the first person they contacted. After the Residents Committee was founded, Ms. Cheng helped make the women's stories politically relevant. Through her participation in coalition meetings and her contacts with the media, Ms. Cheng brought the women's concerns to a wider audience. She was able to generalize individual kinship grievances and lobby for a change in the law. By having a voice in the coalition's strategy, Ms. Cheng was also able to shape how the women's stories were used in the movement.[27]

Although she did not have a formal leadership title, Linda Wong was the critical link between the indigenous women and the broader world. The women were able to tell their stories in the Legislative Council because Linda Wong created the opportunity and showed them how to do it. With the help of other outsiders, she helped frame the women's stories in terms of equality and rights so that they were politically salable. Unlike the indigenous women, who rarely traveled outside of the New Territories, Wong had experience in activism and, like the other outsiders, had a good idea what the media and the public would find appealing. The carefully orchestrated dramas and songs had, in the words of one participant, a "symbolic meeting" that "became an icon for the whole movement" (Chan, interview 2003). Wong also literally translated the Cantonese and Hakka used by the indigenous women into English. Using English ensured that the women's stories reached a wider audience and were taken seriously by elites. In some sense, both Linda Wong and Lai-Sheung Cheng translated "up." They took stories anchored in a local kinship system and talked about them using global rights language.

In the Legislative Council, Anna Wu played quite a different role as a translator. Wu's attention to the Bill of Rights and the ICCPR shows that she was well aware of international law. With help from other legislative councilors, Wu brought international law, a concern mainly expressed by the expatriate layer, into the Legislative Council debate. However, Wu's attempt to codify indigenous women's customary rights shows that she also understood and appreciated the kinship system. In an early meeting between Anna Wu and the indigenous women, for example, Wu suggested that the women might be able to sue male relatives for failing to live up to their responsibilities. Compared with other legislative councilors, the indigenous women came away with a sense that Wu's view of the issue was closest to theirs (Wong, interview 2003). By bringing the kinship system into a dialogue about rights, Wu, to some degree, localized the human rights framework, or translated "down." This localization could have gone further if other legislative councilors had picked up Wu's concern. The issue died quietly because the discussion was dominated by the tradition-versus-rights debate. Unlike Wu, most legislative councilors saw the issue only one way.

In Hong Kong, rights language was adopted, not transformed. Terms like "nondiscrimination," "gender equality," and "human rights" retained their grounding in Western philosophical ideas about individualism, choice, autonomy, and equality, although postrevolutionary Chinese conceptions of gender equality also contributed. These ideas were not imposed but appropriated because they were politically useful. In 1994 Hong Kong, rights language had political currency specifically because it was international. Both citizens and the government were concerned about losing Hong Kong's liberal traditions after the 1997 handover. Allegiance to gender equality and human rights was a sign, both to them and to the outside world, that things in Hong Kong were not going to change — that Hong Kong deserved a place in the "civilized" community of nations.

LOCAL AS A MATTER OF DEGREE

This discussion of layers is implicitly a discussion about what it means to be local and what it means to be global. Clearly, the different layers are, to a greater or lesser degree, global or local. More or less, the degree to which each layer is global corresponds to the degree to which its members see female inheritance in global terms as an international human rights issue. However, the terms "global" and "local" are not particularly useful. Their meaning is ambiguous and they often become a stand-in for social class. To say the indigenous women are local while the expatriates are global is to say that the expatriates are educated, mobile, and rich while the indigenous women are illiterate, fixed and poor. In an international city like Hong Kong, it is not even clear that there is any absolute "local." In Hong Kong, as in many other parts of the world, there are such pervasive global influences that local is a matter of degree.

In particular, the female inheritance movement cannot be separated from the global politics of the 1997 handover and the larger question of Sino-British relations. The years 1989–97 were the high tide of human rights consciousness in Hong Kong (Petersen, interview 2003). The 1991 passage of the Bill of Rights, based on the ICCPR, encouraged everyone, including women, to think in terms of human rights (Petersen and Samuels 2002: 24). Greater awareness of human rights coincided with Patten's democratic reforms, particularly the 1992 reform package and the 1991 introduction of direct elections to the Legislative Council.[28] Democratization, particularly the introduction of directly elected representatives in the Legislative Council, led to increased attention to local problems.[29]

Hong Kong still had two sovereigns: Britain and China. Lobbying these two countries for their support (and subsequently using that support to put pressure on individual legislators) was a separate political game, one played well by the Heung Yee Kuk.[30] Although China's top leaders did not comment on the inheritance question, China was initially supportive of the Kuk. Both the Xinhua news agency, China's de facto embassy in Hong Kong, and the Hong Kong and Macau Affairs office released statements in March 1994 warning the Hong Kong government that the amended NTL(E)O violated the Basic Law (Lui 1997: chaps. 4, 13; Wong 2000: 187).[31] Following up on this momentum, Kuk representatives met China's ambassador in England on April 5 (Tsang and Wan 1994: 10). The ambassador was supportive, but China's support noticeably waned as the vote on the NTL(E)O drew closer. The internal workings of the Chinese Communist Party are opaque, but the party must have decided that international bad press about lack of support for gender equality was not worth the support of the Kuk.[32]

Moreover, the "local" problem of female inheritance was created by the world's ultimate global system — colonialism. The root of the problem was, of course, the preservation of Chinese customary land law under the British, but this was not the source of Heung Yee Kuk opposition to the NTL(E)O. Customs were slowly changing in the New Territories, and it was becoming more and more common for women to inherit money, if not land (Chan 1997: 169). The Kuk were not horrified by the idea of female inheritance per se; they wanted to protect the profits guaranteed under another colonial program, the small-house policy.

Under the terms of the 1972 small-house policy, male villagers who can trace their lineage back to 1898 can obtain a 700-square-foot piece of land, free of land premium, to build within the borders of the village a house that they will own (Chan 2003: 72).[33] All New Territories men are eligible for this once-in-a-lifetime land grant, even those overseas. The original aim of the policy was to replace temporary housing and allow for natural growth in the New Territories, but a glut of small houses has led to rapid development (Hopkinson and Lei 2003: 2). Since 1972, the Lands Department has approved 26,000 small-house applications (Asia Television News 2001). Houses are often rented or sold rather than used by villagers themselves.

Although the small-house policy was originally seen as a privilege that would be abolished if abused, it has come to be seen as a right (Hopkinson and

Lei 2003: 4, 31), Because of rising land values, it is a tremendously valuable right.[34] Although the Kuk cites clan continuity as the primary justification for the policy, houses are often sold or rented to outsiders for a profit (Chan 1999: 238–40). During the female inheritance movement, it was an open secret that the Kuk were concerned that female inheritance would lead to the dismantling of other indigenous rights, particularly the small-house policy (see Chan 2003).[35] Village elder Bruce Kan even said publicly, "the next thing the government would do is cancel our rights on applying for land" (*South China Morning Post,* March 27, 1993).

"Local" is a particularly slippery word because no one in the female inheritance movement is a truly local actor. The indigenous women seem local, but appearances are deceiving. One of the core members of the Residents Committee actually lived in Holland. She found out about the inheritance debate during a visit back to Hong Kong (Wong and Chan, interview). The organization that claims to represent local indigenous people, the Hueng Yee Kuk, is actually a transnational group because so many indigenous villagers have emigrated. Many emigrants have established deep ties in their new communities. In 1981, one lineage bought a four-story house in London's Soho district for HK $1.6 million (Chan 2001: 277). Yet these overseas villagers still retain their New Territories identity. They help pay for celebrations and many come back to reconnect with their village during yearly rituals (Chan 2001: 276). They feel strongly about preserving the past and, as a result, indigenous tradition is largely financed, protected and promulgated by people who no longer live in Hong Kong. Many routinely return for local ritual events (Chan 1996: 28). Some were encouraged to participate in the effort against the female inheritance movement, and the Headquarters for the Protection for the Village and Defense of the Clan even established a UK branch (Tong 1999: 58).

Like the female inheritance movement, the Heung Yee Kuk also used global UN language for political ends. In the late 1960s, the Heung Yee Kuk closely watched Britain's behavior in Gibraltar and learned that indigenous people are entitled to certain rights (Chan 1998: 41). In a 1994 Proclamation, the Kuk appealed to international norms to protect local tradition: "the indigenous inhabitants of any country in the world all have their legitimate traditions and customs well protected by law . . . Therefore the existing provisions in the legislation to safeguard the traditional customs of New Territories indigenous inhabitants are not special favors to them. They are rather a primary obligation of the Hong Kong government" (quoted in Chan 1998: 42). Kuk supporters also recognized the persuasiveness of human rights language. It was a stretch, but during the October 1993 motion debate, one legislative councilor argued that female inheritance would infringe the human rights of ancestors. "There should not be a double standard in human rights," he said, "as we have to respect the human rights of our contemporaries, we have also to respect the human rights of our ancient ancestors" (Hong Kong Hansard 1993: 268).

Thus, the female inheritance movement, like the other case studies in this book, destabilizes any easy assumptions about the meanings of local and global. Those claiming to speak for local tradition had powerful allies in an overseas diaspora, for example, while those asserting global rights included both transnational elites and national political leaders who thought of themselves only in the context of Hong Kong laws and politics.

Conclusion: Taking on Rights

Two important points emerge from this examination of how human rights affect local legal consciousness. First, vulnerable individuals' willingness to adopt a rights framework depends in part on the way institutions respond to their rights claims. If their claims are treated as unimportant, unreasonable, or insignificant, they are less likely to take a rights approach to their problems. On the other hand, if their experience of claiming rights is positive, in that institutional actors support and validate these claims, they are more likely to see themselves as rights-bearing subjects and to claim rights in the next crisis. The case study of women in Hawai'i shows that the support of the courts, the police, and advocates is crucial to transforming their consciousness of themselves as having rights. Poor women think of themselves as having rights only when powerful institutions treat them as if they do.

Second, human rights movements do not require the adoption of a human rights consciousness by individuals at the grass roots. The case study of the female inheritance movement in Hong Kong shows that grassroots individuals can be mobilized to use human rights approaches but that their commitment to rights is not necessarily deep or long lasting. Middle-level women's groups and activists as well as transnational elites who developed the human rights approach were far more committed. Nevertheless, because this movement involved a coalition of groups, even the grassroots women whose orientation to rights was contingent and temporary were able to contribute in critical ways. This example shows that a human rights movement can operate effectively even though it includes groups with quite different levels of commitment to rights.

These case studies show that when grassroots people use the human rights framework, it is appropriated rather than imposed. Rights language is adopted because it offers political possibilities to activists. Activists translate rights claims into frameworks that are relevant to the life situations of grassroots people. Such translations provide a way of communicating grievances broadly that may generate national and international support. In the translation, however, international perspectives are translated "down" more than grassroots perspectives are translated "up." There is a real possibility that women's own experiences are alienated in the process. As rights concepts are translated into local terms, they are not transformed. Vernacular rights are ornamented by local cultural signs and symbols and tailored to local institutions such as court systems or housing authorities. However, their basic assumptions about the values of choice, autonomy, equality, and the protection of the body remain unchanged.

Local human rights activism lies at the conjunction of particular local grievances and transnational social movements and depends on intermediaries with multiple consciousnesses to translate back and forth between them. The human rights frame takes a particular story and makes it general, targeting the state as the responsible agent and source of redress. It is the particular story of grievance and suffering that provides grist for outrage. But an individual story becomes politically efficacious only when it is attached to a larger principle that provides a basis for making alliances and building political coalitions. As the local story is inserted into a more general one, it generates support outside the local community. Among indigenous women in Hong Kong, as well as for women victims of domestic violence in Hilo, redefining the self as having rights requires rethinking one's problem as caused by structural conditions rather than violations of the obligations of kinship or love.

Taking on rights is a difficult process and fraught with ambivalence. Asserting rights often comes at a price. It can antagonize relatives who attack the person for failing to honor family obligations. In Hilo, relatives and neighbors sometimes resented the women's efforts to punish their batterers and ostracized them in various ways. Similarly, in the New Territories, demanding inheritance in the name of rights antagonized the relatives of the women (Chan 1995). The women who protested their inability to inherit land in the New Territories by testifying at the Legislative Council and speaking to the media were often isolated by their families, even though they tried to frame their grievances as those of filial daughters who were affectionate to their fathers. One woman said that she was afraid to go back to her natal village. It was not only men who were threatened by the demands for equal rights to inherit, but also wives whose husbands stood to lose property to their sisters. Just as "good" women in Hilo did not take their batterers to court, so "good" women in the

New Territories did not ask to inherit, but married and stayed with their husbands. Leaders of the women's movement and feminist legislators who rode rights talk to victory had their sense of rights reinforced, but for indigenous women the benefits were less clear. Since the law was not made retroactive, they did not benefit personally. Similarly, those women who called the police and went to court complaining about the violence they experienced in Hawai'i often earned the wrath of their partners and their partner's kin. Such women were told they were not good wives and that they had betrayed their husbands. Nor did the court always punish or reform their batterers.

Thus, seeing oneself as injured by a human rights violation requires entering into a new terrain of opposition and risk. Rights offers a new vision of the self as entitled to protection by the state, but this promise must be made good. Although poor people around the world are gradually learning that they have rights, they are less likely to seize them if the state fails to deliver on their claims. It is not unusual for individuals to retreat from a rights consciousness of grievance to a kin-based one. Nor is it surprising that one would try on this identity, drop it, and try again. A double consciousness, with rights claims layered over claims of social obligations of kinship and community, seems likely to describe the way grassroots groups relate to human rights. Translators, including women's movement activists and advocates in domestic violence programs, bridge the divide between rights principles and kinship principles. As they do so, they are negotiating the interface between globally produced human rights concepts and local grievances.

Conclusions

Human rights are clearly making a significant contribution to global reform projects concerned with violence against women. The ideas produced in global settings through international deliberations are being appropriated by national political leaders and NGO activists in India, China, Fiji, and Hong Kong, and, to a lesser extent, in the United States. Human rights ideas about violence against women are, in a far more limited and fragmentary way, percolating into local communities, primarily through the mediation of activists who translate the global language into locally relevant terms. Traveling theories such as feminism had an enormous impact on local women's movements around the world in the 1980s and 1990s and contributed to important forms of institution building. As the idea that violence against women is a crime spread globally, new forms of social service for battered women and criminalization of offenders spread as well. The global women's movement encouraged the development of a similar repertoire of interventions in India, China, Fiji, Hong Kong, and the United States. Although programs were tailored to local social contexts and languages, their overall approaches and goals were similar. As women encountered the counseling centers, shelters, public education efforts, and legal changes that activists produced, they begin to rethink the violence they experienced. Some probably took on a new understanding of themselves as rights-endowed, as they did in Hilo, but this study did not follow these shifts in local rights consciousness in all the locations. At the same time, the global circulation of human rights ideas led to its own forms of institution-building, such as the ratification of treaties, the growth of human rights advocacy NGOs, and governmentally supported human rights commissions.

These two developments are complementary, despite differences in theory, personnel, and objectives. Service providers for battered women encourage them to think of themselves as having human rights, helping to build human rights consciousness. Conversely, human rights mechanisms build political space for feminist social services and the assertion of women's rights. As countries ratify conventions, lawyers and judges refer to them in decisions and political leaders carry out the responsibility of reporting to treaty bodies; this means that human rights become part of national and local political debate and a more valuable political resource for service providers.

Making Human Rights in the Vernacular

As these ideas are appropriated around the world, they are remade in the vernacular. The concept of vernacularization was developed to explain the nineteenth-century process by which national languages in Europe separated, moving away from the medieval transnational use of Latin and creating a new and more differentiated sense of nationhood in Europe (Anderson 1983). Human rights language is similarly being extracted from the universal and adapted to national and local communities. But, as we have seen, to translate human rights into the vernacular is not to change their fundamental meanings. Instead, the legal basis of human rights and the institutions through which they are implemented retain their grounding in global structures and understandings.

The process of vernacularization is one of appropriation and translation. Human rights ideas and feminist ideas are appropriated by national elites and middle-level social activists and translated into local terms. Those who are most vulnerable, often the subjects of human rights, come to see the relevance of this framework for their lives only through the mediation of middle-level and elite activists who reframe their everyday problems in human rights terms. I watched a woman in a support group in Hilo realizing that her experience with unwanted sex from her partner could be called rape after the leader pointed that out to her. Similarly, women in many parts of the world come to redefine the abuse they suffer as a crime and a rights violation in interactions with others more familiar with the human rights framework. Grassroots women adopt this new framework in a limited and contingent way. The case studies suggest that it is layered over other frameworks, such as fair treatment by kinsmen. Human rights add a new interpretation but do not displace the older ones. Just as battered women in Hilo came to see themselves as having rights to take their partners to court as well as to complain of bad treatment to their relatives, so the indigenous women in Hong Kong came to see themselves as endowed with the right to inherit land as well as entitled to receive care and support from their male kin.

Whether the rights layer of understanding endures or not depends on the institutional response claimants receive. As the Hilo example indicated, women try out these rights conceptions, hesitating to adopt them if the courts, police, and prosecutors trivialize and ignore them. Similarly, the enthusiasm of the women's groups in Hong Kong for a rights framework was reinforced by their victory. For the indigenous women activists, who did not benefit personally from the new law, the commitment to the rights framework was far more limited. The extent to which human rights consciousness is appropriated depends on how successful it is.

Translation requires three kinds of changes in the form and presentation of human rights ideas and institutions. First, they need to be framed in images, symbols, narratives, and religious or secular language that resonate with the local community. When a group of batterers is taught not to hit in Hong Kong, this is presented as part of Confucian ideas of marriage. In Hilo, the same idea is framed as learning to recognize feelings and make choices. Second, they need to be tailored to the structural conditions of the place where they are deployed, including its economic, political, and kinship systems. Shelters focus on getting Hong Kong women into public housing while Delhi and Beijing activists find the concept of shelters less valuable since finding housing outside the family is virtually impossible. Third, the target population needs to be defined. Victims of domestic violence in the United States are typically intimate partners, not necessarily married or heterosexual, whereas in China they are typically members of an extended household of several generations but not necessarily in intimate sexual relationships.

But translation does not mean transformation. Despite changes in the cultural phrasing of human rights ideas and the structural conditions of interventions, the underlying assumptions of person and action remain the same. Human rights are part of a distinctive modernist vision of the good and just society that emphasizes autonomy, choice, equality, secularism, and protection of the body. It envisions the state as responsible for creating these conditions of life and the individual as responsible for making rights claims on the state. It assumes that all people have equal rights, although all do not have equal needs. As human rights are vernacularized, these conceptions of the person, the state, and the community are not changed. In the field of violence against women, the power of the rights framework is its challenge to ideas that gender violence is a normal and natural social practice. Although human rights ideas are repackaged in culturally resonant wrappings, the interior remains a radical challenge to patriarchy. The failure to fully indigenize these ideas impedes their spread, yet to do so would undermine their potential to challenge social inequalities.

This is the paradox of making human rights in the vernacular: in order to be accepted, they have to be tailored to the local context and resonate with the local cultural framework. However, in order to be part of the human rights system, they must emphasize individualism, autonomy, choice, bodily integrity, and equality, ideas embedded in the legal documents that constitute human rights law. These core values of the human rights system endure even as the ideas are translated. Whether this is the most effective approach to diminishing violence against women or promoting global social justice is still an open question. It is certainly an important part of the expansion of a modernist view of the individual and society embedded in the global North.

A prominent body of work in international relations explores the question of the power of human rights from the perspective of social movements and transnational organizations. These scholars focus on how international norms become widespread and generally accepted through the work of social movements and government actors (Keck and Sikkink 1998; Risse, Ropp, and Sikkink 1999; Khagram, Riker, and Sikkink 2002). They define beliefs as shared values held by transnational networks, coalitions, and movements and norms as standards of appropriate behavior held by a critical mass of states. They argue that achieving value consensus in transnational situations with diverse communities and a lack of communication is very difficult. Transnational networks, coalitions, and movements work to frame issues in ways that will generate interest and support. Transnational collective action groups develop shared beliefs while countries working together in international organizations, multinational corporations, or professional groups produce international norms (Khagram, Riker, and Sikkink 2002: 14). These norms become resources for social movement activists in their efforts to develop collective beliefs. Social movement activists often seek to transform their shared beliefs into international norms. Over time, a gradual expansion of norms creates institutional structures, leading ultimately to a norms cascade as the ideas of human rights become widespread and internalized. Rapid and widespread treaty ratification is one indicator of an international norms cascade. Another indicator is the development of soft law and policy guidelines and statements (Khagram, Riker, and Sikkink 2002: 15).

This analysis focuses primarily on the interaction between transnational social movement activists and governments and does not examine the interface between global ideas and those of local groups. My analysis of vernacularization expands and extends this work. Understanding appropriation and translation illuminates the less elite dimensions of the norm change process and highlights areas where norms and ideas are resisted or only temporarily and tentatively adopted. It examines how the success of particular frames depends on features of social class, gender, race, and ethnicity that make up the social hierarchies of modern states. And it shows that norm cascades at the top may not reach poor communities and transform consciousness, particularly if there is no institutional reinforcement for new forms of consciousness.

Conundrums

The conundrums facing the practice of human rights emerge clearly from this study. First, because human rights law sets universal standards through a legal framework, it is inhibited from tailoring these standards to the particular political and social situations of the countries that have ratified conventions. As the dilemma of persuading India to reform its family laws demonstrates, the overall commitment to secularism and universalism defines the system of separate personal laws as inhibiting women's rights and freedoms, even though this insistence on a secular reform risks increasing communal tensions. The legal framework makes it more difficult to tailor human rights standards to local contexts, yet this is also the basis for claiming transnational legitimacy for these standards.

Second, human rights ideas are appropriated and adapted to local circumstances but are not remade in fully indigenous terms, even though this might make them more readily accepted. If the women in the female inheritance movement had asked for better treatment from their male relatives instead of the right to inherit land, their disruption of the existing patriarchal social order would have been far less. However, they had already made those demands of their relatives and received no help, and so turning to a human rights perspective offered them a new and more powerful framework for redressing their grievances. Human rights ideas are more easily adopted if they are packaged in familiar terms and do not disturb established hierarchies, but they are more transformative if they challenge existing assumptions about power relationships.

Third, for human rights ideas to become part of local rights consciousness, they need to be adapted to local circumstances. However, since NGOs and social service programs are often dependent on international foundations or government funding, they need to present their work in a way that will reach a wider audience and have international legitimacy. Transnational human rights principles clearly have a significant strategic value for encouraging international funding and global media support. Local social services and NGOs are pressured by funding and publicity concerns to adopt international human rights language. This may counter the most effective approaches within a local place. When the first women's center was established in Hong Kong in the 1980s, for example, in order to diminish public opposition it focused on the treatment of women, not the assertion of their rights.

Fourth, individuals' willingness to adopt a human rights consciousness depends on their success with making these claims. If institutions respond to these demands, a human rights approach to social justice will be reinforced. In the event that they fail to respond, a human rights approach will seem useless. Battered women in Hilo were reluctant to accept rights unless they were institutionally reinforced. Similarly, the indigenous women in Hong Kong were less enthusiastic about human rights than middle-level and elite activists who forged the movement and saw its success. This is a dialogic process: to promote individual rights-consciousness, institutions have to implement rights effectively. But if there is little rights consciousness, there will be less pressure on institutions to take rights seriously and implement them effectively.

Fifth, as the discussion of the transplantation of human rights institutions indicates, the effectiveness of human rights approaches is intimately linked to state action. If a state sets up these institutions and promotes human rights ideas, there will be wider support for claims by NGOs and citizens. If a country ratifies treaties, takes the monitoring process seriously, and collaborates with NGOs in the report-writing process, it will incorporate human rights thinking more extensively in the governing process. Clearly, there are states that ignore these processes and make little effort to comply with the human rights regime. Thus, despite the assumption that the human rights system challenges states' authority, the central focus of human rights activism is the state. It may strengthen the state's regulatory control over the population. NGOs make claims on the state to pass laws, develop criminal justice institutions, establish shelters, and punish offenders. Despite worries that the international human rights system will weaken state sovereignty, the state remains the focus of action, both in the processes of document production and in the implementation of human rights reforms.

Legitimacy and Transnational Consensus Building

International consensus building is critical to the legitimacy of the human rights system. Much of the writing in the field of human rights is concerned with establishing the legitimacy of a set of universal values as the basis for human rights. Some use philosophical approaches, others cross-cultural ones, others the search for basic values such as agency (e.g., Ignatieff 2001). These are all ways of responding to the problems of legitimacy and the resistance of those who say that human rights is a Western system and irrelevant to their lives. But there is a more pragmatic basis for the global legitimacy of human rights. The processes of production through consensus building guarantee that they reflect some level of international agreement and incorporate ideas from around the world.

Human rights ideas still have difficulty, however, crossing the divide between their global sites of production and local sites of appropriation. Local and national ideas and issues enter the process of international document creation, but they are subject to the smoothing out required by transnational consensus building. Particular concerns of individual countries or subgroups within those countries are rarely included in final documents. Coalition building among regional or economic groups such as G-77 or JUSCANZ makes it more likely that issues and concerns of these coalitions will be incorporated into final documents. The horse trading of document creation also makes possible the introduction of one or another specific issue into the process, such as dowry murders, or the deletion of others, such as the right to protection of sexual minorities. Insofar as decisions are made by democratic processes, larger coalitions are more effective than smaller ones.

The vast global inequality in resources is always a subtle factor behind these deliberations. Despite officially equal sovereignty, wealthier and larger countries are more powerful participants in transnational consensus building. Although government and NGO representatives from around the world participate in these international forums, they participate unequally. Larger and wealthier countries can afford to send larger delegations that can be more active in working on documents. Small countries may send no representatives at all. Similarly, NGOs from poorer countries typically attend only when they are funded by international donors who wish to send them there. Since these donors' agendas are shaped by transnational goals and values, they implicitly determine which NGO representatives are able to participate in the international deliberations. In general, the human rights system operates in a context of formally equal sovereignty but vastly unequal levels of national power and resources. Indeed, by basing participation on a set of standards for statehood derived from the European experience, the UN system maintains a colonial predominance of European institutions by excluding many groups that are not states and requiring states to assume a European form of sovereignty in order to participate (Otto 1999a: 145–80). Finally, since document production takes place in English, even though speeches and documents are translated into six languages, those countries whose representatives are fluent English speakers are clearly better able to participate in the process. Although local and national ideas do enter into discussions and shape outcomes, particularities are often lost.

Moreover, alternative visions of social justice based on religious, communitarian, or socialist models do not fit readily into the existing framework. There are continuing gaps between global standards and local, contextualized ways of addressing problems. When representatives of this global legal order engage in monitoring the compliance of member nations, they resort to more general legal principles and are unable to consider the range of particular features of a country's history and current situation that affect compliance. Wary of excuses, CEDAW experts are not willing to grant dispensation for many of the reasons countries claim. A civil war or major natural disaster are certainly recognized as reasons why a country cannot comply, but other excuses, such as a national culture of patriarchy, are far less willingly accepted. Even in situations in which the transnational principle produces an outcome different from what the CEDAW experts want, such as providing fuel for anti-Muslim politics in India, the CEDAW Committee stands by its transnational principles. They are also bound to do so to uphold the international legal convention. Thus, legal rationality requires the even-handed implementation of these principles, regardless of the political crises surrounding the uniform civil code in India or the cultural nationalist defense of bulubulu in Fiji. The reliance on a transnational legal order makes it more difficult to reinterpret human rights in the vernacular.

Human Rights, Culture, and Imperialism

These case studies demonstrate that human rights are generally adopted rather than imposed. Does this mean that the spread of human rights is not a form of imperialism? In some ways, the process of introducing global human rights law parallels the introduction of imperial law during nineteenth- and early twentieth-century European and American colonialism. As in the case of colonial legal transplants, the introduced law differs from existing local law and is dedicated to transforming family structure, land, and labor relations and the tie between the individual and the state. The proponents of human rights are the former colonial powers of Europe and North America and many of the targets of their human rights initiatives are their former colonies in Africa, Asia, Latin America, and the Pacific. Like colonialism, human rights discourse contains implicit assumptions about the nature of civilized and backward societies, often glossed as modern and traditional. Concepts of civilization and savagery, rationality and passion, that were fundamental binaries of thinking during the imperialist era creep back into debates over human rights and social justice. The practice of human rights is burdened by a colonialist understanding of culture that smuggles nineteenth-century ideas of backwardness and savagery into the process, along with ideas of racial inferiority. Rather than using these clearly retrograde terms, however, human rights law focuses on culture as the target of critique, often understood as ancient tradition.

Although the human rights system does not simply replicate imperialism, there are certainly some similarities. There are abiding tensions between the transnational certainty of standards and the local contingencies produced by history, structure, and serendipity. While local context is critical to understanding the application of either colonial policies or human rights, those promoting universal standards tend to see local context as irrelevant and even a hindrance. During colonialism, law was seen as the gift of the colonizers to societies viewed as chaotic and arbitrary. The move to human rights as the dominant language of social justice similarly empowers the state to serve as the final arbiter of justice and the central site of struggle over social justice. It establishes the terrain of social justice as the law and the state, not religion or community. At the same time, it imports through the back door assumptions about oppositions between rights and culture that were fundamental during imperialism and are still embedded in human rights rhetoric.

Moreover, the human rights system is deeply shaped by power and resource inequalities between the global North and the global South, as was the imperial system. These inequalities determine the flow of funding for innovative programs, research, support for attending international meetings, and the creation of new governmental and private reform initiatives. Since NGOs require funds to operate, they must depend on membership dues, government subsidies, or donors. These donors include private foundations such as the Ford Foundation as well as governmental aid funds, particularly from the United States, Canada, Japan, Australia, New Zealand, and northern European countries. Donors focus on reforming particular practices rather than changing economic and political structures that generate global inequality. They often promote reforms that further neoliberalism and capitalist expansion rather than diminishing social class inequality.

Yet, the expansion of human rights also differs from the legal transplants of European colonialism. First, human rights documents come from transnational and relatively consensual deliberations, not from prototypes developed in a single colonial state. The creation of human rights is now a global process, not an exclusively Western one. In significant ways it is under the control of transnational elites from around the world, albeit largely English-speaking ones. Despite vast differences in resources and power, in at least some settings countries participate as equals. On the floor of the UN General Assembly, each country has one vote.

Second, human rights are being appropriated around the globe by national and local actors who see the potential benefits of a human rights framework and redefine their agendas in these terms. This framework provides an international audience for local problems. Thought of as human rights violations, local problems become issues that a global audience can understand. Donors are more readily obtained for such problems, particularly foreign donors, as well as allies. Moreover, the human rights perspective offers a new cultural framework that breaks with past ways of understanding behavior. Such a break is critical in changing behavior such as wife battering that was long accepted as normal but must be redefined as offensive in order to diminish its frequency. This is a process of appropriation rather than imposition. It suggests that these ideas have legitimacy for at least some local and national groups.

Third, human rights law is far from being a consistent and coercive system of law. Rather, it is a fragmentary and largely persuasive mechanism very much in the making. It exists in constant negotiation with nation-state law. States may contest, ignore, or adopt features of international human rights law. In fact, the focus of activists is typically the state, with the international community a source of support rather than coercion. Human rights law is embodied in international conventions, but these take effect only when ratified by states. They are also articulated in a series of policy statements such as declarations by the UN General Assembly, outcome documents from major world conferences, such as the Beijing Conference on Women, and resolutions passed by UN commissions, such as the Commission on Human Rights and the Commission on the Status of Women, all of which are constituted by state representatives. These documents articulate standards, rules, and visions of a just society. Some are widely accepted as policy statements, some are conventions ratified by a significant number of states, and some are sets of principles so broadly accepted that they are viewed as international customary law analogous to the customary law of small scale societies. Like state law, these documents define offenses and articulate desirable standards of behavior. But they do not contain rules whose infractions result in punishment of noncompliant nations.

International human rights law has relatively few sanctions. It grows out of a compact among sovereign nations so that its ability to force recalcitrant states to comply is quite limited. Although legal frameworks govern the practice of human rights, implementation depends on complex interactions among international and national NGOs, governments, UN officials, and a wide array of economic and social pressures. It relies on international social pressure and shame, often mobilized by nonstate actors. Recalcitrant states feel pressure because of concerns about belonging to the international community. Compliance with the terms of the international community affects foreign aid and investment, tourism, participation in global sporting events, and national reputation including the status of leaders. States differ in their vulnerability to this social pressure. Poor nations with small and vulnerable economies are more subject to international pressure than wealthier ones. Those with a more vibrant NGO community and more democratic governance face greater internal pressures to go along than those that have a more repressive form of governance. Many human rights scholars and practitioners bemoan the lack of more direct enforcement.

Adopting an anthropological view of culture avoids the othering and denigration of culture characteristic of the colonial past and promotes a more complex understanding of the interactions between local and transnational culture. Rather than viewing culture simply as an obstacle to change, a more dynamic understanding of culture recognizes its capacity to innovate, appropriate, and create local practices. This understanding of culture challenges those who claim that reforms violate their culture at the same time as it encourages activists to take seriously meaning and practice within local contexts. Local leadership, working in conjunction with global movements, can foster productive dialogues in which translation across the global-local divide takes place. Human rights are themselves a cultural practice, with embedded values of autonomy and choice, protection of the body, equality as the route to social justice, and the responsibility of the state to promote social justice. In language, procedures, and forms of transnational social organization, the human rights system has developed a global cultural world with a distinctive vision of social justice.

Instead of viewing human rights as a form of global law that imposes rules, it is better imagined as a cultural practice, as a means of producing new cultural understandings and actions. The human rights legal system produces culture by developing general principles that define problems and articulate normative visions of a just society in a variety of documents ranging from lawlike ratified treaties to nonbinding declarations of the General Assembly. The myriad transnational NGOs give these documents much of their life and power: they do the research on which documents are constructed, publicize the completed documents, and pressure their governments to conform to them. NGOs work in collaboration with UN agencies to produce reports on human rights violations, encourage victims to complain to UN bodies, and provide services to local populations that increase their understanding of their human rights. These processes are central to the knowledge practices of the human rights regime — its technologies for fixing truth in universal and legalistic forms. Global law is produced as these documents are written, disseminated, and understood by local populations around the world.

Intermediaries play a critical role in translating human rights concepts to make them relevant to local situations. These ideas become localized through the work of individuals who serve as translators between transnational and local arenas. They are people who hold a double consciousness, combining both human rights conceptions and local ways of thinking about grievances. They move between them, translating local problems into human rights terms and human rights concepts into approaches to local problems. They may be local activists, human rights lawyers, feminist NGO leaders, or a host of other people who have one foot in the transnational community and one at home. On the one hand, they have to speak the language of international human rights that the international donors prefer in order to get funds. On the other hand, they have to present their initiatives in cultural terms that will be acceptable to at least some of the local community. As they scramble for funds, they often need to select issues that the international donors are interested in, such as female genital cutting, women's empowerment, or trafficking, even though local populations may be more interested in clean drinking water, changed inheritance laws, or good roads.

Localizing human rights does not typically change the meaning and structure of human rights. The human rights approach retains its distinctive cultural conception of the person, embedded in the human rights documents, which values autonomy, security of the body, and equality. The case studies suggest that they produce human rights consciousness among people at the bottom of the social hierarchy from time to time, but that in the absence of success or reinforcement, this consciousness can fade. It seems likely that the process of human rights creation and appropriation is different for women's rights than for other spheres of rights. Protecting vulnerable womanhood has long been part of imperial reform movements, denigrating the way of life of the target society while legitimating military and political intervention. More recently, the image of the vulnerable woman victim of violence has proved politically useful in promoting military invasion, as it did in Afghanistan, or in dramatically increasing rates of incarceration in the United States (see Garland 2002). The story of the innocent young girl trafficked into the sex trade by villainous crime figures is currently legitimating an increased intensity of policing and border control in the global North. Women's rights seem to be a relatively nonpolitical domain of rights. They appear not to challenge the growing global inequalities produced by race, class, and capitalism, although these inequalities impinge on women more than men. The villain is the individual brown or black man, not the system of global economic inequality or racism. The focus on women both underscores older ideas about differential levels of civilization and offers a relatively innocuous way to foster the expansion of rights-based conceptions of social justice and the rule of law. It deflects attention from systemic problems such as lack of clean water or environmental degradation to the inadequacies of different cultures.

There are clearly ways in which the current conception of women as bearers of human rights supports market-based capitalism. Some argue that rights reforms seek to resituate women within existing regimes of power without challenging the regimes themselves. Dianne Otto has pointed out the limitations of the transformative potential of an approach which seeks to relocate women with relationship to men but not to transform the institutions that produce hierarchy in society itself. The model of woman developed within the international human rights movement of the 1990s, particularly in the Beijing conference, exemplifies this limitation, which Otto attributes to the rupture between the women's rights agenda and the development agenda. By Beijing, there was a fundamental separation between women as bearers of human rights and women and development. The image of woman being protected by human rights is compatible with the individualistic, family-centered assumptions of neoliberalism and the expansion of the market economy. She notes that in the Platform for Action where women's experience is the same as men's, women are granted access to human rights in the same way as men. Where the Platform refers to female-specific experiences, however, such as violence against women, the language is more equivocal (Otto 1999b: 132). Violence against women is recognized as impairing or nullifying women's enjoyment of human rights rather than as a violation of those human rights (par. 131, Otto 1999b: 132). On the other hand, violence against women resulting from harmful traditional or customary practices, cultural prejudices, and extremism is identified explicitly as a human rights violation (par. 232(g), 1999b: 132). Thus, the focus of the document is on women's oppression by culture rather than class or capitalism.

The absence of attention to the effects of the globalization of capital and a class-based awareness of the importance of economic and social rights means, Otto argues, that the women's rights as human rights agenda is in danger of being coopted by global capital, as the women's development agenda was earlier (1999b: 133). Restricting women's issues to the paradigm of equality prohibits transformative change and fails to contest the institutions that reproduce gender hierarchies. The equality paradigm silences women's diversities by confining rights entitlements to those who fit the model of woman of legal discourse (1999b: 135). In order to escape the homogeneity of the woman who is being protected by international human rights law—a woman living in a heterosexual family but increasingly committed to employing her skills to promote market-driven development—Otto advocates conceptualizing diversity in terms of cultural specificity rather than relativism (1999b: 130–31). Her fundamental point is that the narrow post–Cold War dominant discourse on human rights and equality should be rejected because of its allegiance to the interests of the West and global capital (1999b: 125). Instead, it is essential to develop a framework that recognizes difference and specificity but also enables a shared language of equity and justice, recognizing its contingency in various locations (1999b:135). Including women in such a framework is a step toward disrupting the patriarchal shape of that framework.

Clearly, there are powerful linkages between women's human rights activism and the interests of global capital, links that may account for the similarities in reform strategies across countries. Nevertheless, these efforts provide some opening for change. As women achieve more autonomy over their bodies and lives, they may unleash new demands for change. Human rights is a powerful language in contemporary political discourse, one that evokes notions of law and legality and confers membership in the international community of "civilized" nations. Despite drawbacks in the way the concept of human rights has been developed and used, it is still the only global vision of social justice currently available. With all its flaws, it is the best we have. It provides at least some constraint on the operation of markets and offers a potentially powerful tool to those who learn to use it. Like the language of law itself, it serves those in power but is always in danger of escaping its bounds and working in a genuinely emancipatory way.

Notes

Chapter One

1. News sources include Blair 2002: 15 and Fisher 2002: 3.

2. For example, a report issued by an African NGO group at the 2000 global meeting on women, Beijing Plus Five, recommends, in an echo of colonial rhetoric, that governments "legislate against customary laws and traditional practices that are repugnant to natural justice and which are incompatible with other objectives of the African and Global Platforms for Action, as well as other international and human rights instruments" (Okello and Wambui 2000: 1).

3. A 1979 seminar of the WHO Regional Office in Khartoum recommended forming the Inter-African Committee on Traditional Practices Affecting the Health of Women and Children, and in 1983 the Subcommission of the Human Rights Commission set up a Working Group on Traditional Practices Affecting the Health of Women and Children (High Commissioner for Human Rights n.d.).

4. The concept of the nation as an imagined community, an idea born in the nineteenth century, also emphasizes a shared system of beliefs and values (Anderson 1983).

5. This understanding of culture migrated into early US anthropology through the work of Franz Boas in the early twentieth century.

6. This argument was presented in 1993 by the Asian regional preparatory meeting for the Vienna Conference on Human Rights. The Bangkok Declaration stated: "while human rights are universal in nature they must be considered in the context of a dynamic and evolving process of international norm-setting, bearing in mind the significance of national and regional particularities and various historical, cultural and religious backgrounds" (Final Declaration of the Regional Meeting for Asia of the World Conference on Human Rights, adopted 7 April 1993, UN Doc A/Conf.157/ASRM/8-A/CONF.157/

234

PC/59 [1993]: 3-8) Similarly, when Singapore presented its report to the Women's Convention committee at the UN in 2001, the head of the delegation defended Singapore's reservations to the convention — articles that it refused to ratify — by asserting that Singapore's laws and policies must reflect its particular economic, social, and geopolitical constraints and realities. Moreover, the government had to be sensitive to the different cultural and religious beliefs of its people (Press Release WOM/1293, July 13, 2001 Convention on the Elimination of Discrimination against Women, 25th session, 522nd meeting (AM): p. 1).

All UN documents are available in UN depository libraries and most recent documents are also available on the UN website, www.un.org.

7. Indeed, women's NGOs in Nigeria have worked hard to protect widows from persecution and to provide them a fair share of the property left by their husbands, resulting in laws passed protecting widows in three states, Oyo, Enugu, and Edo (womensrightswatch-nigeria@kabissa.org email 6/24/02). The movement, according to the NGO in southern Nigeria that runs this listserve, focuses on inheritance rights but also identifies a variety of customs and traditions concerning widowhood as harmful cultural practices.

8. Annelise Riles's account of document production in Fiji and in the run-up to the 1995 Beijing Conference on Women, which focuses on the creation of the document itself, reveals striking parallels to the process I observed in other international settings (1998).

9. For example, a conference called the Color of Violence in Santa Cruz, California in 2000 brought together hundreds of indigenous leaders from the United States and the Pacific and minority communities in the United States and Canada. A conference on violence and culture in the Asia-Pacific region in Sydney, Australia pulled together 450 people to hear about approaches to violence against women in India, China, Canada, Australia, New Zealand, Vanuatu, Fiji, Papua New Guinea, the United States, and a variety of other Asia-Pacific nations.

In 2003, the Wellesley Centers for Women held an international conference called Violence against Women, which brought together over one hundred scholars and activists from around the world.

10. takeaction.amnestyusa.org/Newsletter/?nlid=20&nlaid=81, visited November 23, 2004.

11. See also Office of the United Nations High Commissioner for Human Rights, World Conference on Human Rights (June 1993), http://www.unhchr.ch/html/menu5/ wchr.htm.

12. Hanna Roberts, *The Human Rights of Women in the United Nations: Developments 1993–1994,* at www.amnesty.se/women/23ae.htm.

13. United Nations Department of Public Information, *Women and Violence* (1996), at www.un.org.rights/dpi1772e.htm.

14. Rhoda Howard-Hassman describes the resistance of judges in Northern Nigeria to the Canadian critique of stoning and whipping as punishments for adultery (2004). In response to the international outcry, one judge carried out the flogging penalty more quickly.

15. The Declaration by the General Assembly of 1993 is similarly clear in its condemnation of culture as a justification for violence against women. It explicitly denies that

any notion of cultural relativism permits violence against women and prohibits states from using tradition to skirt compliance. It allows individual states to be held accountable for their failure to protect female citizens from violence (Ulrich 2000: 652). Ulrich thinks this declaration makes progress in moving toward seeing that it is essential to demolish social, economic, and cultural power structures that have kept women dominated for centuries (Ulrich 2000: 653).

16. For example, in the 1998 version of the Commission on Human Rights resolution on violence against women, it was the only "traditional or customary practice" listed (par. 11), while resolutions in subsequent years expanded the list. Female genital cutting, as it is less pejoratively called (see Boyle 2002), is a form of genital surgery that is widely seen as having harmful health consequences such as infections, painful urination and menstruation, difficulties in childbirth, and other complications.

17. The Working Group on Traditional Practices was formed by the Human Rights Commission in 1986 (Bernard 1996: 78). In 1989, in response to NGO activism, the Subcomission on the Prevention of Discrimination and Protection of Minorities of the Human Rights Commission created the Special Rapporteur on Traditional Practices Affecting the Health of Women and Children (Report of the Special Rapporteur on Traditional Practices affecting the Health of Women and Children UN Doc E/CN.4/Sub .2/1990/44). In 1990, the CEDAW Committee, being gravely concerned "that there are continuing cultural, traditional and economic pressures which help to perpetuate harmful practices, such as female circumcision," adopted a general recommendation (number 14) that suggested that states parties should take measures to eradicate the practice of female circumcision (Bernard 1996: 78).

18. This campaign orchestrates events by over one thousand groups and individuals from over one hundred countries. It maintains an electronic listserve with 600 participants.

19. Email from lmclarke@rci.retgers.edu August 20, 2002: "2002 Campaign Announcement."

Chapter Two

1. For example, NGOs expecting to address the High Commission on Human Rights, meeting in March–April 2003, were required to submit their written statements before February 3, 2003.

2. First Information Note for nongovernmental organizations participating in the fifty-ninth session of the Commission on Human Rights, November 22, 2002.

3. For example, at the CSW meetings, NGOs in the highest status, general consultative status, are entitled to 2000 words, those in special consultative status may have 1500 words, and those in the lowest status roster, can only submit statements if requested. NGOs may also make oral statements at certain places in the agenda if there is time, such as in the discussions after the panels, but in order to do so NGOs must complete a form which gives the name of the speaker, organization, topic to be addressed, names of groups that endorse the statement, and 17 copies of the statement itself no later than 5:00 PM the evening before the NGO representative expects to speak. A maximum of five NGO representatives can be called on to speak during the panel discussion, and they must submit their names to the NGO Liaison Officer 12 hours before the panel

discussion. NGOs are encouraged to collaborate in producing these statements so that they speak for more than their own organization. Consequently, NGOs are not free to make spontaneous contributions during the discussion of panels, unlike member states (Information from the NGO Committee on the Status of Women, New York, distributed via email December 18, 2001).

4. The website for the Conference of NGOs in Consultative Status with the United Nations Economic and Social Council (CONGO) describes the process of gaining consultative status as follows: "The basis for the consultative relationship between the United Nations and non-governmental organizations was set forth most recently following an extensive intergovernmental review that culminated in ECOSOC Resolution 1996/31. This relationship is the principal means through which ECOSOC receives input from NGOs into its deliberations at public meetings and in its subsidiary bodies as well as in UN international conferences and their preparatory bodies. Each year the approximately 2000 NGOs now holding consultative status receive the provisional agenda of ECOSOC. They have certain privileges to place items on the agenda of ECOSOC and its subsidiary bodies; they may attend meetings, where they may submit written statements and make oral presentations to governments" (www.congo.org/ngopart/constat.htm).

5. Examples of women's NGOs in general consultative status are Soroptomist International, Rotary International (which describes itself as an organization of business and professional leaders who provide humanitarian service and help to build goodwill and peace in the world, a total of 1.2 million members in 30,462 Rotary clubs in 162 countries (E/CN.6/2002/NGO/6:3), and Zonta International. Other organizations with this status include HelpAge International, International Alliance of Women, International Council of Women, and International Federation of Business and Professional Women. My observations suggest that these organizations typically send one or more staff members to attend the meetings. Many are large membership-based international organizations.

Organizations in special consultative status include European Women's Lobby, International Federation of University Women, Italian Centre of Solidarity, National Council of German Women's Organizations, Salvation Army, Socialist International Women, Fédération européenne des femmes actives au foyer, and Mother's Union, an Anglican voluntary organization with one million members (E/CN.6/2002/NGO/12). The European Union of Women and International Association for Counseling are both roster organizations. Such organizations are less likely to be able to afford to send a staff member to the conference, although many send volunteers. For example, the Women's International League for Peace and Freedom has a volunteer who attends the CSW every year.

6. A large red electronic sign at the front of the room records the elapsed time for each speaker and signals when the time is up. NGOs are allowed to speak on the floor, although their speaking time is far shorter than that of government representatives. Member countries are allocated 10 minutes each per item on the agenda, observers, including other governments, intergovernmental organizations, specialized agencies, and NGOs, five minutes per item. If NGOs present collaboratively, they may have more time: for example, 6–10 NGOs collectively may speak for 10 minutes. For each item on the agenda, there is a speaker's list for member states, for observers, and for NGOs, in

that order. While NGOs are making their presentations to the commission, the noise level usually rises as delegates wander around and talk to each other. The chair frequently admonishes those in the room to be quiet. This activity suggests that NGO speeches receive less attention than government ones. ("First information note for non-governmental organizations participating in the fifty-ninth session of the Commission on Human Rights," UN Office at Geneva, November 22, 2002.)

7. In my observations of the commission in 2001 and 2002, it seemed that much of the formal meeting time was devoted to statements from government representatives and from NGOs. Country representatives typically use the time to portray their country's efforts to promote human rights in the best light. For example, in the discussion of violence against women in 2001, Egypt noted that it has a new Shari'a law on divorce that stipulates the equality of men and women and the political will to emphasize these aspects of Islamic law (April 9, 2001). Heads of state or high-ranking ministers of government also address the commission. The CHR is a body of governments, and the rank of the speakers within their governments carries weight. One chair introduced a speech by a head of state by saying "It shows how important our work is that a head of state wants to address us." At least five heads of state did in the 2001 meeting. Allocations of time are carefully demarcated and laid out in UN document E/CN.4/2001.CRP.1, p. 2.

8. She also presented reports on her visits to Sierra Leone and Colombia (E/CN.4/2002/83 and Adds. 1–3).

9. The staff support for the CSW is the Division for the Advancement of Women, which also provides staff support for the expert committee that monitors CEDAW.

10. From article in Punch, March 4, 2002, by Clara Nwachukwu, Owerri, circulated by womensrightswatch-nigeria@kabissa.org, March 14, 2002.

Chapter Three

1. For example, Bayefsky argues that "If rights are not followed by remedies, and standards have little to do with reality, then the rule of law is at risk" (2001: 7). Byrnes and Connors point out that women-specific human rights tend to have less effective implementation procedures than other human rights, an indication of a pervasive second-class status to women's human rights (1996: 679). However, some argue that human rights do not depend only on enforcement. In her study of the impact of the human rights system on China, Rosemary Foot notes that there is a debate about the way norms are diffused in the global system, with some emphasizing the role of constraint and fear of consequences for noncompliance, whereas others stress the constitutive role of norms and the symbolic significance of compliance for a nation's self-identity (Foot 2000: 5–6). She concludes that both are important for China.

2. This is, however, not always so straightforward. For example, Joan Fitzpatrick argues that equal treatment fails to protect women from violence by police since women's special vulnerabilities to gender-based violence may be buried in the larger category of police abuse (Fitzpatrick 1994: 545).

3. Some countries have produced 20 or more reports to all the treaty monitoring bodies and the most frequently reporting country, the UK, has produced 38 (Bayefsky 2001: 244–51).

4. Complaints and inquiry procedures are particularly important for the High Com-

mission on Human Rights, which has, since 1978, appointed special rapporteurs, representatives, and working groups to carry out investigative procedures (see Foot 2000: 34–36).

5. The CEDAW Committee has said that Articles 2 and 16 are core provisions of the convention and that reservations which challenge central principles are contrary to the provisions of the convention and to general international law. "Reservations to articles 2 and 16 perpetuate the myth of women's inferiority and reinforce the inequalities in the lives of millions of women throughout the world. The Committee holds the view that article 2 is central to the objects and purpose of the Convention. . . . [R]eservations to article 16, whether lodged for national, traditional, religious, or cultural reasons, are incompatible with the Convention and therefore impermissible" (from CEDAW, A/53/38/ Rev.1, pars. 6, 8, 15, 16, 17, quoted in Bayefsky 2001: 69).

6. They are paid only $3000 a year for 8 weeks of meeting time and considerable preparation between meetings (Bayefsky 2001: 99).

Chapter Four

1. I am grateful to Mark Goodale for pointing out the importance of alternative visions of social justice.

2. Coomaraswamy notes that women's rights commonly lose out to communal politics (1994: 53–54).

3. The Rashtra Swayamsevak Sangh, for example, was founded in 1925 as an alternative to the mass anticolonial struggles and its only activism was anti-Muslim violence. The women's wing was formed in 1936 (Sarkar 1995: 183).

4. The Hindu right uses concepts of secularism and equality to attack minority rights and to reinscribe a modernized but patriarchal family in which women participate as mothers and wives (Sarkar 1995: 187–89; Kapur and Cossman 1996: 235–36). Using the concept of equal rights, the Hindu right argues for equal respect for all religions and against any special treatment for religious minorities. Minority rights are attacked as "special rights" that violate secularism and equality. Secularism requires not recognizing religious differences, including separate personal laws. Creating a uniform civil code is a way to treat all minorities exactly the same.

5. The Hindu Succession Act (1956), for example, changed the system from one that allowed a daughter virtually no inheritance rights to one that allowed equal shares to sons, daughters, widows, and mothers if a Hindu male died intestate, but discrimination remains with regard to inheritance of the ancestral property, which is inherited patrilineally (Kapur and Cossman 1996: 134–35). Hindu laws concerning maintenance can be modified or rescinded if the applicant remarries or if the wife commits adultery, while under Muslim law a woman has the right to maintenance for three months after divorce and during marriage unless she "refuses herself to him or is disobedient" (Kapur and Cossman 1996: 140).

6. The situation in India is similar to that of other South Asian countries, in which majority law (Hindu in India, Muslim in Bangladesh and Pakistan, for example) has been reformed but minority law remains as it was crystallized during the colonial era (Hossain 1994: 476). South Asian states justify their retention of personal laws as an aspect of a policy of pluralism and protection of minority and ethnic communities but in doing so,

they accept the arrogation by so-called community leaders of the right to represent the community and ignore women's voices that point to an underlying unity of oppression and subordination within the family (Hossain 1994: 483). Some argue that this is a polit- ical strategy to guarantee the votes and political support of minorities.

7. International standards are of course important in India. The country is a very active and articulate participant in all the human rights meetings I have attended. In an article on a new domestic violence bill in a major English-language Indian daily, the *Times of India*, the author notes that the Vienna Accord of 1994 and the Beijing Platform of Action of 1995 have acknowledged the existence of domestic violence as a problem. Moreover, the article continues that the intervention of the state to protect women against violence, especially in the family, has been strongly recommended by the UN committee on CEDAW (Times of India, January 7, 2002, p. 7). This article, in the main- stream press, indicates that international documents are recognized and seen as impor- tant in defining problems and legitimating, if not directing, their solution.

8. I am grateful to Paul Geraghty, Karen Brison, Steven Ratuva, Letitia Hickson, An- drew Arno, and Martha Kaplan for suggestions and insights on this discussion.

9. The committee monitoring the Convention on Racial Discrimination issued con- cluding comments to Fiji in 2003 sternly critical of its coups and its failure to promote a multiethnic society (CERD/C/62/CO/3, June 2, 2003).

10. Two other members of the Women's Ministry were also present at the meeting I had with the assistant minister, neither of whom had attended the New York CEDAW meeting. They were concerned about the use of bulubulu for rape although not about the custom itself. But they were more concerned about the effects of Christianity. One woman said that a woman's brothers and cousins would challenge her husband if he abused her, but now, because of Christian concepts, they say, "You stay with him." The other woman agreed that Christian teaching was the problem. This teaching talks about a woman becoming a martyr to Christian heroism, insisting that she stay with her hus- band at all costs. She said that she read the Bible through the lens of feminism and found that it was not necessarily that way in the Bible. This is a selective interpretation of Christianity, she thinks. But both agreed that it is hard for a woman to flee back to her family because it is too hard for them to feed her. Ultimately she has to go back to her husband. As Kaplan argues (2004), Christianity is fundamental to Fijian conceptions of land rights and indigenous claims and has become in some ways connected to the notion of the nation itself.

11. In Fiji Women's Rights Movement's draft Sexual Offences Legislation, they rec- ommended a minimum five-year sentence for sexual offenses and seven years for aggra- vated sexual assault (2000: 26).

12. He agreed to make changes, according to a 1991 article, including imposing com- pulsory counseling for rapists in jail and ruling against accepting alcohol or "traditional reconciliation" in mitigation (Bromby 1991: 19).

13. She is being interviewed by Patty Orofino in a program called Pacific Women (tape courtesy of Letitia Hickson, Center for Pacific Islands Studies, Univ. of Hawai'i, Manoa).

14. There are efforts to recuperate Fijian traditions of reconciliation to deal with the current ethnic crisis. Ratuva suggests using some of the widely used forms of apol- ogy and forgiveness for peace-building between Fijians and Indo-Fijians. "Through the

240

ceremonial discourse, differences are put on the table for collective scrutiny and then 'buried' in an atmosphere of openness and trust. Both groups agree to be the guardians of future peace" (Ratuva 2002). This process might provide restorative justice and long-term peace-building in intercommunal conflicts. However, unlike other processes of mutual self-humbling, forgiveness, and community convergence, bulubulu is one sided, good for restoring relations between groups but not for addressing the suffering of an individual as in situations of rape (Ratuva 2002). The apology may or may not benefit the victim. There are clearly strengths in these processes for the maintenance of a cooperative local community.

Chapter Five

1. In her comparative study of government responses to domestic violence and sexual assault in 36 democratic countries, Weldon observes a similar repertoire of interventions. She finds that they are most extensive in Australia, Canada, and the United States (2002: 143–54).

2. Rong Weiyi, "The interaction between the police and the community," DVRIP conference 2002, trans. by Wei-ying Lin.

3. "Social Work and Support for victims of Domestic Violence," presented at DVRIP International Conference 2002 (trans. by Wei-ying Lin), p. 4.

4. The MS program straddles the government-NGO divide, claiming either identity as it seems helpful (Sharma, forthcoming). It functions in the autonomous fashion of a nongovernmental organization in some contexts and as a government program in others. Personnel are paid by the government and sometimes emphasize their official roles, while other branches of government view them as relatively powerless (Sharma, forthcoming). The full-time local women organizers are paid, but only slightly more than the government-stipulated minimum for skilled work (Sharma, forthcoming, n. xi).

5. Seventeen women were given paralegal training by the MS program with a feminist critique of the legal system to develop alternate definitions of violence against women, divorce, and the like (ICRW 2002: 49).

6. A major study of Chinese women's social status conducted in 2001, updating a 1990 survey, by the ACWF of 19,512 people in urban and rural areas showed that in the last ten years, despite improvements of women's social status and a great increase in consciousness of women's rights and acceptance of gender equality, the income gap between men and women is widening every year (*China Women's News,* September 5, 2001, Wei-ying Lin, trans.).

7. Sakshi offers training in addressing violence, intervention, and the law to women's groups, police, medial and legal personal, government functionaries, judges, parents, and individual women as well as conducting feminist legal research on violations of women's human rights (www.mnet.fr/webparticulier/a/aiindex/sakshi.html, September 24, 2001).

Chapter Six

1. Each of these interviews was done in person and lasted between one and two and a half hours. I did twelve of the interviews and my research assistants did the rest. Fourteen of the women's interviews were conducted by Leilani Miller, six by Marilyn Brown,

seven by Madelaine Adelman, and three by me. Leilani Miller's method was to read her text back to the interviewee to verify that she expressed their views while Madelaine Adelman taped the interviews. I interviewed nine men, Leilani Miller interviewed six, Linda Andres talked to three, Marilyn Brown two, and Joy Adapon one. These interviews were conducted between 1991 and 1994, the years of the greatest expansion of gender violence cases in the courts. The interviews included both partners in six couples, although each member was interviewed separately. Interviews were solicited by researchers who attended the men's and women's groups and invited participants to volunteer in exchange for a small stipend. Although interviewees were told that the research was an independent project, it is very likely that they saw the project as closely connected to the Alternatives to Violence program (ATV) itself.

2. Since the 1980s, under pressure from groups demanding a more activist police force and mandatory arrest policies, there has been a vast increase in the number of cases of domestic violence in court, for example, going up 60-fold per capita in California between 1981 and 1995. Arrests in California for spousal assault jumped from 757 in 1981 to 60,279 in 1995 (Rosenbaum 1998: 412). After Denver's mandatory arrest policy was implemented in 1984, arrests increased tenfold in ten years (St. Joan 1997: 264). The number of restraining orders issued in Massachusetts nearly tripled between 1985 and 1993, then began to level off (Ptacek 1999: 62).

3. This analysis was developed in collaboration with Rachel Stern, who served first as my research assistant and then coauthor of a longer article on the movement. We relied on ethnographic studies done at the time of the movement and carried out subsequent field research in 2002–2003. Rachel Stern did most of the ethnographic research. After spending a year in Hong Kong, she returned twice in 2003 to interview many of the leaders of the movement. I joined her for a period of interviewing in 2001. These interviews took place nearly ten years after the movement. While they provided insight into how people saw the issue, we have relied heavily on secondary sources to reconstruct a timeline of events. Eliza Chan's master's thesis in anthropology at the Chinese University of Hong Kong is a particularly important source because Chan spent significant time with the indigenous women during the movement and, among those who studied the movement, put the greatest emphasis on how these women perceived events at the time. Chan developed an analysis of the difference between the way the indigenous women saw the movement and the way it was understood by others (1995). It was her insightful analysis that started us on a further exploration of the female inheritance movement as a way of understanding the process of localizing human rights.

4. Ms. Cheng told her story to Rachel Stern and to the media; this account relies on both sources.

5. Wills are considered bad luck in traditional Chinese culture because of their association with death. For this reason, wills detailing division of property are rare. However, men would occasionally leave "voice from the grave" wills that exhorted family members to behave well or gave a widow permission to remarry (Selby 1991: 72–73; see also Wong 2000: 173).

6. Governor Patten did, in fact, reply, although he did not take any action (Cheng interview 2003).

7. There were calls for a bill of rights prior to 1989, but the proposal was not endorsed by the government until after Tiananmen (Petersen 1996: 350). In a tricky bit of legisla-

tive drafting, Hong Kong's Bill of Rights was modeled on the ICCPR to make it harder to repeal after the handover. China had already agreed in the Joint Declaration (the document outlining the terms of the handover) that the ICCPR would remain in force (Petersen 1996: 350).

8. The Hong Kong Council of Women was formed in 1947. Due to an explosion in the number of local women's groups during the 1980s, membership in the early 1990s was limited to a small number of expatriate women.

9. This oversight was a gross piece of negligence by the colonial government. In 1986, the government set up a working group to investigate the application of Chinese custom in the New Territories and consider the need for amendments to the New Territories Ordinance (Selby 1991: 45). If the working group realized that urban parts of the New Territories were also subject to Chinese customary law, they failed to report their findings. They also failed to consult any women in preparing their report.

10. By the time the news broke, the Hong Kong Council of Women had already informed the government of the problem. In June 1993, the government started automatically exempting all new grants of lands (with the exception of land grants to indigenous villagers) from the New Territories Ordinance (*South China Morning Post,* November 3, 1994).

11. There was almost no public consultation on this bill. The only group the government consulted was the Heung Yee Kuk (Home Affairs Branch 1993: 4). The Kuk supported a change in law, as long as it did not apply to indigenous residents.

12. The exact number of members of the Residents Committee is unclear. Chan cites six active members, although one is a news reporter without a grievance (1995: 39). Wong and Chan (interview 2003) list seven core members. Most likely, there was some flux over time.

13. This is a matter of dispute. In a 2003 interview, Ms. Cheng claimed that the women knew that the law had to be changed from the start.

14. In some cases, affection and kinship were valid criteria for female inheritance. Chan (1997) discusses a case from the 1970s in which a village council ruled that a daughter could become trustee of her father's land because she was the person closest to her father (155–59). Celestine Nyamu-Musembi reports a similar pattern in Kenya: Akamba women argue that daughters should inherit land, even though they are not generally entitled to, if they have been "dutiful" and diligent in helping their parents (2002: 133–34).

15. All Chinese terms are in Mandarin. For a more extended discussion of what it means to be a "last of line" daughter, see Chan 1995: 40, 60–63.

16. It is not clear from her thesis if Chan asked all the women this question. Chan (1995) writes: "When I interviewed the women, they expressed their willingness to give up their inheritance rights, should they have brothers in their immediate families" (72). One of the members of the Anti-Discrimination Female Indigenous Residents Committee thought that there was a difference in attitude between the older and younger women. The older women's claims did not involve property while the younger women wanted a fair share of their father's land (Chan, interview 2003).

17. For a broader discussion of how claims are framed to garner official and public support, see O'Brien 1996: 31–55.

18. In 1996, some of the members of this group were critical in getting the Convention on the Elimination of Discrimination against Women (CEDAW) extended to

Hong Kong. One member of this group, Andrew Byrnes, was a law professor who had been active in promoting CEDAW for many years.

19. This debate took place in both English and Cantonese, the two official languages of Hong Kong.

20. The Hong Kong Federation of Women, a conservative women's group founded in 1993, also favored a more gradual approach. In a statement, the federation wrote "we aim at progress without upsetting stability" (Hong Kong Federation of Women 1994). Peggy Lam, a founding member of the Hong Kong Federation of Women as well as a legislative councilor, advocated passing the government's original version of the NTL(E)O and dealing with female inheritance as a separate issue. Lam argued that haste to pass the amended NTL(E)O caused anxiety and conflict that could have been avoided (Hong Kong Hansard 1994: 4548–49).

21. The Hong Kong women's movement has a history of working in coalitions. Wong documents 16 coalitions between 1985 and 1996 (2000: 61–62).

22. Some later criticized the female inheritance movement because it failed to offer a fundamental challenge to patriarchy (Lui 1997: 22).

23. In general, the May Fourth movement (1919) was a move away from Confucian tradition toward gender equality, vernacular literature and reliance on science.

24. Fanny Cheung, the founder of the Hong Kong Federation of Women's Centres, says that the HKFWC has a "community approach" that differs from Western feminism. In addition to mobilizing community resources, this approach seeks to avoid the confrontation and militancy associated with Western feminism (Lee 2000: 253).

25. Of the seven indigenous women who formed the core of the Residents Committee, four were illiterate. None were educated beyond secondary school (Wong and Chan, interview).

26. There may be more translators. This is not meant as an exhaustive list, but as an illustration of the way layers communicated.

27. To a large extent, the female inheritance movement grew out of Ms. Cheng's commitment to the cause. A growing body of literature discusses the importance of risk-takers like Ms. Cheng (sometimes called "political entrepreneurs") in Chinese popular resistance movements. See O'Brien and Li 2005 and Diamant 2005.

28. In 1991, eighteen (of sixty) Legislative Council seats were elected for the first time. The 1992 reform package broadened the electorate by lowering the voting age to 18 and provided for the direct election of half the Legislative Council.

29. A great deal of literature has examined the connection between democratization and increased support for women's rights. See Fischler 2000, Lui 1997, Tong 1999.

30. The tactic of appealing to China continued even after the NTL(E)O was passed. In 1997, the Heung Yee Kuk lobbied the Preparatory Committee, the body reviewing Hong Kong's laws in preparation for the handover, to repeal female inheritance in the rural New Territories. When the Preparatory Committee let the NTL(E)O stand, the Kuk appealed to the National People's Congress (NPC). Ultimately, this tactic also failed.

31. Negotiated by Britain and China, the Basic Law is Hong Kong's constitution following the handover.

32. At the time, China was under a lot of international pressure because of its human rights record. In contrast, China had a relatively good record on gender equality and this must have been something that the CCP wanted to preserve (Petersen, interview).

33. In 1995, the UN Committee on Economic and Social Rights complained that the small-house policy discriminates against women (Hopkinson and Lei 2003: 23). Although the small-house policy has been under review since 1996, extending the policy to include women is not seen as an option because there is simply not enough land. For an excellent discussion of the small-house policy, see Hopkinson and Lei 2003.

34. Smart and Lee (2003) document the rapid expansion of the Hong Kong real estate market during this period.

35. In private, Heung Yee Kuk admitted that the real issue was not female inheritance, but the small-house policy (Loh, interview; see also Petersen, interview 2003).

References

All UN documents are available in UN depository libraries and most recent documents are also available on the UN website, www.un.org.

Abdullah, Hussaina J. 2002. "Religious Revivalism, Human Rights Activism and the Struggle for Women's Rights in Nigeria." In Abdullahi An-Naʿim, ed., *Cultural Transformation and Human Rights in Africa,* pp. 151–91. London: Zed Books.

Afsharipour, Afra. 1999. "Empowering Ourselves: The Role of Women's NGOs in the Enforcement of the Women's Convention." *Columbia Law Review* 99: 129–73.

Agnes, Flavia. 1995. "Redefining the Agenda of the Women's Movment within a Secular Framework." In Tanika Sarkar and Urvashi Butalia, eds., *Women and Right-Wing Movements: Indian Experiences,* pp. 136–58. London: Zed Books.

———. 1996a. "The Domestic Applications of International Human Rights Norms Relevant to Womee Human Rights: Strategies of Law Reform in the Indian Context." In Andrew Byrnes, Jane Connors, and Lum Bik, eds., *Advancing the Human Rights of Women: Using International Human Rights Standards in Domestic Litigation,* pp. 101–13. London: The Commonwealth Secretariat.

———. 1996b. "The Hidden Agenda beneath the Rhetoric of Women's Rights." In Madhusree Dutta, Flavia Agnes and Neera Adarkar, eds., *The Nation, the State, and Indian Identity,* pp. 68–95. Calcutta: Samya.

Alston, Philip. 1992. "The Commission on Human Rights." In Philip Alston, ed., *The United Nations and Human Rights: A Critical Appraisal,* pp. 126–210. Oxford: Clarendon Press.

Amnesty International. 2001. *Broken Bodies, Shattered Minds: Torture and Ill-treatment of Women.* London: Amesty International.

Anderson, Benedict. 1983. The Imagined Community: Reflections on the Origin and Spread of Nationalism. New York: Verso.

An-Naʻim, Abdullahi Ahmed, 1990. "Problems of Universal Cultural Legitimacy for Human Rights." In Abdullahi Ahmed An-Naʻim and Francis Deng, eds., *Human Rights in Africa: Cross-Cultural Perspectives,* pp. 331–68. Washington, D.C.: Brookings Institution.

——. 1992a. "Introduction." In Abdullahi Ahmed An-Naʻim, ed., *Human Rights in Cross-Cultural Perspectives: A Quest for Consensus,* pp. 1–18. Philadelphia: Univ. of Pennsylvania Press.

——. 1992b. "Toward a Cross-Cultural Approach to Defining International Standards of Human Rights: The Meaning of Cruel, Inhuman, or Degrading Treatment or Punishment." In Abdullahi Ahmed An-Naʻim, ed., *Human Rights in Cross-Cultural Perspectives: A Quest for Consensus,* pp. 19–44. Philadelphia: Univ. of Pennsylvania Press.

——. 1994. "State Responsibility Under International Human Rights Law to Change Religious and Customary Laws." In Rebecca J. Cook, ed., *Human Rights of Women: National and International Perspectives,* pp. 167–88. Philadelphia: Univ. of Pennsylvania Press.

——, ed. 2002. *Cultural Transformation and Human Rights in Africa.* London: Zed Books.

An-Naʻim, Abdullahi Ahmed, and Jeffrey Hammond. 2002. "Cultural Transformation and Human Rights in African Societies." In Abdullahi An-Naʻim, ed., *Cultural Transformation and Human Rights in Africa,* pp. 13–38. London: Zed Books.

Anon. 1999. "Fighting Violence against Women." *Tok Blong Pacific* 53 (1/2): 28.

Anti-Discrimination Female Indigenous Residents Committee. 1994. "Submission on the Green Paper on Opportunities for Women and Men." Unpublished.

Appadurai, Arjun. 1996. *Modernity at Large: Cultural Dimensions of Globalization.* Minneapolis: Univ. of Minnesota Press.

——, ed. 2001. *Globalization.* Durham and London: Duke Univ. Press.

Arno, Andrew. 1976. "Ritual of Reconciliation and Village Conflict Management in Fiji." *Oceania* 47 (1): 49–65.

——. 1980. "Fijian Gossip as Adjudication: A Communication Model of Informal Social Control." *Journal of Anthropological Research* 36 (3): 343–60.

——. 1993. *The World of Talk on a Fijian Island: An Ethnography of Law and Communicative Causation.* Norwood, NJ: Ablex Publishing.

Asia Television News. 2001. "A Fight for Rights in the New Territories." Aired February 27, 2001.

Association for the Advancement of Feminism. 1993. "New Territories Women Denied Right to Inherit." *Women's News Digest* 29: 13–14.

Aucoin, Pauline McKenzie. 1990. "Domestic Violence and Social Relations of Conflict in Fiji." In *Pacific Studies: Special Issue on Domestic Violence in Oceania* 13 (3): 23–43.

Basu, Amrita. 1995. "Feminism Inverted: The Gendered Imagery and Real Women of Hindu Nationalism." In Tanika Sarkar and Urvashi Butalia, eds., *Women and Right-Wing Movements: Indian Experiences,* pp. 158–80. London: Zed Books.

——. 1999. "Hindu Women's Activism in India and the Questions it raises." In Patricia Jeffery and Amrita Basu, eds., *Resisting the Sacred and the Secular: Women's Activism and Politicized Religion in South Asia,* pp. 167–84. New Delhi: Kali for Women.

Bauer, Joanne R., and Daniel A. Bell, eds. 1999. *The East Asian Challenge for Human Rights.* London and New York: Cambridge Univ. Press.

Bayefsky, Anne F. 2001. *The UN Human Rights Treaty System: Universality at the Crossroads.* Ardsley, NY: Transnational Publishers.

Beattie, David, Sir. 1994. *The Commission of Inquiry on the Courts.* Republic of Fiji.

Bernard, Desiree. 1996. "The Work of the Committee on the Elimination of Discrimination against Women: Its Focus on Nationality, Custom, Culture and the Rights of the Girl-Child." In Andrew Byrnes, Jane Connors, and Lum Bik, eds., *Advancing the Human Rights of Women: Using International Human Rights Standards in Domestic Litigation,* pp. 72–85. London: The Commonwealth Secretariat.

Blair, David. 2002. "Everyone laughed at me. I cried for someone to save me, no one helped . . ." *The Daily Telegraph* (London), July 26, 2002, p. 15.

Boyle, Elizabeth Heger. 2002. *Female Genital Cutting: Cultural Conflict in the Global Community.* Baltimore and London: Johns Hopkins Univ. Press.

Brison, Karen J. 2001. "Constructing identity through ceremonial language in rural Fiji." *Ethnology* 40: 309 (19).

Bromby, Robin. 1991. "Door Opened on Domestic Violence." *Pacific Islands Monthly* 61(1): 17–10.

Bunch, Charlotte. 1990. "Women's Rights as Human Rights: Toward a Re-Vision of Human Rights." *Human Rights Quarterly* 12: 489–498.

———. 1997. "The Intolerable Status Quo: Violence against Women and Girls." *The Progress of Nations 1997.* New York: UNICEF Publication.

Bush, Diane Mitsch. 1992. "Women's Movements and State Policy Reform aimed at Domestic Violence against Women: A Comparison of the Consequences of Movement Mobilization in the U.S. and India." *Gender and Society* 6: 587–608.

Butegwa, Florence. 2002. "Mediating Culture and Human Rights in Favour of Land Rights for Women in Africa: A Framework for Community-level Action." In Abdullahi An-Naʿim, ed., *Cultural Transformation and Human Rights in Africa,* pp. 108–25. London: Zed Books.

Butler, Judith. 1990. *Gender Trouble: Feminism and the Subversion of Identity.* New York: Routledge.

Byrnes, Andrew. 1994. "Toward More Effective Enforcement of Women's Human Rights Through the Use of International Human Rights Law and Procedures." In Rebecca J. Cook, ed., *Human Rights of Women: National and International Perspectives,* pp. 189–227. Philadelphia: Univ. of Pennsylvania Press.

———. 1996. "Human Rights Instruments Relating Specifically to Women, with Particular Emphasis on the Convention on the Elimination of all forms of Discrimination against Women." In Andrew Byrnes, Jane Connors, and Lum Bik, eds., *Advancing the Human Rights of Women: Using International Human Rights Standards in Domestic Litigation,* pp. 39–57. London: The Commonwealth Secretariat.

———. 1999. "CEDAW and Violence against Women: Implications for Hong Kong." *A World Free of Violence against Women: Conference Proceedings.* March 20, 1999. Hong Kong Convention and Exhibition Center.

Byrnes, Andrew, Jane Connors, and Lum Bik, eds. 1996. *Advancing the Human Rights of Women: Using International Human Rights Standards in Domestic Litigation.* London: The Commonwealth Secretariat.

Byrnes, Andrew, and Jane Connors. 1996. "Enforcing the Human Rights of Women: A

Complaints Procedure for the Women's Convention? Draft Optional Protocol to the Convention on the Elimination of all Forms of Discrimination against Women." *Brooklyn Journal of International Law* 21: 679–797.

Centre for Women's Law Studies and Legal Services of Peking University. 2001. *Theory and Practice of Protection of Women's Rights and Interests in Contemporary China.* Beijing: Workers Publishing House of China.

Cerna, Christina M., and Jennifer C. Wallace. 1999. "Women and Culture." In Kelly D. Askin and Dorean M. Koenig, eds., *Women and International Human Rights Law,* 1: 623–51. Ardsley, NY: Transnational Publishers.

Chan, Eliza Chong-lai. 1995. "Negotiating Daughterhood: A Case Study of the Female Inheritance Movement in the New Territories, Hong Kong." M.Phil. diss., Anthropology, Chinese Univ. of Hong Kong.

Chan, Selina Ching. 1996. "Negotiating Coloniality and Tradition: The Identity of Indigenous Inhabitants in Hong Kong." Department of Sociology, National University of Singapore Working Paper No. 131.

———. 1997. "Negotiating Tradition: Customary Succession in the New Territories of Hong Kong." In Grant Evans and Maria Tam, eds., *Hong Kong: The Anthropology of a Metropolis.* Honolulu: University of Hawai'i Press.

———. 1998. "Politicizing Tradition: The Identity of Indigenous Inhabitants of Hong Kong." *Ethnology* 37: 39–54.

———. 1999. "Colonial Policy in a Borrowed Place and Time: Invented Tradition in the New Territories of Hong Kong." *European Planning Studies* 7 (2): 231–42.

———. 2001. "Selling the Ancestor's Land: A Hong Kong Lineage Adapts," *Modern China* 27 (2): 262–84.

———. 2003. "Memory Making, Identity Building: The Dynamics of Economics and Politics in the New Territories of Hong Kong." *China Information* 17 (1): 66–91.

Chan Ko Ling. 2000a. "Study of the Impact of Family Violence on Battered Women and Their Children." Hong Kong: Christian Family Service Center and Department of Social Work and Social Administration, Univ. of Hong Kong, Resource Paper Series No. 38.

———. 2000b. "Unraveling the Dynamics of Spousal Abuse through the Narrative Accounts of Chinese Male Batterers." Ph.D. diss., Univ. of Hong Kong.

———. 2001. An Evaluative Study of Group Therapy for Male Batterers Cum Intervention Strategies. Hong Kong: Hong Kong Family Welfare Society.

Chanock, Martin. 2002. "Human Rights and Cultural Branding: Who Speaks and How?" In Abdullahi An-Na'im, ed., *Cultural Transformation and Human Rights in Africa,* pp. 151–91. London: Zed Books.

Charlesworth, Hilary. 1994. "What are 'Women's International Human Rights?'" In Rebecca J. Cook, ed., *Human Rights of Women: National and International Perspectives,* pp. 58–84. Philadelphia: Univ. of Pennsylvania Press.

Cheung, Choi Wan. 1994. "New Territories Indigenous Women Reclaimed Inheritance Rights." *Women's News Digest* 32–33: 6–7.

China Working Group against Domestic Violence, ed. 2000a. *A Review of Governmental Efforts against Domestic Violence in China.* Project for Beijing+5. Founded by the Hong Kong Oxfam. 17 pp., booklet in English and Chinese.

——, ed. 2000b. *China: Actions Undertaking against Domestic Violence.* Project for Beijing+5. Founded by the Hong Kong Oxfam. 36 pp., booklet in English and Chinese.

Choi Po-king. 1995. "Identities and Diversities: Hong Kong Women's Movement in 1980s and 1990s." *Hong Kong Cultural Studies Bulletin* 4:95–103.

Chowdhury, Gouri, Shakun Kannabiran, and Kalpana Kannabiran. 1996. *"The Challenge of Communalism to Gender Issues." In Madhusree Dutta, Flavia Agnes and Neera Adarkar, eds.,* The Nation, the State, and Indian Identity, pp. 95–127. Calcutta: Samya.

Cohn, Bernard S. 1996. *Colonialism and its Forms of Knowledge.* Princeton: Princeton Univ. Press.

Collier, Jane Fishburne. 1997. *From Duty to Desire: Remaking Families in a Spanish Village.* Princeton: Princeton Univ. Press.

Comaroff, Jean, and John L. Comaroff. 1999. "Occult economies and the violence of abstraction: notes from the South African postcolony." *American Ethnologist* 26: 279–303.

Comaroff, John L. 1998. "Reflections on the Colonial State, in South Africa and Elsewhere: Factions, Fragments, Facts and Fictions." *Social Identities* 4 (3): 321–361.

Comaroff, John L., and Jean Comaroff. 1997. *Of Revelation and Revolution: The Dialectics of Modernity on a South African Frontier,* vol. 2. Chicago: Univ. of Chicago Press.

Connell, R. W. 1995. *Masculinities.* Berkeley: Univ. of Calif Press.

Connors, Jane. 1996. "General Human Rights Instruments and their Relevance to Women." In Andrew Byrnes, Jane Connors, and Lum Bik, eds., *Advancing the Human Rights of Women: Using International Human Rights Standards in Domestic Litigation,* pp. 27–39. London: The Commonwealth Secretariat.

Cook, Rebecca J. 1990. "Reservations to the Convention on the Elimination of All Forms of Discrimination against Women." *Virginia Journal of International Law* 30: 643.

——. 1993. "Women's International Human Rights Law: The Way Forward." *Human Rights Quarterly* 15: 230–61.

——. 1994a. *Human Rights of Women: National and International Perspectives.* Philadelphia: Univ. of Pennsylvania Press.

——. 1994b. "State Responsibility for Violations of Women's Human Rights." *Harvard Human Rights Journal* 7: 125–175.

——. 1994c. "State Accountability Under the Convention on the Elimination of All Forms of Discrimination against Women." In Rebecca J. Cook, ed. , *Human Rights of Women: National and International Perspectives,* pp. 228–57. Philadelphia: Univ. of Pennsylvania Press.

Coomaraswamy, Radhika. 1994. "To Bellow like a Cow: Women, Ethnicity, and the Discourse of Rights." In Rebecca J. Cook, ed., *Human Rights of Women: National and International Perspectives,* pp. 39–57. Philadelphia: Univ. of Pennsylvania Press.

Coomaraswamy, Radhika, and Lisa M. Kois. 1999. "Violence against Women." In Kelly D. Askin and Dorean M. Koenig, eds., *Women and International Human Rights Law,* 1: 177–217. Ardsley, NY: Transnational Publishers.

Copelon, Rhonda. 1994. "Intimate Terror: Understanding Domestic Violence as Torture." In Rebecca J. Cook, ed., *Human Rights of Women: National and International Perspectives,* pp. 116–152. Philadelphia: Univ. of Pennsylvania Press.

Cowan, Jane K., Marie-Benedict Dembour, and Richard Wilson, eds. 2001. *Culture and Rights*. Cambridge: Cambridge Univ. Press.

Cowan, Jane K. 2001. "Ambiguities of an emancipatory discourse: the making of a Macedonian minority in Greece." In Jane K. Cowan, Marie-Benedict Dembour, and Richard Wilson, eds., *Culture and Rights*, pp. 152–177. Cambridge: Cambridge Univ. Press.

Diamant, Neil J. 2005. "Hollow Glory: The Politics of Rights and Identity among PRC Veterans." In Neil J. Diamant, Stanley B. Lubman, and Kevin O'Brien, eds., *Engaging the Law in China: State, Society and Possibilities for Justice*. Stanford, CA: Stanford University Press.

Division for the Advancement of Women. 1991. "Report: South Pacific Seminar on CEDAW." Vienna, UN Office, 2 April 1991. SPS/CEDAW/1991/2. UN DAW reference room, New York.

———. 2000. *Assessing the Status of Women: A Guide to Reporting under the Convention on the Elimination of All Forms of Discrimination against Women*. New York: United Nations Department of Economic and Social Affairs.

Domestic Violence in China: Research, Intervention and Prevention. *Newsletter*, No. 3. No date, approximately 2001.

Donnelley, Jack. 2003. *Universal Human Rights in Theory and Practice*. Second Ed. Ithaca, NY: Cornell Univ. Press.

Economic and Social Commission for Asia and the Pacific (ESCAP). 1997. *Human Rights and Legal Status of Women in the Asian and Pacific Region*. Studies on Women in Development 1. By Savitri Goonesekere. New York: United Nations.

———. 2000. *Using CEDAW at the Grass Roots: Convention on the Elimination of All Forms of Discrimination against Women in the Pacific*. New York: United Nations, ST/ESCAP/2095.

Ecumenical Centre for Research, Education and Advocacy. 2002. *An NGO Report on the International Convention on the Elimination of All Forms of Racial Discrimination: Submission to the Fiji Country Report*. January. 32 pp.

Egyptian Non-Governmental Organizations Coalition. 2000. *CEDAW: The Shadow Report*. December, 2000.

Eide, Asbjorn. 1992. "The Sub-Commission on Prevention of Discrimination and Protection of Minorities." In Philip Alston, ed., *The United Nations and Human Rights: A Critical Appraisal*, pp. 211–64. Oxford: Clarendon Press.

Elias, Norbert. 1978 [1939]. *The Civilizing Process: The History of Manners and State Formation and Civilization*. Trans. By Edmund Jephcott. Oxford: Blackwells.

Emberson-Bain, 'Atu. 1994. "The Status of Fiji women." *Pacific Islands Monthly*, May, p. 32.

Engel, David M., and Frank W. Munger. 2003. *Rights of Inclusion: Law and Identity in the Life Stories of Americans with Disabilities*. Chicago: Univ. of Chicago Press.

Erickson, Moana, and Andrew Byrnes. 1999. "Hong Kong and the Convention on the Elimination of All Forms of Discrimination Agaisnt Women." Hong Kong Law Journal 29: 350–369.

Ewick, Patricia, and Susan Silbey. 1998. *The Common Place of Law*. Chicago: Univ. of Chicago Press.

Fanon, Frantz. 1963. *Wretched of the Earth*. New York: Grove.

Ferree, Myra Marx. 2003. "Resonance and Radicalism: Feminist Framing in the Abortion Debates of the United States and German." *American Journal of Sociology* 109 (2): 304–44.

Ferraro, Kathleen J., and Lucille Pope. 1993. "Irreconcilable Differences: Battered Women, Police, and the Law." In N. Zoe Hilton, ed., *Legal Responses to Wife Assault*, pp. 96–127. Newbury Park: Sage.

Fiji Women's Crisis Centre. 1996. *Report on the Second Regional Meeting on Violence against Women in the Pacific.* Suva, Fiji.

———. C. 2000. *The Incidence, Prevalence and Nature of Domestic Violence and Sexual Assault in Fiji: A research project of the Fiji Women's Crisis Centre.* Supported by the UNIFEM Trust Fund New York, Asia Foundation, Government of Fiji- Department for Women. No date provided but approximately 2000.

Fiji Women's Rights Movement. 2000. *Herstory: A Profile of the Fiji Women's Rights Movement.* Suva, Fiji: Fiji Women's Rights Movement.

Fineman, Martha. 1995. *The Neutered Mother, the Sexual Family, and Other Twentieth-Century Tragedies.* New York: Routledge.

Fischler, Lisa Collynn. 2000. "Women at the Margin: Challenging Boundaries of the Political in Hong Kong." Ph.D. diss., Political Science, Univ. of Wisconsin at Madison.

Fisher, Ian. 2002. "Account of Punjab Rape Tells of a Brutal Society." *New York Times* July 17, 2002, sec. A, p. 3, col. 1, Foreign Desk.

Fitzpatrick, Joan. 1994. "The Use of International Human Rights Norms to Combat Violence against Women." In Rebecca J. Cook, ed., *Human Rights of Women: National and International Perspectives,* pp. 532–71. Philadelphia: Univ. of Penn Press.

Foot, Rosemary. 2000. *Rights Beyond Borders: The Global Community and the Struggle over Human Rights in China.* Oxford: Oxford Univ. Press.

Friedman, Elisabeth. 1995. "Women's Human Rights: The Emergence of a Movement." In Julie Peters and Andrea Wolper, eds., *Women's Rights, Human Rights: International Feminist Perspectives,* pp. 18–35. New York: Routledge.

Garland, David. 2002. The Culture of Control: Crime and Social Order in Contemporary Society. Chicago: Univ. of Chicago Press.

Geraghty, Paul. 2002. "Traditional Fijian Reconciliation." Draft on file with author.

Goldberg-Hiller, Jonathan, and Neal Milner. 2003. "Rights as Excess: Understanding the Politics of Special Rights." *Law and Social Inquiry* 28 (4): 1075–1118.

Goldberg-Hiller, Jonathan. 2002. The Limits to Union: Same-Sex Marriage and the Politics of Civil Rights. Ann Arbor: Univ. of Michigan Press.

Goodale, Mark. 2002. "Legal Ethnography in an Era of Globalization: The Arrival of Western Human Rights Discourse to Rural Bolivia." In June Starr and Mark Goodale, eds., *Practicing Ethnography in Law: New Dialogues, Enduring Methods,* pp. 50–72. New York: Palgrave Macmillan.

Green, December. 1999. *Gender Violence in Africa: African Women's Responses.* New York: St. Martin's Press.

Greenberg, Jonathan D. 2003. "Does Power Trump Law?" *Stanford Law Review* 55: 1789–1821.

Gunning, Isabelle. 1991–2. "Arrogant Perception, World-Traveling and Multicutlural Feminism: The Case of Female Genital Surgeries." *Columbia Human Rights Law Review* 23: 189–248.

———. 1999. "Women and Traditional Practices: Female Genital Surgery." In Kelly D. Askin and Dorean M. Koenig, eds., *Women and International Human Rights Law*, 1: 651–683. Ardsley, NY: Transnational Publishers.

Guo Jianmei. 2000. "A Research Report of the Legal Aid Cases Undertaken by the Center for Women's Law Studies and Legal Services under the Law School of Peking University (1996–2000)." Typescript.

Gupta, Akhil, and James Ferguson, eds. 1997. *Culture Power Place: Explorations in Critical Anthropology.* Durham N.C.: Duke Univ. Press.

Hajjar, Lisa. 2004. "Religion, State Power, and Domestic Violence in Muslim Societies: A Framework for Comparative Analysis." *Law and Social Inquiry* 29 (1): 1–38.

Hameed, Syeda Saiyidain. N.d. *Voice of the Voiceless: Status of Muslim Women in India.* Delhi: National Commission for Women.

Hannerz, Ulf. 1992. *Cultural Complexity: Studies in the Social Organization of Meaning.* New York: Columbia Univ. Press.

Hasan, Zoya. 1999. "Gender Politics, Legal Reform, and the Muslim Community in India." In Patricia Jeffery and Amrita Basu, eds., *Resisting the Sacred and the Secular: Women's Activism and Politicized Religion in South Asia,* pp. 71–89. New Delhi: Kali for Women.

Hatch, Elvin. 1997. "The Good Side of Relativism." *Journal of Anthropological Research* 53: 371–81.

Hecht, Jonathan. 1998. "Women's Rights, States' Law: The Role of Law in Women's Rights Policy in China." In John D. Montgomery, ed., *Human Rights: Positive Policies in Asia and the Pacific Rim,* pp. 71–96. Hollis, NH: Hollis Publishing Co.

Hathaway, Oona. 2002. "Do Human Rights Treaties Make a Difference?" *Yale Law Journal* 111: 1935–2042.

Hickson, Letitia. 1975. "The I Soro: Ritual Apology and Avoidance of Punishment in Fijian Dispute Settlement." Ph.D. diss., Department of Social Anthropology, Harvard Univ.

High Commissioner for Human Rights. N.d. *Harmful Traditional Practices Affecting the Health of Women and Children.* Fact Sheet No. 23. www.unhchr.ch/html/menu6/2/fs23.htm (8/8/2003).

Hobsbawm, Eric, and Terrence Ranger, eds. 1983. *The Invention of Tradition.* Cambridge: Cambridge Univ. Press.

Home Affairs Branch. 1994. Submission to the Bill Committee Meeting on January 13, 1994. Reference: HAB CR 8/26/21 III.

Hong Kong Federation of Women's Centres. 1994. *Annual Report: 1993–1994.* Hong Kong: Hong Kong Federation of Women's Centres.

Hong Kong Hansard. 1993. *Proceedings of the Legislative Council.* <www.legco.gov.hk/yr93–94/english/lc_sitg/hansard/h931013.pdf>.

———. 1994. *Proceedings of the Legislative Council.* <www.legco.gov.hk/yr93–94/english/lc_sitg/hansard/h940622.pdf>.

Hong Kong Women Christian Council, ed. 1995. *Uncertain Times: Hong Kong Women Facing 1997.* Hong Kong: Hong Kong Women Christian Council.

Hopkinson, Lisa, and Mandy Lao Man Lei. 2003. *Rethinking the Small House Policy.* Hong Kong: Civic Exchange.

Hossain, Sara. 1994. "Equality in the Home: Women's Rights and Personal Laws in South

Asia." In Rebecca J. Cook, ed., *Human Rights of Women: National and International Perspectives,* pp. 465–95. Philadelphia: Univ. of Pennsylvania Press.

Howard, Rhoda E. 1995. *Human Rights and the Search for Community.* Boulder: Westview Press.

Howard-Hassman, Rhoda E. 2004. "The Flogging of Bariya Magazu: Nigerian Politics, Canadian Pressures, and Women's and Children's Rights." *Journal of Human Rights* 3: 3–21.

Howarth, Carla, Carol Jones, Carole Petersen, and Harriet Samuels. 1991. *Report by the Hong Kong Council of Women on the Third Periodic Report by Hong Kong under Article 40 of the International Covenant on Civil and Political Rights.* Hong Kong: Hong Kong Council of Women.

Human Rights in China. 1998. *Report on Implementation of CEDAW in the People's Republic of China: A Report with Recommendations and Questions for the Chinese Government Representatives.* New York: Asia Monitor Resource Centre, China Labour Bulletin, and Hong Kong Christian Industrial Committee.

Human Rights in China. 1995. *Caught between Tradition and the State: Violations of the Human Rights of Chinese Women.* New York: Human Rights in China.

ICRW (International Center for Research on Women). 1999–2002. *Domestic Violence in India,* vols. 1–5. Washington, DC: USAID/India.

——. 2002. *Women-Initiated Community Level Responses to Domestic Violence: Domestic Violence in India: Exploring Strategies, Promoting Dialogue 5.* Washington, DC: USAID/India.

Ignatieff, Michael. 2001. *Human Rights as Politics and Idolatry.* Princeton: Princeton Univ. Press.

——. 2002. "American Exceptionalism and Human Rights." Ms. on file with author.

Initial Reports of States Parties: Guinea. 2001. "Consideration of Reports Submitted by States Parties under Article 18 of the Convention on the Elimination of All Forms of Discrimination against Women." United Nations CEDAW/C/GIN/1.

International Initiative for Justice in Gujarat. 2003. *Threatened Existence: A Feminist Analysis of the Genocide in Gujarat.* Bombay: New Age Printing Press, for Forum against Oppression of Women, Bombay.

International Women's Tribune Center. 2000. "Moving Ahead from the Final PrepCom to the Beijing Plus Five Special Session." From "300 Religious Right Representatives Attend Beijing Plus Five Preparatory Committee Meeting." By Jennifer Butler, Ecumenical Women 2000. *Preview 2000* (4 May): 1–11. New York: International Women's Tribune Center.

Jacobson, Roberta. 1992. "The Committee on the Elimination of Discrimination against Women." In Philip Alston, ed., *The United Nations and Human Rights: A Critical Appraisal,* pp. 444–72. Oxford: Oxford Univ. Press.

Jalal, Patricia. 1988. "The Urban Woman: Victim of a Changing Social Environment." In Leatuailevao Ruba Va'a and Joan Martin Teaiwa, eds., *Environment and Pacific Women: From the Globe to the Village,* pp. 30–37. Suva, Fiji: UH Manoa Library.

Jethmalani, Rani, ed. 1995. *Kali's Yug: Empowerment, Law and Dowry Deaths.* New Delhi: Har-Anand Publications.

——, ed. 2001. "Kali's Yug." *Women and Law Journal* (March), Special Issue: Bride Burning and Dowry. WARLAW.

Kaplan, Martha. 2004. "Promised Lands: From Colonial Law-giving to Postcolonial Takeovers in Fiji." In Sally Engle Merry and Donald Brenneis, eds., *Law and Empire in the Pacific: Hawai'i and Fiji*, pp. 153–87. Sante Fe: School of American Research Press.

Kapur, Ratna, and Brenda Cossman. 1996. *Subversive Sites: Feminist Engagements with Law in India*. New Delhi: Sage Publications.

Keck, Margaret E., and Kathryn Sikkink. 1998. *Activists beyond Borders: Advocacy Networks in International Politics*. Ithaca: Cornell Univ. Press.

Kelly, John D. 1991. *A Politics of Virtue: Hinduism, Sexuality, and Countercolonial Discourse in Fiji*. Chicago: Univ. of Chicago Press.

———. 1997. "Gaze and Grasp: Plantations, Desires, Indentured Indians, and Colonial Law in Fiji." In Lenore Manderson and Margaret Jolly, eds., *Sites of Desire, Economies of Pleasure: Sexualities in Asia and the Pacific*, pp. 72–99. Chicago: Univ. of Chicago Press.

Kerr, Joanna, ed. 1993. *Ours by Right: Women's Rights as Human Rights*. London: Zed Books.

Khagram, Sanjeev, James V. Riker, and Kathryn Sikkink, eds. 2002. *Restructuring World Politics: Transnational Social Movements, Networks, and Norms*. Minneapolis: Univ. of Minnesota Press.

Koh, Harold Hongju. 2003. "On American Exceptionalism." *Stanford Law Review* 55: 1479–1527.

Krishnamurthy, Mekhala. 2002. "In the Shadow of the State, in the Shade of a Tree: The Politics of the Possible in Rural Gujarat." BA thesis, Harvard University. Ms. on file with the author.

Kumar, Radha. 1999 [1995] "From Chipko to Sati: The Contemporary Indian Women's Movement." In Amrita Basu, ed., *The Challenge of Local Feminisms: Women's Movements in Global Perspective*, pp. 58–87. With the assistance of C. Elizabeth McGrory. Boulder: Westview Press. Reprinted Delhi, India: Kali for Women, 1999.

Kuper, Adam. 1999. *Culture: The Anthropologists' Account*. Cambridge, MA: Harvard Univ. Press.

Lal, Brij V. 1992. *Broken Waves: A History of the Fiji Islands in the Twentieth Century*. Honolulu: Univ. of Hawai'i Press.

———. 2002. "Making History, Becoming History: Reflections on Fijian Coups and Constitutions." *The Contemporary Pacific* 14 (1): 148–68.

Lawyers' Collective. 1992. *Legal Aid Handbook* 1: *Domestic Violence*. Delhi: Kali for Women.

Lazarus-Black, Mindie, and Susan Hirsch, eds., 1994. *Contested States: Law, Hegemony, and Resistance*. New York: Routledge.

Lazarus-Black, Mindie. 1994. *Legitimate Acts and Illegal Encounters: Law and Society in Antigua and Barbuda*. Washington, D.C.: Smithsonian Institution Press.

Leary, Virginia. 1990. "The Effect of Western Perspectives on International Human Rights." In Abdullahi Ahmed An-Na'im and Francis Deng, eds., *Human Rights in Africa: Cross-Cultural Perspectives*, pp. 15–31. Washington, D.C.: Brookings Institution.

Lee, Ching Kwan. 2000. "Public Discourses and Collective Identities: Emergence of Women as a Collective Actor in the Women's Movement in Hong Kong." In Stephen Wing Kai Chiu and Tai Lok Lui, eds., *The Dynamics of Social Movement in Hong Kong*. Hong Kong: Hong Kong University Press.

Leung, Elsie. 2002. "Women for a Better Tomorrow." Speech by the Secretary for Justice at a Luncheon of the Women's Commission Conference 2002 on May 11, 2002.

Li Hongxiang. 2000. "Definition of Domestic Violence in Law Theory." In China Law Society et al., eds., *Research on Prevention and Control of Domestic Violence,* pp. 75–82. Beijing: Qunzhong Publishing House.

Liu Donghua. C. 2001. "Five-year Consulting Report." Center for Women's Law Studies and Legal Service of Peking University.

Liu Meng and Cecelia Chan. 1999. "Enduring Violence and Staying in Marriage: Stories of Battered Women in Rural China." *Violence against Women* 5 (12): 1469–92.

——. 2000. "Family Violence in China: Past and Present." *New Global Development* 16: 74–87.

Liu Meng and Zhang Li-Xi. 2002. "Current Situation, Attitude, and Prevention Survey Report on Domestic Violence in China (National Survey subproject DVRIP)." Translated by Wei-Ying Lin. 12 pp. on file with author.

Lui, Yuk-lin. 1997. "The Emergence and Development of the Feminist Movement in Hong Kong from the Mid-1980s to the Mid-1990s." M.A. thesis, Government and Public Administration, Chinese University.

McCann, Michael W. 1994. Rights at Work: Pay Equity Reform and the Politics of Legal Mobilization. Chicago: Univ. of Chicago Press.

MacKinnon, Catharine. 1989. Toward a *Feminist Theory of the State.* Cambridge: Harvard Univ. Press.

Man Chung Chiu. 2001. "Politicising Han-Chinese Masculinities: A Plea for Court-Mandated Counselling for Wife Abusers in Hong Kong." *Feminist Legal Studies* 9: 3–27.

Marcus, George. 1998. *Ethnography through Thick and Thin.* Princeton: Princeton Univ. Press.

Menon, Nivedita. 2000. "State, Community and the Debate on the Uniform Civil Code in India." In Mahmood Mamdani, ed., *Beyond Rights Talk and Culture Talk: Comparative Essays on the Politics of Rights and Culture,* pp. 75–96. New York: St. Martin's Press.

Merry, Sally Engle. 1990. *Getting Justice and Getting Even: Legal Consciousness among Working-Class Americans.* Chicago: Univ. of Chicago Press.

——. 1995a. "Wife Battering and the Ambiguities of Rights." In Austin Sarat and Thomas Kearns, eds., *Identities, Politics, and Rights,* pp. 271–307. Amherst Series in Law, Jurisprudence, and Social Thought. Ann Arbor: Univ. of Michigan Press.

——. 1995b. "Gender Violence and Legally Engendered Selves." *Identities: Global Studies in Culture and Power* 2:49–73.

——. 2000. *Colonizing Hawai'i: The Cultural Power of Law.* Princeton: Princeton Univ. Press.

——. 2001a. "Rights, Religion, and Community: Approaches to Violence against Women in the Context of Globalization." *Law and Society Review* 35: 39–88.

——. 2001b. "Changing Rights, Changing Culture." In Jane Cowan, Marie-Benedicte Dembour, and Richard Wilson, eds., *Culture and Rights.* London: Cambridge Univ. Press.

——. 2003. "Rights Talk and the Experience of Law: Implementing Women's Human Rights to Protection from Violence." *Human Rights Quarterly* 25 (2) 343–81.

Merry, Sally Engle, and Donald Brenneis, eds. 2004. *Law and Empire in the Pacific: Hawai'i and Fiji.* Santa Fe: School of American Research Press.

Messer, Ellen, 1997. "Pluralist Approaches to Human Rights." *Journal of Anthropological Research* 53: 293–317.

Milner, Neal. 1986. "The Dilemmas of Legal Mobilization: Ideologies and Strategies of Mental Patient Liberation." *Law and Policy* 8: 105–29.

Mohapatra, Arun Ray. 2001. *National Human Rights Commission of India: Formation, Functioning, and Future Prospects.* New Delhi: Radha Publications.

Moore, Henrietta. 1994. "The Problem of Explaining Violence in the Social Sciences." In Penelope Harvey and Peter Gow, eds., *Sex and Violence: Issues in Representation and Experience,* pp. 138–55. London: Routledge.

Morrow, Betty Hearn. 1994. "A Grass-roots Feminist Response to Intimate Violence in the Caribbean." *Women's Studies International Forum* 17: 579–92.

Nagengast, Carole, and Terence Turner. 1997. "Introduction: Universal Human Rights versus Cultural Relativity." *Journal of Anthropological Research* 53: 269–72.

National Commission for Women. 2001. *Sexual Harassment at Workplace.* New Delhi: National Commission for Women.

Nizioki, Akinyi. 2002. "The Effects of Land Tenure on Women's Access and Control of Land in Kenya." In Abdullahi An-Na'im, ed., *Cultural Transformation and Human Rights in Africa,* pp. 218–61. London: Zed Books.

Nyamu-Musembi, Celestine. 2002. "Are Local Norms and Practices Fences or Pathways? The Example of Women's Property Rights." In Abdullahi An-Na'im, ed., *Cultural Transformation and Human Rights in Africa,* pp. 126–50. London: Zed Books.

O'Brien, Kevin. 1996. "Rightful Resistance." *World Politics* 49 (1):31–55.

O'Brien, Kevin, and Lianjiang Li. 2005. "Suing the State: Administrative Litigation in Rural China." In Neil J. Diamant, Stanley B. Lubman, and Kevin O'Brien, eds., *Engaging the Law in China: State, Society and Possibilities for Justice.* Stanford, CA: Stanford University Press.

Ofei-Aboagye, Rosemary Ofeibea. 1994. "Altering the Strands of the Fabric: A Preliminary Look at Domestic Violence in Ghana." *Signs: Journal of Women in Culture and Society* 19: 924–38.

Okello, Rosemary, and Mercy Wambui. 2000. "Progress Marred by Crises: NGO Report." Flame/Flamme: The African Daily Newspaper of Women 2000: Gender Equality, Development, and Peace for the 21st Century. 5 (June): 1.

Oller, Lucrecia. 1994. "Domestic Violence: Breaking the Cycle in Argentina." In Miranda Davies, ed., *Women and Violence,* pp. 229–34. London: Zed Books.

Omaha World Herald (Nebraska). Editorial: "Crime and Punishment: Scratch the Surface, and Some Pakistanis Can Be Barbaric." July 7, 2002, p. 68.

Ong, Aihwa. 1999. *Flexible Citizenship: The Cultural Logics of Transnationality.* Durham and London: Duke Univ. Press.

Otto, Dianne. 1999a. "Subalternity and International Law: The Problems of Global Community and the Incomensurability of Difference." In Eve Darian-Smith and Peter Fitzpatrick, eds., *Laws of the Postcolonial,* pp. 145–80. Ann Arbor: Univ. of Michigan Press.

———. 1999b. "A Post-Beijing Reflection on the Limitations and Potential of Human Rights Discourse for Women." In Kelly D. Askin and Dorean M. Koenig, eds., *Women and International Human Rights Law,* 1: 115–35. Ardsley, NY: Transnational Publishers.

Parish, William L., Tianfu Wang, Edward O. Laumann, Suiming Pan, and Ye Luo. 2004. "Intimate Partner Violence in China: National Prevalence, Risk Factors and Associated Health Problems." *International Family Planning Perspectives* 30 (4): 174–81.

Pence, Ellen, and Michael Paymar. 1993. *Education Groups for Men Who Batter: The Duluth Model.* New York: Springer Publishing Co.

Petersen, Carole. 1996. "Equality as a Human Right: The Development of Anti-Discrimination Law in Hong Kong." *Columbia Journal of Transnational Law* 34: 335–87.

Petersen, Carole, and Harriet Samuels. 2002. "The International Convention on the Elimination of All Forms of Discrimination against Women: A Comparison of Its Implementation and the Role of Non-Governmental Organizations in the United Kingdom and Hong Kong." 26 *Hastings International and Comparative Law Review* 1–51.

Pollis, Adamantia. 1996. "Cultural Relativism Revisited: Through a State Prism." *Human Rights Quarterly* 18: 316–44.

Poonacha, Veena, and Divya Pandey. 1999. *Responses to Domestic Violence in the States of Karnataka and Gujarat.* Mumbai: Research Centre for Women's Studies, SNDT Women's Univ.

Prasad, Satendra, ed. 1989. *Coup and Crisis: Fiji—a Year Later.* North Carlton, Victoria, Australia: Arena Publications.

Preis, Ann-Belinda S. 1996. "Human Rights as Cultural Practice: An Anthropological Critique." *Human Rights Quarterly* 18: 286–315.

Ptacek, James. 1999. *Battered Women in the Courtroom: The Power of Judicial Responses.* Boston: Northeastern Univ. Press.

Radio Television Hong Kong. 1986. "An Indigenous Village: A Case for Concern." Aired June 20, 1986.

Rajagopal, Balakrishnan. 2003. *International Law from Below: Development, Social Movements, and Third World Resistance.* Cambridge: Cambridge Univ. Press.

Rasmussen, Joyce. 1980. "Memorandum on Subregional Follow-up Meeting for Pacific Women of the World Conference of the UN Decade for Women." Library of the University of the South Pacific.

Ratuva, Steven. 2002. "Re-inventing the Cultural Wheel: Re-conceptualizing Restorative Justice and Peace-building in Ethnically Divided Fiji." Draft on file with author.

Razack, Sherene H. 1998. *Looking White People in the Eye: Gender, Race, and Culture in Courtrooms and Classrooms.* Toronto: Univ. of Toronto Press.

———. 2004. *Dark Threats and White Knights: The Somalia Affair, Peacekeeping, and the New Imperialism.* Toronto: Univ. of Toronto Press.

Reanda, Laura. 1992. "The Commission on the Status of Women." In Philip Alston, ed., *The United Nations and Human Rights: A Critical Appraisal,* pp. 265–304. Oxford: Clarendon Press.

Renteln, Alison Dundes. 1988. "Relativism and the Search for Human Rights." *American Anthropologist* 90:56–72.

———. 1990. *International Human Rights: Universalism Versus Relativism.* Newbury Park, CA: Sage Publications.

Report of the Secretary-General. 1995. *From Nairobi to Beijing: Second Review and Appraisal of the Implementation of the Nairobi Forward-Looking Strategies for the Advancement of Women.* New York: United Nations.

Resnik, Judith. 2001. "Categorical Federalism: Jurisdiction, Gender, and the Globe." *Yale Law Journal* 111: 619–80.

Riles, Annelise. 1998. "Infinity within the Brackets." *American Ethnologist* 25: 378–98.
———. 2001. *The Network Inside Out.* Ann Arbor: Univ. of Michigan Press.

Risse, Thomas, Stephen C. Ropp, and Kathryn Sikkink, eds. 1999. *The Power of Human Rights: International Norms and Domestic Change.* Cambridge: Cambridge Univ. Press.

Ristock, Janice L. 2002. No More Secrets: Violence in Lesbian Relationships. New York: Routledge.

Rodriguez, Noelie Maria. 1988. "A Successful Feminist Shelter: A Case Study of the Family Crisis Shelter in Hawai'i." *Journal of Applied Behavioral Science* 24: 235–50.

Romany, Celia. 1994. "State Responsibility Goes Private: A Feminist Critique of the Public/Private Distinction in International Human Rights Law." In Rebecca J. Cook, ed., *Human Rights of Women: National and International Perspectives*, pp. 85–115. Philadelphia: Univ. of Pennsylvania Press.

Rosenbaum, Michael D. 1998. "To Break the Shell without Scrambling the Egg: An Empirical Analysis of the Impact of Intervention into Violent Families." *Stanford Law and Policy Review* 9: 409–27.

Sakshi. 1996. Gender and Judges: A Judicial Point of View. New Delhi: Sakshi.
——— 1997. *Report: Regional Perspectives on Gender Equality* (January 4–5). New Delhi: Sakshi.

Samuels, Harriet. 1994. "Chairwoman's Report." *Hong Kong Council of Women Newsletter* 29: 5–7.

Sarat, Austin, and Thomas Kearns, eds. 1993. *Law and Everyday Life.* Ann Arbor: Univ. of Michigan Press.

Sarkar, Tanika. 1995. "Heroic Women, Mother Goddesses: Family and Organization in Hindutva Politics." In Tanika Sarkar and Urvashi Butalia, eds., *Women and Right-Wing Movements: Indian Experiences*, pp. 181–215. London: Zed Books.

Sarkar, Tanika. 2001. Hindu Wife, Hindu Nation: Community, Religion, and Cultural Nationalism. London: Hurst and Co.

Sarkar, Tanika, and Urvashi Butalia, eds. 1995. *Women and Right-Wing Movements: Indian Experiences.* London: Zed Books.

Sassen, Saskia. 1994. *Cities in a World Economy.* Thousand Oaks: Pine Forge Press.
———. 1996. *Losing Control?* New York: Columbia University Press.
———. 1998. *Globalization and Its Discontents.* New York: New Press.

Schechter, Susan. 1982. *Women and Male Violence: The Visions and Struggles of the Battered Women's Movement.* Boston: South End Press.

Scheingold, Stuart A. 1974. The Politics of Rights: Lawyers, Public Policy, and Political Change. New Haven: Yale Univ. Press.

Schneider, Elizabeth M. 2000. *Battered Women and Feminist Lawmaking.* New Haven: Yale Univ. Press.
———. 2004. "Transnational Law as a Domestic Resource: Thoughts on the Case of Women's Rights." *New England Law Review* 38 (3): 689–724.

Scheper-Hughes, Nancy. 1995. "Primacy of the Ethical: Propositions for a Militant Anthropology." *Current Anthropology* 36 (6): 409–20.

Schöpp-Schilling, Hanna Beate. 2000. "CEDAW: A Key Instrument for Promoting Human Rights of Women." Talk delivered in St. Petersburg, Nov. 13.

258

Schuler, Margaret, ed. 1992. Freedom from Violence: Women's Strategies from Around the World. New York: UNIFEM.

Secretariat of the Pacific Community. 1998. *Joint SPC/ESCAP/UNDP Consultative Meeting on the Implementation of the CEDAW Mechanisms in the Pacific: Nadi, Fiji, 20–23 July 1998.* Noumea, New Caledonia: Secretariat of the Pacific Community.

Secretary-General Report. 2001. "Status of Submission of Reports by States Parties under Article 18 of the Convention." CEDAW, United Nations. CEDAW/C/2001/II/2.

Selby, Stephen. 1991. "Everything You Wanted to Know about Chinese Customary Law (But Were Afraid to Ask)." *Hong Kong Law Journal* 21: 45–77.

Sen, Amartya. 1999. *Development as Freedom.* Westminster, MD: Knopf.

Shamsie, Kamila. 2002. "Women: Child Abuse in Belgium 'Shocks the Nation'— So Why Is Gang Rape in Pakistan 'a Cultural Issue'?" *The Guardian,* September 6, G2, p. 7.

Sharma, Aradhana. Forthcoming. "Cross-breeding Institutions, Breeding Struggle: Women's 'Empowerment,' Neoliberal Govenmentality, and Engendered Statehood in India." *Cultural Anthropology.*

Silard, Kathy. 1994. "Helping Women to Help Themselves: Counselling against Domestic Violence in Australia." In Miranda Davies, ed., *Women and Violence,* pp. 239–46. London: Zed Books.

Singh, Debbie. 1992. "Workshop on the Convention of the Elimination of All Forms of Discrimination against Women, 3–6 March 1992." Library of the University of the South Pacific.

Singh, Kirti. 1994. "Obstacles to Women's Rights in India." In Rebecca J. Cook, ed., *Human Rights of Women: National and International Perspectives,* pp. 375–96. Philadelphia: Univ. of Pennsylvania Press.

Singh-Wendt, Debbie, for Fiji Women's Crisis Centre. 1991. National Workshop on Violence against Women, 10–20 August 1991, Coral Coast Christian Camp, Deuba. Funded by Canada Fund.

Sitaraman, Bhavani. 2002. "Policing Poor Families: Domestic Dispute Resolution in All-Women Police Stations." Paper presented at the Law and Society Association Meeting, Vancouver.

Smart, Alan, and James Lee. 2003. "Financialization and the Role of Real Estate in Hong Kong's Regime of Accumulation." *Economic Geography* 79 (1): 153–71.

Snow, David, E. Burke Rochford, Jr., Steven K. Worden, and Robert D. Benford. 1986. "Frame Alignment Processes, Micromobilization, and Movement Participation." *American Sociological Review* 51 (4): 464–81.

Speed, Shannon, and Jane Collier. 2000. "Limiting Indigenous Autonomy in Chiapas, Mexico: The State Government's Use of Human Rights." *Human Rights Quarterly* 22: 877–905.

Spiro, Peter J. 2000. "The New Sovereigntists: American Exceptionalism and Its False Prophets." *Foreign Affairs* 79 (6): 9.

St. Joan, Jacqueline. 1997. "Sex, Sense, and Sensibility: Trespassing into the Culture of Domestic Abuse." *Harvard Women's Law Journal* 20: 263–308.

Tang, Catherine So-Kum. 1999a. "Wife Abuse in Hong Kong Chinese Families: A Community Survey." *Journal of Family Violence* 14 (2): 173–91.

———. 1999b. "Marital Power and Aggression in a Community Sample of Hong Kong Chinese Families." *Journal of Interpersonal Violence* 14 (6): 586–602.

259

Tang, Catherine So-kum, Antoinette Lee, and Fanny Mui-ching Cheung. 1999. "Violence against Women in Hong Kong." In Fanny M. Cheung, Malavika Karlekar, Aurora De Dios, Juree Vichit-Vadakan, Lourdes R. Quisumbing, eds., *Breaking the Silence: Violence against Women in Asia*, pp. 38–58. Hong Kong: Equal Opportunities Commission in collaboration with Women in Asian Development and UNESCO National Commission of the Philippines.

Tang, Catherine So-Kum, Day Wong, Fanny M. C. Cheung, and Antoinette Lee. 2000. "Exploring How Chinese Define Violence against Women: A Focus Group Study in Hong Kong." *Women's Studies International Forum 23: 197–209.*

Tarrow, Sidney. 1998. Power in Movements: Social Movements and Contentious Politics. 2d ed. Cambridge: Cambridge Univ. Press.

Task Force on Women 2000: India. 2000. *What Has Changed for Women and Girls Since 1995? The NGO Country Report on Beijing Plus Five from the Indian Women's Movement.* Delhi: National NGO Core Group for the Beijing Plus Five Review.

Tate, Winifred. 2005. "Counting the Dead: Human Rights Claims and Counter-Claims in Colombia." Ph.D. diss., Department of Anthropology, New York Univ.

Tatsuo, Inoue. 1999. "Liberal Democracy and Asian Orientalism." In Joanne R. Bauer and Daniel A. Bell, eds., *The East Asian Challenge for Human Rights,* pp. 27–60. London and New York: Cambridge Univ. Press.

Thomas, Cheryl. 1999. "Domestic Violence." In Kelly D. Askin and Dorean M. Koenig, eds., *Women and International Human Rights Law* 1: 219–56. Ardsley, NY: Transnational Publishers.

Thomas, Dorothy, and Michele Beaseley. 1993. "Domestic Violence as a Human Rights Issue." *Human Rights Quarterly* 15: 36–62.

Thomas, Dorothy Q. 1994. "In Search of Solutions: Women's Police Stations in Brazil." In Miranda Davies, ed., *Women and Violence,* pp. 32–43. London: Zed Books.

Thomas, Dorothy Q., and Robin S. Levi. 1999. "Common Abuses against Women." In Kelly D. Askin and Dorean M. Koenig, eds., *Women and International Human Rights Law,* 1: 139–76. Ardsley, NY: Transnational Publishers.

Thomas, Nicholas. 1994. *Colonialism's Culture: Anthropology, Travel and Government.* Princeton: Princeton Univ. Press.

Tong, Irene. 1999. "Re-inheriting Women in Decolonizing Hong Kong." In Jill M. Bystydzienski and Joti Sekhon, eds., *Democratization and Women's Movements,* Bloomington: Indiana University Press.

———. N.d. "The Women's Movement in Hong Kong's Transition." Department of Politics and Public Administration, University of Hong Kong, Hong Kong. Pp. 643–59.

Toren, Christina. 1994. "All Things Go in Pairs, or the Sharks Will Bite: The Antithetical Nature of Fijian Chiefship." *Oceania* 64 (3): 197.

Tsang Gar Yin and Chi Kie Wan. 1994. "Campaign for Equal Inheritance Rights." *Women's News Digest* 32–33: 8–13.

Turner, Terence. 1997. "Human Rights, Human Difference: Anthropology's Contribution to an Emancipatory Cultural Politics." *Journal of Anthropological Research* 53: 273–91.

Ulrich, Jennifer L. 2000. "Confronting Gender-Based Violence with International Instruments: Is a Solution to the Pandemic within Reach?" *Indiana Journal of Global Legal Studies* 7: 629–54.

UNICEF. 1999. *Transforming Private Rage into Public Action: Strategy Meetings on Gender and Violence against Women and Girls: Perspectives on the Future Role of UNICEF in South Asia.* August 16–18, 1999, Central Godavari Resort, Kathmandu, Nepal.

United Nations. 1995. "Beijing Declaration and Platform for Action: Platform 3." *The IV World Conference on Women, 1995 — Beijing, China: Official Documents.* gopher://gopher .undp.org: 70/oo/uncofns/women/off/platform.3.25 October 1995.

United Nations General Assembly. 2000. *Report of the Committee on the Elimination of Discrimination against Women: Twenty-second Session (17 January–4 February 2000), Twenty-third Session (12–30 June 200).* Supplement No. 38 (A/55/38). New York: United Nations.

Van Bueren, Geraldine. 1995. "The International Protection of Family Members' Rights as the 21st Century Approaches." *Human Rights Quarterly* 17: 732–65.

Volpp, Leti. 2000. "Blaming Culture for Bad Behavior." *Yale Journal of Law and Humanities* 12: 89–117.

Walley, Christine J. 1997. "Searching for 'Voices': Feminism, Anthropology, and the Global Debate over Female Genital Operations." *Cultural Anthropology* 12 (3): 405–38.

Wambui, Mercy. 2000. "NGOs in the Conference, But out of the Loop, Battle to Maintain Ground." *Flame/Flamme: The African Daily Newspaper of Women 2000: Gender Equality, Development, and Peace for the 21stCentury,* June 6, 2000: 2.

Wang Kairong. C. 2001. "Observation of a Court Trial over a Domestic Violence Case." *Newsletter* 3: 4–6. Domestic Violence in China: Research, Intervention, and Prevention Program, China Law Society Project Group, Beijing, China.

Wang Xingjuan. 1999a. "Why Are Beijing Women Beaten by Their Husbands? A Case Analysis of Family Violence in Beijing." *Violence against Women* 5: 1493–1504.

———. 1999b. "Domestic Violence in China." In Fanny M. Cheung, Malavika Karlekar, Aurora De Dios, Juree Vichit-Vadakan, Lourdes R. Quisumbing, eds., *Breaking the Silence: Violence against Women in Asia,* pp. 13–37. Hong Kong: Equal Opportunities Commission in collaboration with Women in Asian Development and UNESCO National Commission of the Philippines.

Watson, James L. 1983. "Rural Society: Hong Kong's New Territories," *China Quarterly* 95 (September): 480–90.

Watson, Rubie S. 1985. *Inequality among Brothers: Class and Kinship in South China.* Cambridge: Cambridge University Press.

Weissman, Deborah M. 2004. "The Human Rights Dilemma: Rethinking the Humanitarian Project." *Columbia Human Rights Law Review* 35 (2): 259–336.

Weldon, S. Laurel. 2002. *Protest, Policy, and the Problem of Violence against Women: A Cross-National Comparison.* Pittsburgh: Univ. of Pittsburgh Press.

Wesley-Smith, Peter. 1994. *The Sources of Hong Kong Law.* Hong Kong: Hong Kong Univ. Press.

Wilson, Richard A. 1996. "Introduction: Human Rights, Culture, and Context." In Richard A. Wilson, ed., *Human Rights, Culture, and Context: Anthropological Perspectives.* London: Pluto Press.

Wittner, Judith. 1998. "Reconceptualizing Agency in Domestic Violence Court." In Nancy A. Naples, ed., *Community Activism and Feminist Politics: Organizing across Race, Class, and Gender,* pp. 81–104. New York: Routledge.

Wong, Pik Wan. 2000. "Negotiating Gender: The Women's Movement for Legal Reform in Colonial Hong Kong," Ph. D. diss., Political Science, Univ. of California at Los Angeles.

Wu, Anna. 1994. Letter to the Members of the Bills Committee Considering the New Territories Land (Exemption) Bill. Unpublished letter.

Yeung Chan So-tuen Caroline, and David Lok Ping-pui. 2001. *An Exploratory Study on Children's Accounts of Wife Abuse in Hong Kong: A Research Monograph.* Hong Kong: Harmony House and City Univ. of Hong Kong.

Yeung, Caroline. 1991. "Wife Abuse: A Brief Historical Review on Research and Intervention." *Hong Kong Journal of Social Work* 25: 29–36.

Zechenter, Elizabeth M. 1997. "In the Name of Culture: Cultural Relativism and the Abuse of the Individual." *Journal of Anthropological Research* 53: 319–47.

Index

Ayana
Woodward
- 2603228044